I0810165

IMAGES
of America

PLATTEKILL

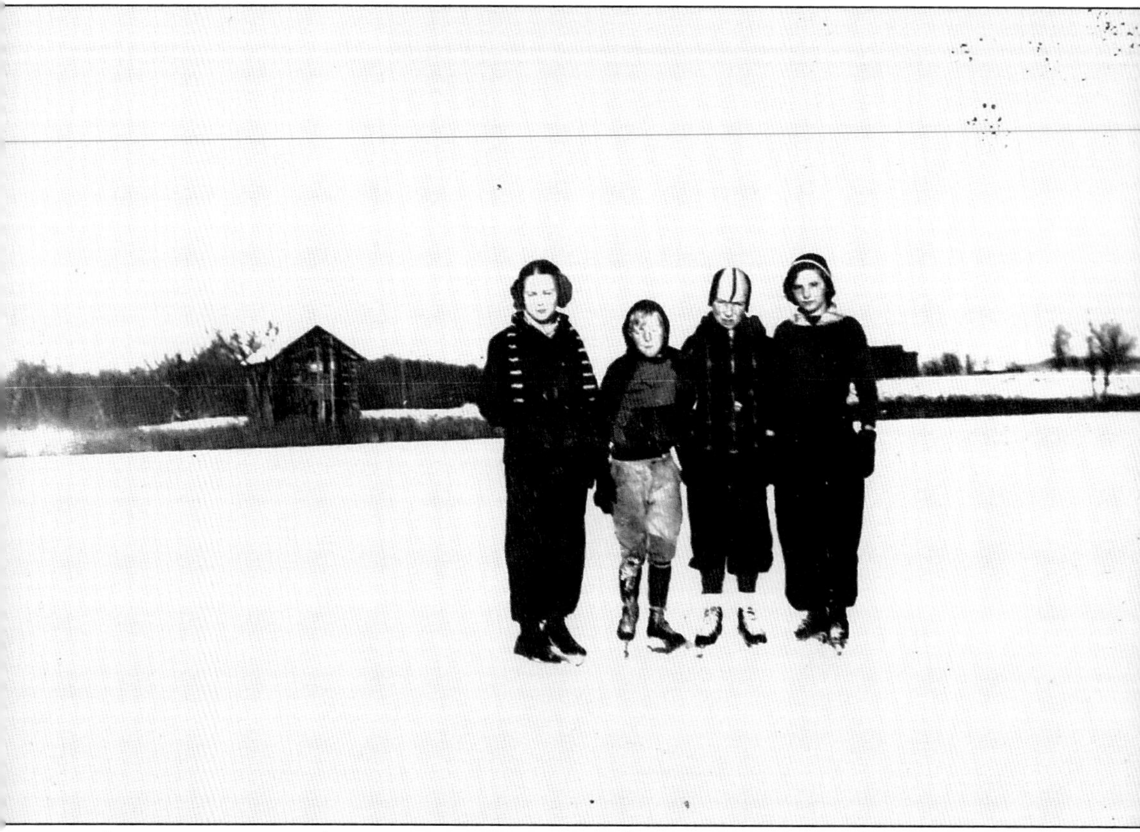

At one time, a popular winter pastime was ice skating on Modena Lake, today commonly referred to as Lembo Lake. Modena children, from left to right, Gloria Corwin, Russ Coy, Al Corwin, and Carrie Doolittle are shown here skating on the lake, around 1935. At the time, Modena Lake was part of the Hasbrouck property. The icehouse can be seen in the background. (Courtesy of Russ Coy.)

On the cover: Members of the Feldt family and their friends take a hayride along South Street in Plattekill, around 1947. Daniel Feldt, the young boy pictured in the center, remembers the neighbors getting together each year for such rides. The wagon was hitched to a tractor. (Courtesy of Daniel and Carol Feldt.)

IMAGES
of America

PLATTEKILL

Elizabeth Werlau

ARCADIA
PUBLISHING

ISBN 978-0-7385-5714-4

Published by Arcadia Publishing
Charleston SC, Chicago IL, Portsmouth NH, San Francisco CA

Printed in the United States of America

Library of Congress Catalog Card Number: 2007941017

For all general information contact Arcadia Publishing at:
Telephone 843-853-2070
Fax 843-853-0044
E-mail sales@arcadiapublishing.com
For customer service and orders:
Toll-Free 1-888-313-2665

Visit us on the Internet at www.arcadiapublishing.com

This book is dedicated to my mother, Joan Feldt Werlau, and to my grandmother Jennie Albano Feldt, both of whom loved the town of Plattekill for its people and all of its stories.

CONTENTS

ACKNOWLEDGMENTS

A project like this would not have come together without the help of an entire community. I am grateful to the many people who have shared their photographs, documents and most importantly, their stories with me.

My editor at Arcadia Publishing, Rebekah Collinsworth, was a great help to me during the process of writing this book. I would also like to thank Carl Aiello, owner and publisher of the *Times Community* newspapers, who has allowed me to tell those stories for several years and to reprint photographs that originally appeared in the *Southern Ulster Times.*

In addition, I would like to thank past editors Bruno Battistoli, Debbie Kwiatoski, and Andrew Hackmack, who allowed me the opportunity to write about Plattekill's current events while encouraging me to dig deeper into its past.

I am indebted to Shirley Anson, president of the Plattekill Historical Society, and Muriel "Micki" Obermeyer, the town of Plattekill historian, who both spent countless hours sharing pictures from their collections and answering my endless questions. Many of the pictures in this book first appeared in Anson's book *Friends and Neighbors: A Pictorial History of the Town of Plattekill and Southwest Lloyd.* Many others are from her own collection, the Town of Plattekill's collection, and Obermeyer's family collection. Plattekill is fortunate to have two people so knowledgeable in history and so willing to share what they know.

Library director James Cosgrove and the staff at the Marlboro Free Library should be commended for maintaining and supporting an extensive local history collection. I would also like to thank Russ Coy, Sonny Wager, Danny and Carol Feldt, Chief Jeff Zupan and the members of the Modena Fire Rescue Department, Valerie Smith, Sue Coy Doyle, Betty Hurd, Bruce Loertscher, Walt Davidson and Plattekill Boy Scout Troop 179, Jeff and Jo Ann Kraus of www.antiquephotograpghics.com, and the many others who took the time to work with me or to track down others who would be able to help with this project.

Finally, to Glen, Dad, and John, thank you for your continual love and support.

INTRODUCTION

In their 1959 history, *The Village of Clintondale: From its Beginning to 1959*, authors Ralph and Alice Van Siclen and Jerome and Elizabeth Hurd note that, "the longer we worked on this record the more we realized how impossible it is to document all the phases of life in a village—even one as small as Clintondale." The same theory applies to the greater town of Plattekill, which in addition to the hamlet of Clintondale, includes the hamlets of Modena, Plattekill, Ardonia, and New Hurley, as well as several neighborhoods such as Unionville and Tuckers Corners. The town spans four school districts, has three fire departments and post offices, and is home to numerous churches and volunteer organizations, and yet, a sense of community remains strong as evidenced by mutual celebrations, parades, and community projects.

Plattekill sits about halfway between the greater New York City area and the New York State capitol in Albany. It lies between the Shawangunk Mountains to the west and the Hudson River to the east and is bounded by the towns of Shawangunk, Gardiner, New Paltz, Lloyd, and Marlborough and by Orange County to the south.

The earliest settlers to the Plattekill area most likely arrived in the early to mid-1700s from the Westchester area, although a lack of major water features in the town would have halted some settlement and made the region closer to the nearby Hudson River more desirable. Settlers constructed homes made of log and stone, which have long since disappeared. Among the earliest families are the Thomases, the Gerows, the Hasbroucks, the Relyeas, the Ostranders, and the Dusinberres. Descendants of these early families still reside in the town and in nearby communities.

Most of the land that is present-day Plattekill was part of the New Marlborough precinct. On March 8, 1800, a special meeting was held to determine the division of Marlborough and Plattekill, and it was determined that "the new Town of the West side of the mountains be called the Town of Patteekiln; and the first Town meeting be held at the home of Robert Gilmore." According to the 1800 census, the new community had 1,625 residents, 20 of whom were slaves. By 1875, the town had already grown to accommodate more than 2000 residents. Today the town is comprised of more than 10,000 residents living on approximately 22,000 acres.

Records show that by the early 1800s stores had been set up throughout the new community. Churches came early to the town as well. Early settlers met in neighboring homes, but by the 1770s, the Dutch Reformed Church had organized in New Hurley and by the 1780s, the first Quaker meetinghouse had been constructed in the Unionville area.

The arrival of the railroad in the late 1880s changed the face of the town. Because of its train station, Modena became the unofficial business center for the area. Farmers from the surrounding communities would bring wagonloads of goods to the station to be loaded on the trains. Businesses such as lumber and coal yards sprung up along the rail line. With the railroad's decline in the mid-20th century came the disappearance of many of those businesses.

As Nathanial Bartlett Sylvester pointed out in his 1880 *History of Ulster County, New York*, "The principal occupation of the inhabitants of Plattekill has always been the cultivation of the soil," and in fact, the 1875 census showed that 19,828 apple trees existed in the town, while 348,995 pounds of grapes had been raised in 1874. Agriculture continues to be a mainstay for the town, as shown by the numerous orchards and family farms that still dominate Plattekill's landscape. At various points in its history, crops such as currents, pears, cherries, plums, peaches, grapes, and apples have been grown in Plattekill, with grapes and apples being the dominant crops. Grape production tapered off in the late 1890s after Ulster County was hard hit by a grape rot, and apples became and remain the dominant crop.

The business base in town continues to grow, as does tourism. Plattekill and the surrounding communities have long been day, weekend, or even summer destinations for tourists seeking to spend time in the country. Tourism reached its peak in the mid-1960s to mid-1970s, as thousands of visitors would shut down Plattekill's main roads each weekend in the summer. Today visitors still come to camp and to stay long-term, while day guests arrive on buses for apple and pumpkin picking or to enjoy the fall foliage.

In the year 2000, the town of Plattekill celebrated its 200-year anniversary and continues to look to the future by attracting new business, adding on to the current town park, and learning to balance new development with the town's existing rural character.

One

Hamlets and Neighborhoods

The town of Plattekill is made up of the five small hamlets known as Plattekill, Modena, Clintondale, Ardonia, and New Hurley. At other points in the town's history, the neighborhoods known as "The Flint," Sylva, Unionville, and Tucker's Corners were more active. Each of the neighborhoods within the town has its own unique character.

Unlike many of the towns and landmarks in this part of New York State that derive their names from Native American or Old Dutch words, the history of names in the town of Plattekill seems to be influenced primarily by the residents of the town itself. Since at least 1743, when the area now known as the towns of Marlborough and Plattekill came to be called the Highlands Precincts, the evolving names within the town have reflected its unique character and changing face.

Many of the Plattekill hamlets, including Clintondale, Modena, Ardonia, and Sylva (located where present-day New Hurley and Forest Roads meet Route 32) were given their present-day names when post offices were established in the area, and the meaning behind the name choice is documented. Plattekill was derived from the Platte Kill that runs through the town, while Modena's name is based in legend. The name "Clintondale" was specially chosen in honor of a governor, while Ardonia's name, if popular legend has any basis in fact, was merely chosen from a geography book.

Other neighborhoods, such as Tucker's Corners, were named for well-known residents, while the origin of the names "Unionville," located in the area of the present-day Old and New Unionville Roads, and "Flint" or "The Flint," located in the area of the present-day intersection of New Hurley and Plains Roads, remains a mystery.

Today only Plattekill, Modena, and Clintondale retain their post offices, although many of the names bestowed by the arrival of that office still remain.

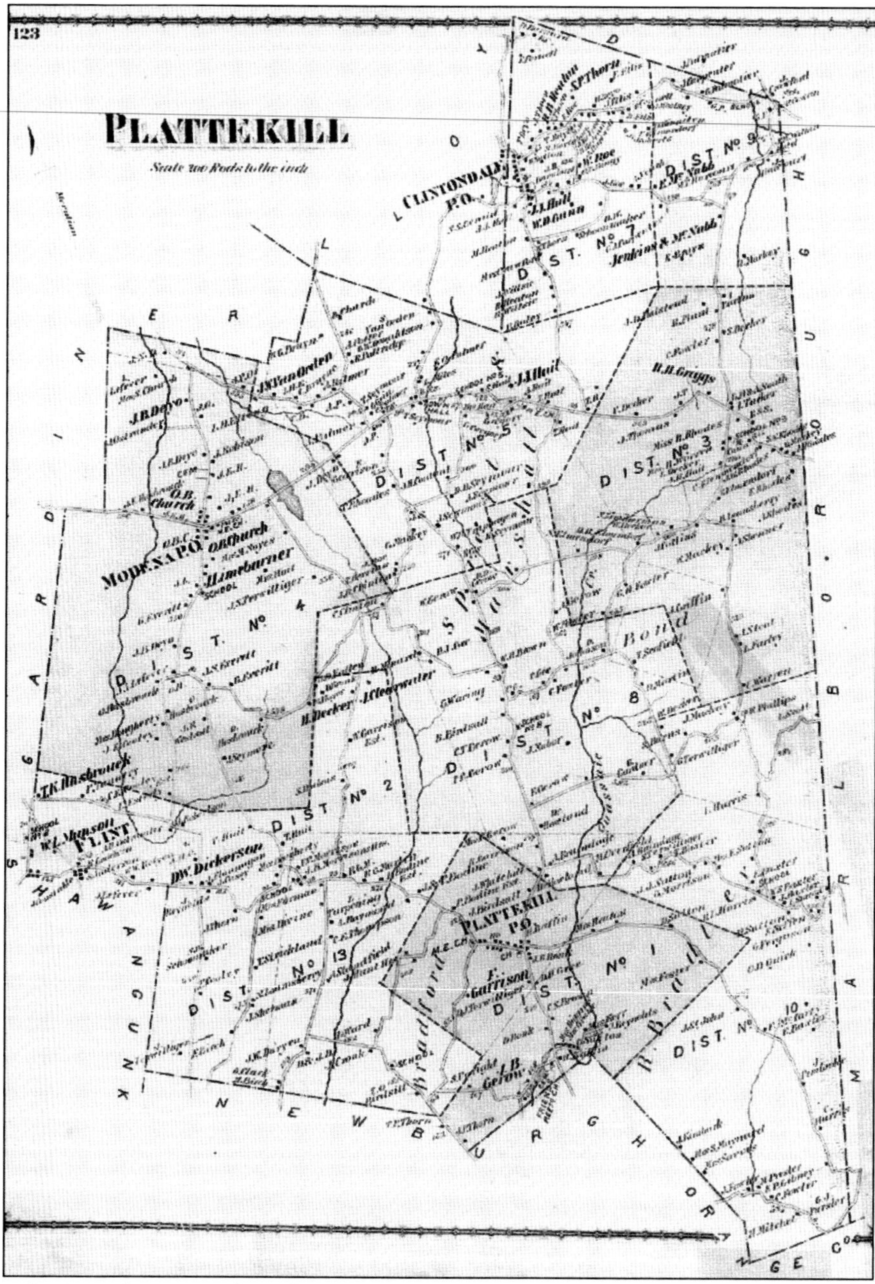

In March 1800, the town of Marlborough was divided, and Plattekill became Ulster County's ninth township. Prior to that time, settlers in the area traveled to the hamlet of Lattingtown for official business, although the mountain that divides Marlborough and Plattekill made such a trip difficult. The town of Plattekill was most likely was referred to as the "Valley" or "Pleasant Valley" when it was still part of the precinct of New Marlborough. After an act of the state legislature allowed for the division of the land into two towns, the new community was named for the Platte "kill," or "stream," which ran through it. The present-day town of Plattekill is bordered by Orange County to the south, the towns of Gardiner and Shawangunk to the west, Lloyd to the north, and Marlborough to the east.

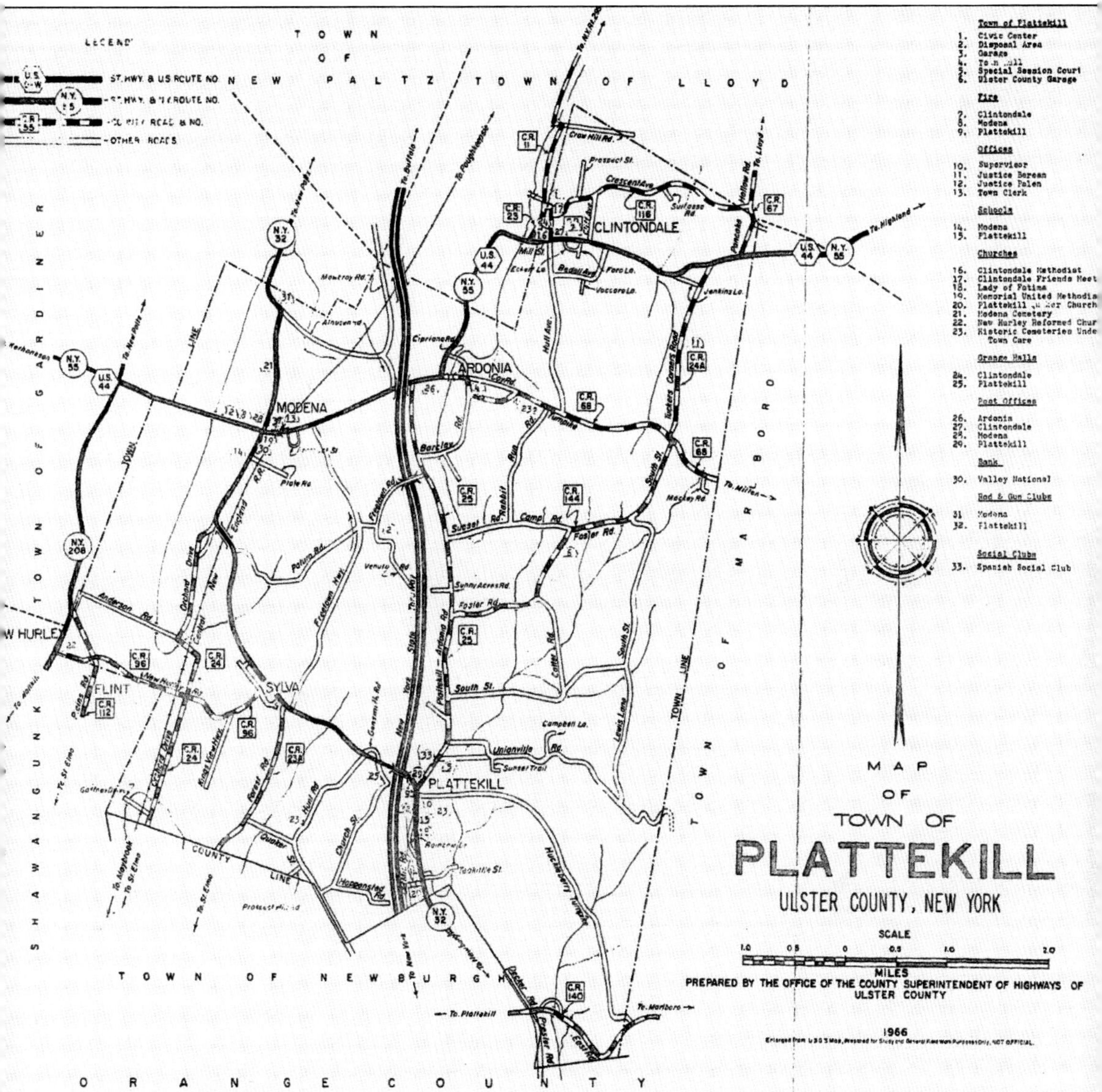

A 1966 map published by the office of the county superintendent of highways of Ulster County shows many changes to the town of Plattekill, including the New York State Thruway running through the town and the naming of many of the smaller roads, both of which occurred in the 1950s. The Central New England Railroad line, which was in its waning years, is also visible. This is one of few maps in which the town's hamlets, including (clockwise) New Hurley, Modena, Ardonia, Clintondale, Unionville, Sylva, and Flint, are all depicted. At the time, Modena, Ardonia, Clintondale, and Plattekill all had active post offices; today the Ardonia Post Office is long gone. (Courtesy of the Office of the Plattekill Town Historian.)

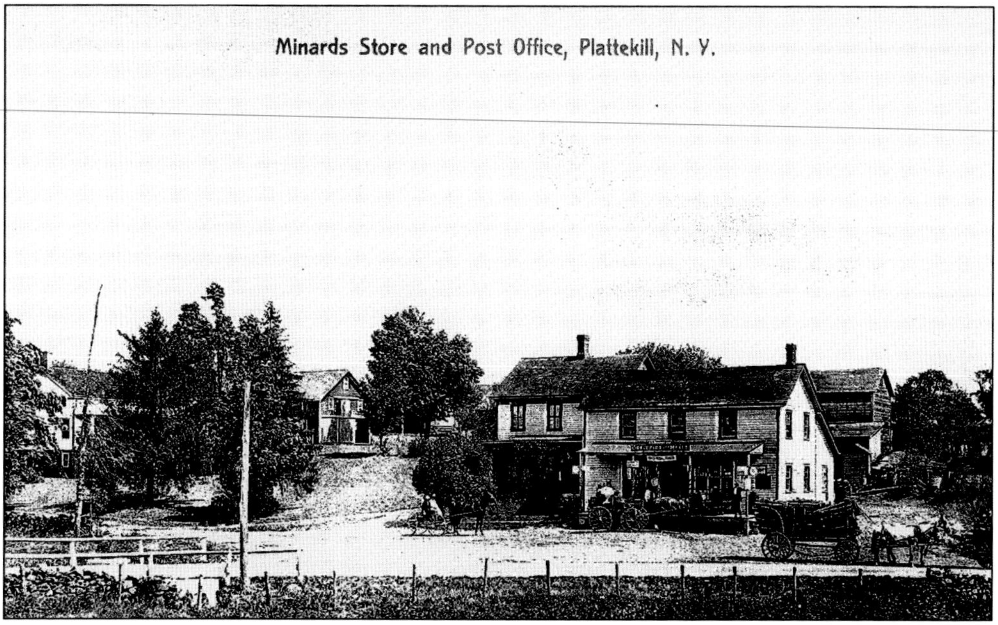

This view shows the intersection of Plattekill-Ardonia Road, Route 32, and Huckleberry Turnpike (at the top). Before the construction of the New York State Thruway during the 1950s, Route 32 would have run just past this store; today it is offset to the west. The neighborhood of Unionville is located off of Plattekill-Ardonia Road, northeast of this intersection. (Courtesy of author's collection.)

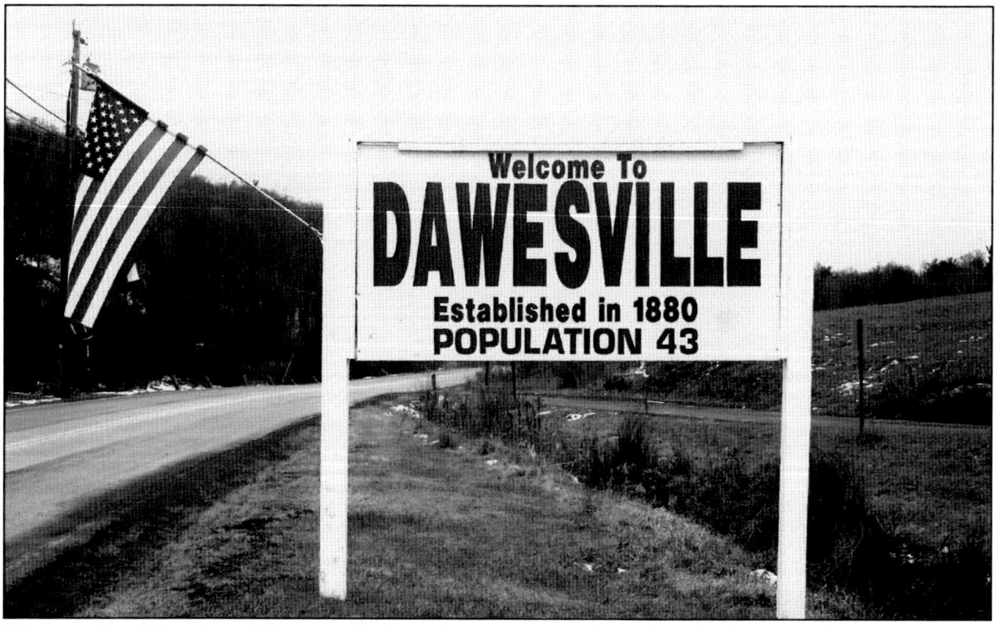

The unofficial hamlet of Dawesville lies along East Road in Plattekill, although residents have Marlborough mailing addresses and Newburgh phone numbers. The Dawes family first settled here in the 1870s, but the "Dawesville" name evolved as a joke after a business sign erected in the 1990s was deemed unsightly by the county. The sign was repainted and has served as a welcome to the area ever since. (Photograph by Elizabeth Werlau.)

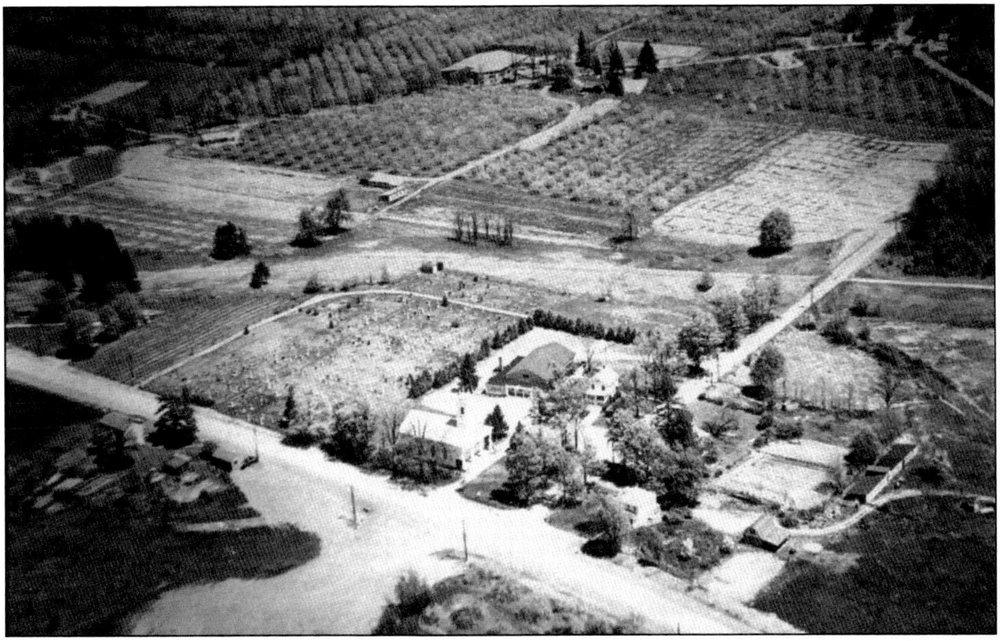

Concerning the neighborhood of Flint, Nathaniel Bartlett Sylvester points out in his 1880 *History of Ulster County, New York* that "at some periods it has been quite an active little place," with both a store and a post office. This aerial view, taken in the 1960s, shows Flint, or "The Flint," to the right, at the four corners of New Hurley Road and Plains Road. (Courtesy of *Friends and Neighbors: A Pictorial History of the Town of Plattekill and Southwest Lloyd.*)

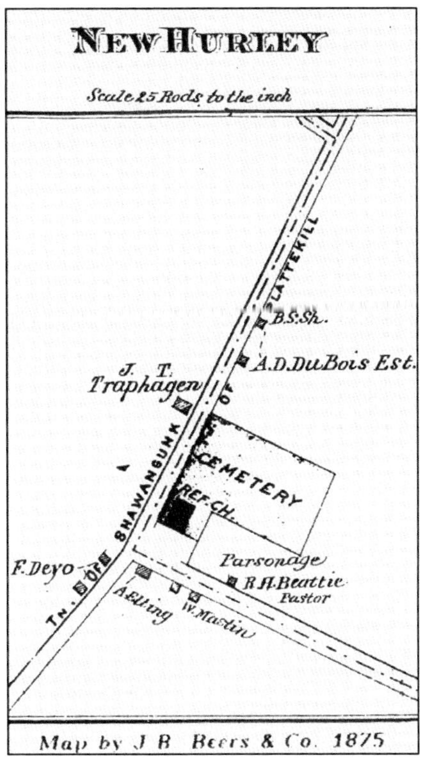

The New Hurley Post Office was actually located in Flint, and was the third post office to open within the town. It was established on January 23, 1834, with Benjamin Traphagen serving as the first postmaster. The post office was closed in 1905, at which time residents received delivery service from the town of Gardiner. (Courtesy of the F. W. Beers *Atlas*, 1875.)

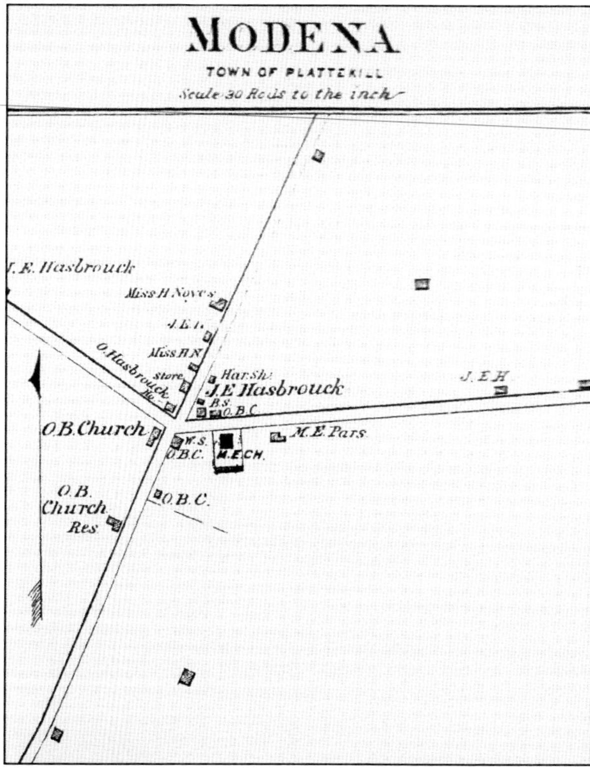

According to local legend, Modena was once called "Money Stumps." During Revolutionary War times, settlers along the Hudson River fled for the protection of the Shawangunk mountains as British forces arrived, hiding their valuable possessions in the stumps of trees just east of their destination. The hamlet was later known as "Clarke's Corners," after resident Thomas Clarke, the town clerk from 1831 to 1834. (Courtesy of the F. W. Beers *Atlas*, 1875.)

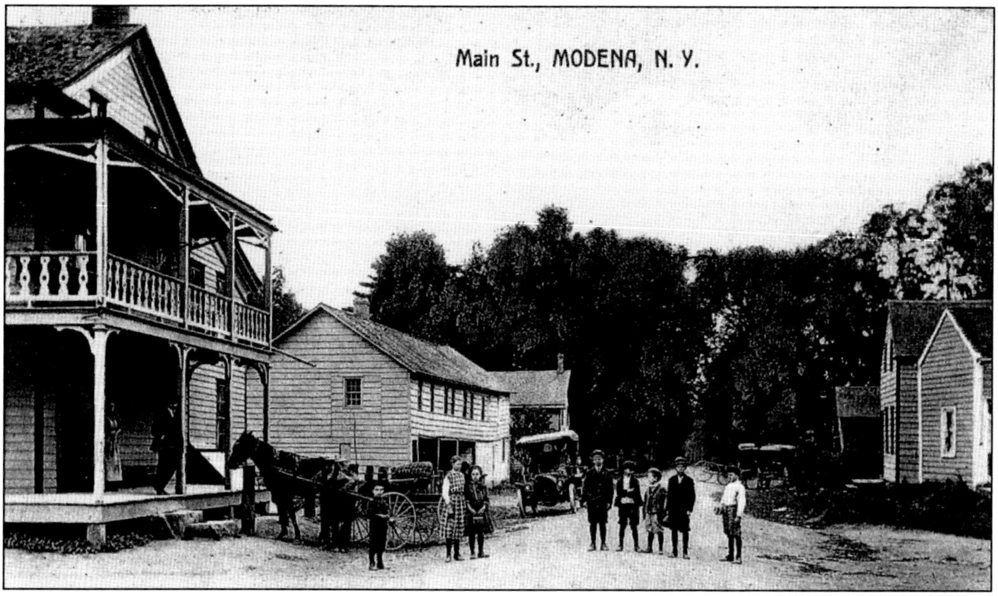

This *c.* 1906 postcard shows the four corners at Modena. Like many other Hudson Valley hamlets, Modena earned its official name with the arrival of the post office. In his 1949 *History of Modena*, Kenneth Hasbrouck wrote that "Modena," derived from a Latin word meaning "fortress" or "protected," was "a very appropriate name, as the earliest settlers, protecting their valuables in the money stump, would testify." (Courtesy of *Friends and Neighbors: A Pictorial History of the Town of Plattekill and Southwest Lloyd*.)

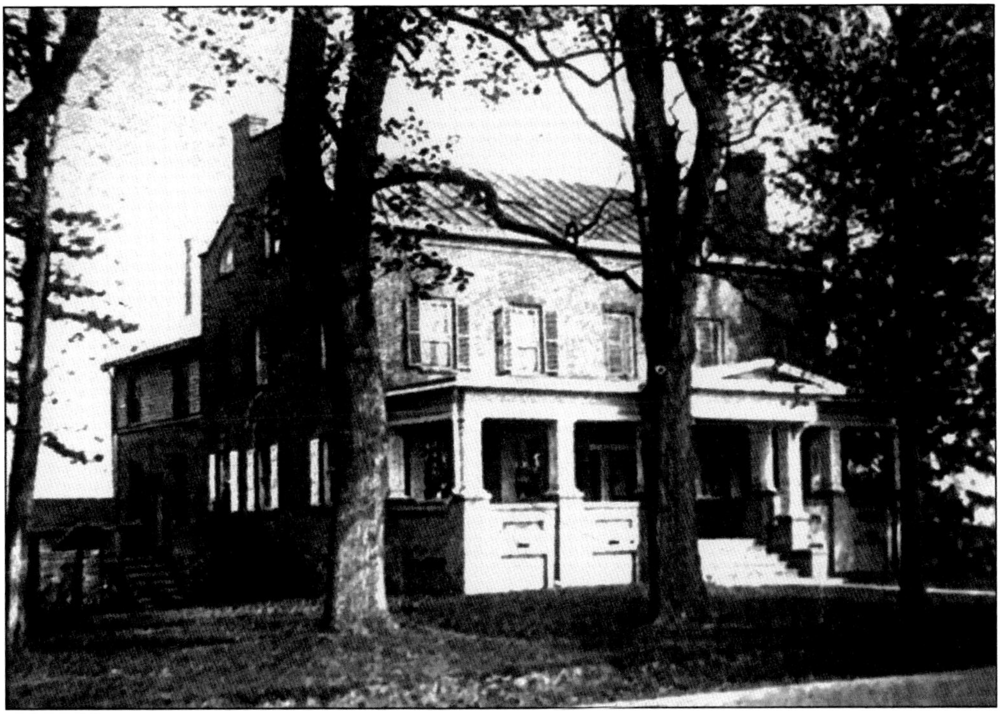

A 1905 postcard shows the Hasbrouck family home north of the Modena corners. The house was built in the early 1800s by the Cole family. Joseph E. Hasbrouck Sr. married into the family, and the house, which is still owned by his descendants, was added on to as businesses owned by the family expanded. (Courtesy of the Office of the Plattekill Town Historian.)

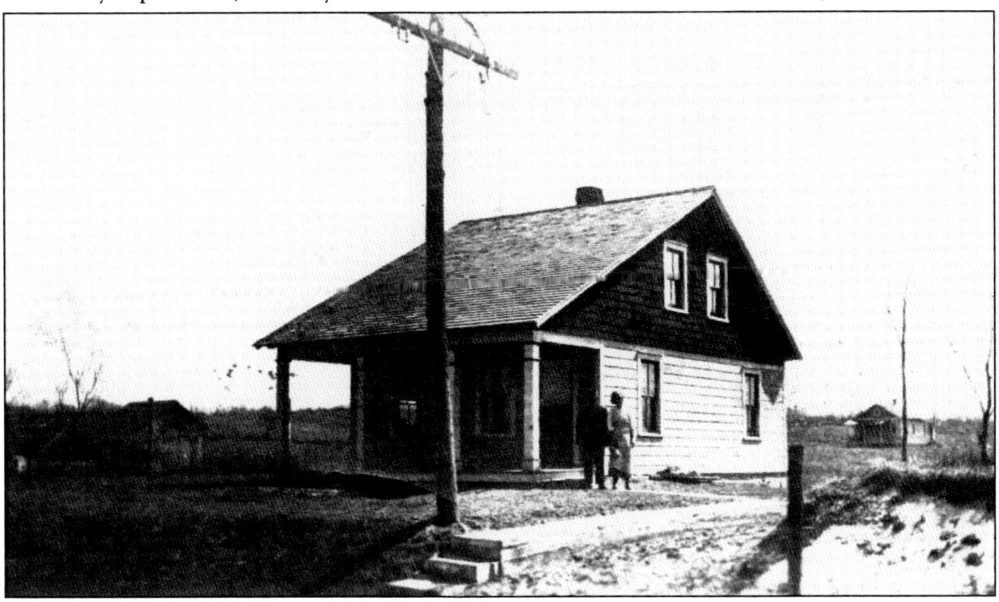

Richard and Dora Coy stand in front of their Modena home in 1911. The house remains standing today. Where the steps are located is now Route 44/55, and the property in the background is part of Prospect Street. Seen in the rear of the picture is the Doolittle home, which also still stands today. (Courtesy of Russ Coy.)

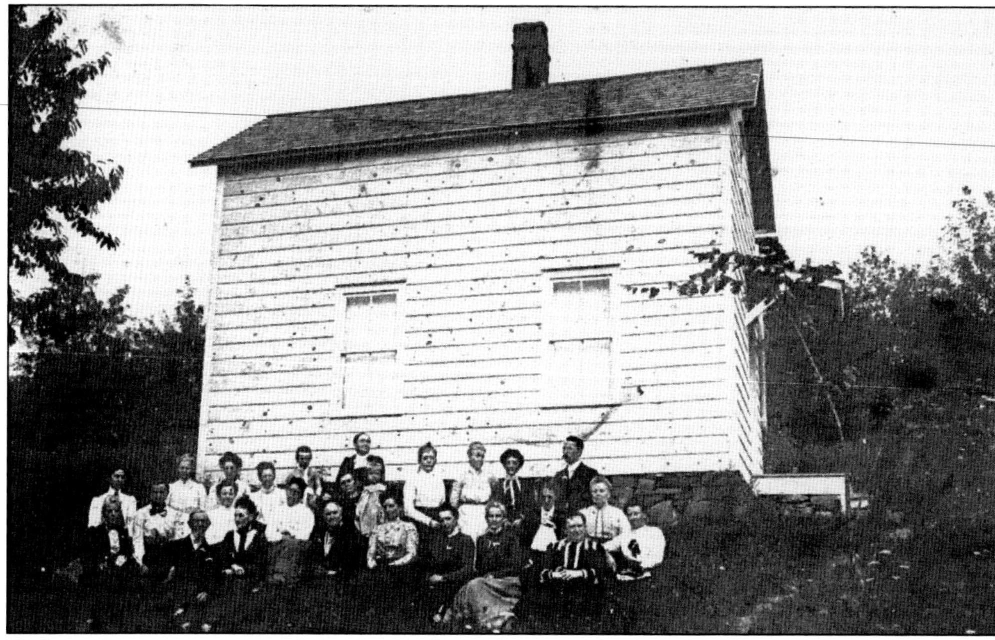

Tuckers Corners was named for Ira Tucker, who owned a large farm and general store near the present-day intersection of Tucker's Corners Road, Milton Turnpike, and South Street. The school (pictured here with an unidentified group) was built in 1883 along South Street and closed in 1945 when students began attending school in Highland. Today the area, still in Plattekill, is part of the Marlboro School District. (Courtesy of Shirley Anson.)

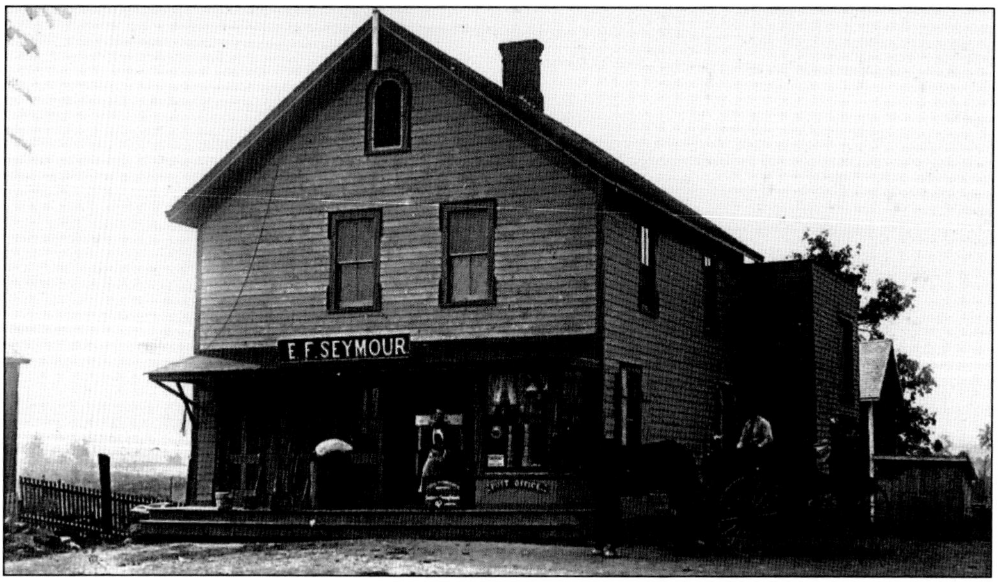

A line in the March 6, 1885, *New Paltz Independent* newspaper read, "Ardonia is making steady growth and already claims to be quite as much of a place as Modena." The Seymour Store, pictured here around 1892, was a general store first operated by George Seymour and located near the present-day intersection of Route 44/55 and Milton Turnpike. The building burned in the early 1900s. (Courtesy of *Friends and Neighbors: A Pictorial History of the Town of Plattekill and Southwest Lloyd.*)

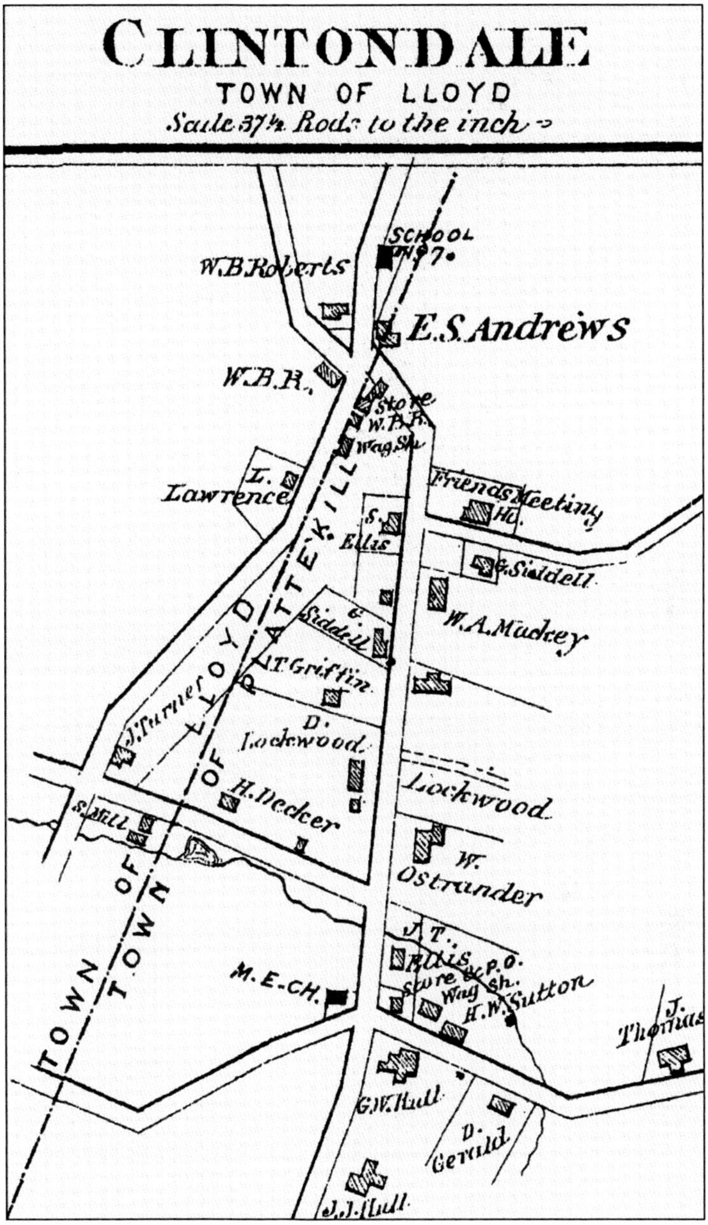

The hamlet of Clintondale is unique in that it lies partially within the town of Plattekill and partially in Lloyd. Children living in Clintondale may attend school in Highland, Marlboro, or New Paltz. In the late 1700s, the area that is now Clintondale was known as Elting and Lefevre's Corners, as it was part of the northeast corner of the Elting and Lefevre patent. Later it became known as Quaker Street for the many Quaker settlers in the South Street area. The name Clintondale, in honor of Gov. DeWitt Clinton, was settled upon in 1849 with the arrival of the post office. In their 1959 Clintondale history, historians Jerome and Elizabeth Hurd, and Ralph and Alice Van Siclen wrote that "a village bounded by school district lines is appropriately named for a man so interested in education." Town of Lloyd historian and well-known poet Warren Sherwood noted the naming in his poem, "Out Clintondale Way," "The place was named Clintondale / For the builder of the 'Big Ditch.'" (From the F.W. Beers *Atlas*, 1875.)

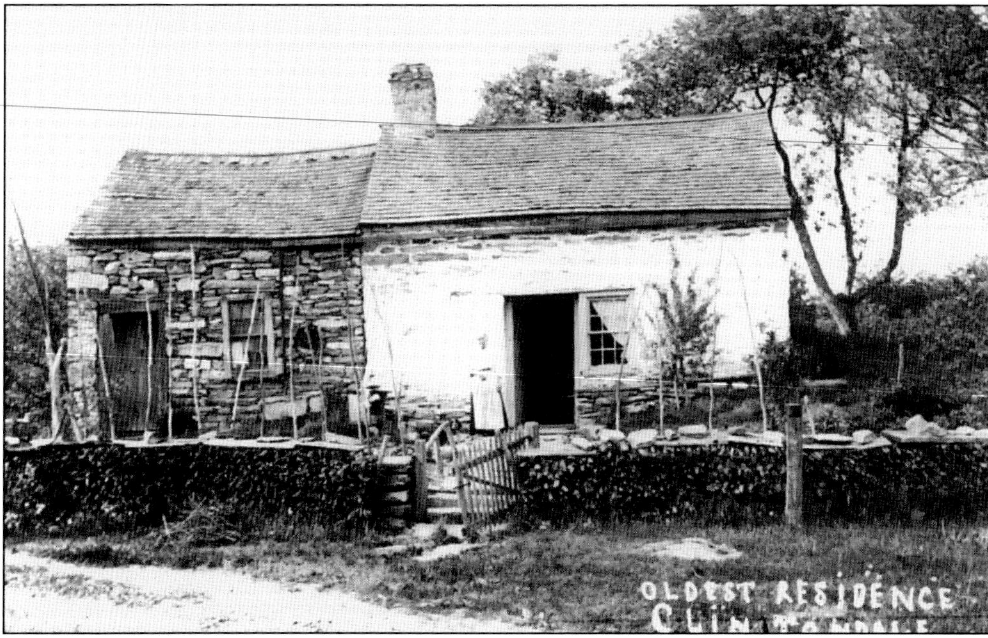

An early postcard shows the "oldest residence in Clintondale," a stone house located along Basket Street. Today the Basket Street area is part of the northern portion of Crescent Avenue. Historians Jerome and Elizabeth Hurd and Ralph and Alice Van Siclen suggest that the earliest residents in this area were squatters who gathered swamp ash and made baskets for a living. (Courtesy of Shirley Anson.)

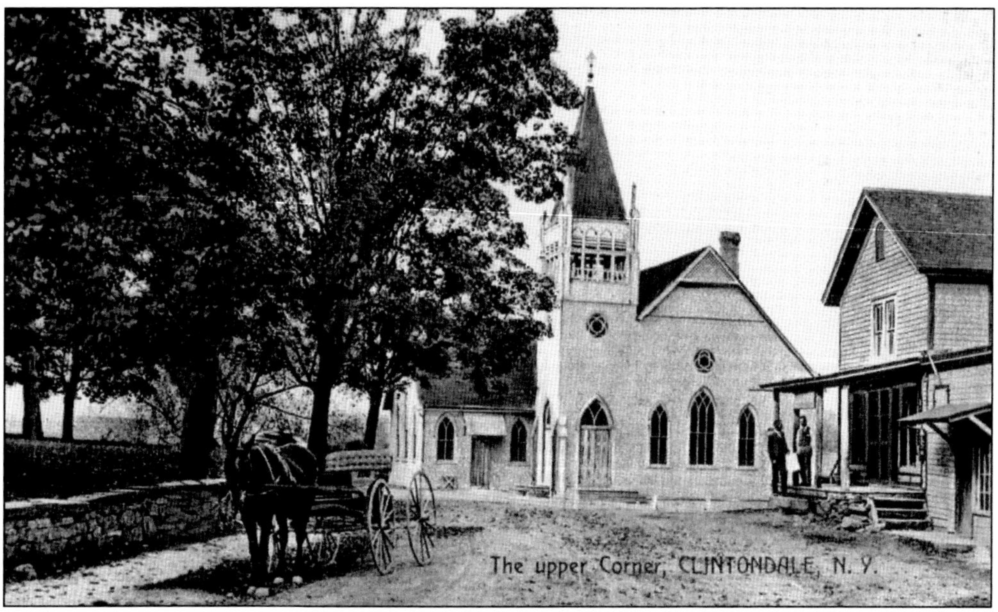

A *c.* 1909 postcard depicts Clintondale's "Upper Corner," with the Clintondale Methodist Episcopal Church and Garrison's store on the right. For many years, the "Lower Corner," at the intersection of South Street, Maple Avenue, and Hurds Road, was considered the center of the village, but by the early 1900s, many businesses were located in the Upper Corner. (Courtesy of *Friends and Neighbors: A Pictorial History of the Town of Plattekill and Southwest Lloyd.*)

Two

The Roads, the Railroad, and the Aqueduct

Many of the main roads in Plattekill follow trails set out by early settlers. Today State Route 44/55 provides an east-west route through Modena and Clintondale, while State Route 32 provides north-south passage through Plattekill and Modena. The New York State Thruway, established in the mid-1950s, cuts through the town as well, although the closest access is from New Paltz to the north or Newburgh to the south.

Milton Turnpike, once known as the "Road to Platte Kill" and later "Farmer's Turnpike and Bridge Company Road" was an early road providing access to the Hudson River in Milton and the Shawangunk Mountains to the west. During the mid-1950s, many of the smaller roads received their official names. In a 1955 article for the *Newburgh News*, reporter Albina Orlowski remarked that "All the country roads leading off Routes 32 and 44/55 are identified for the first time in 195 years." Among the roads named at the time were Teakettle, Hunt, and Forest Roads.

The Hudson Connecting Railroad came through the town of Plattekill in 1889. The line was at different points in its history controlled by the Philadelphia, Reading and New England Railroad Company, the Central New England Railroad (CNE), the New York, New Haven and Hartford Railroad, and the Penn Central Railroad. Both freight and passenger lines through the town ran until 1930, when the line was only used for freight. By the mid-1980s, the trains were discontinued, and the rails were removed.

Aqueducts running near and through the town of Plattekill have carried water from reservoirs in Ulster and nearby counties to New York City since the early 1900s. In 1937, after work was completed on the Rondout Reservoir, tunnels were created to allow the water to flow underneath the Hudson River, eventually connecting to the West Branch Reservoir in Putnam County. Two shafts are located within the town: shaft No. 4 in New Hurley, near the New Hurley Church, and shaft No. 5 in Plattekill, near the Plattekill Elementary School. In 1998, historian Shirley Anson interviewed Alfred Cole of Highland, a former aqueduct worker at shaft No. 5. The information about and pictures of the aqueduct work in this chapter is a result of that meeting.

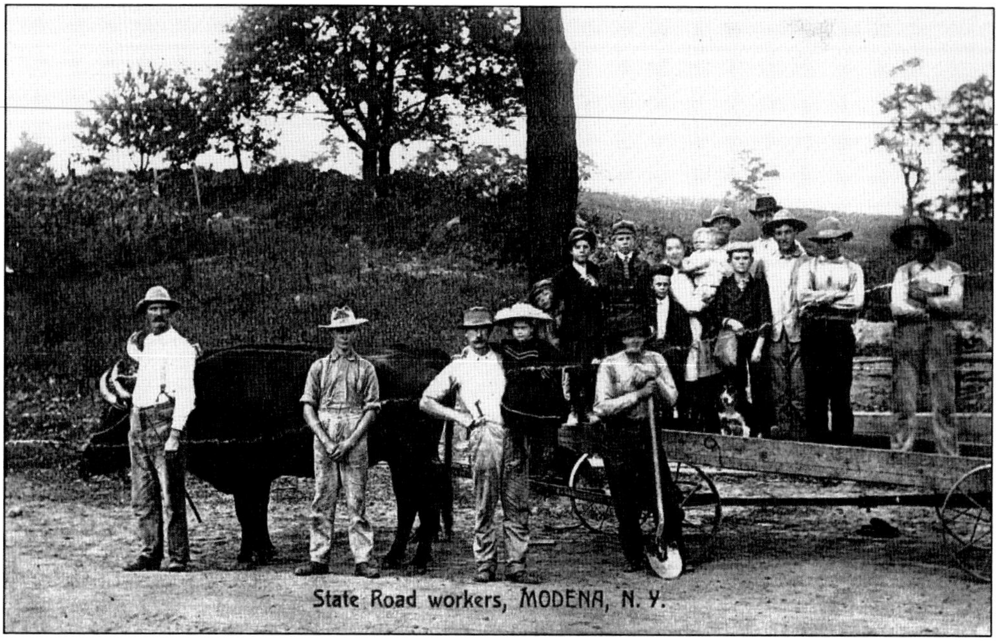

State road crews, such as the one pictured here in 1911, surfaced the Highland-Modena Turnpike when it became State Road Route 44/55. Modena resident John Leonard Coy (boy in black next to tree) was injured while playing near the road after he was accidentally buried by a load of stone. Workers helped dig him out using whatever tools they could find, including their bare hands. (Courtesy of *Friends and Neighbors: A Pictorial History of the Town of Plattekill and Southwest Lloyd.*)

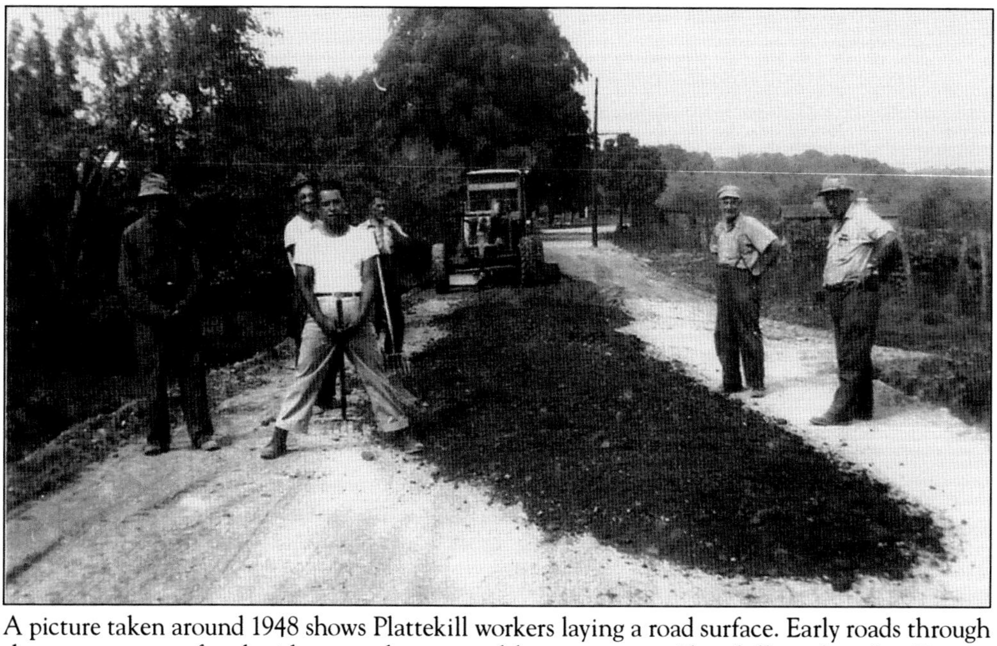
A picture taken around 1948 shows Plattekill workers laying a road surface. Early roads through the town were surfaced with tar and stone and later concrete. Plattekill road worker Eugene Coppola is in the foreground, holding a rake. (Courtesy of George Dougherty and the Town of Plattekill Highway Department.)

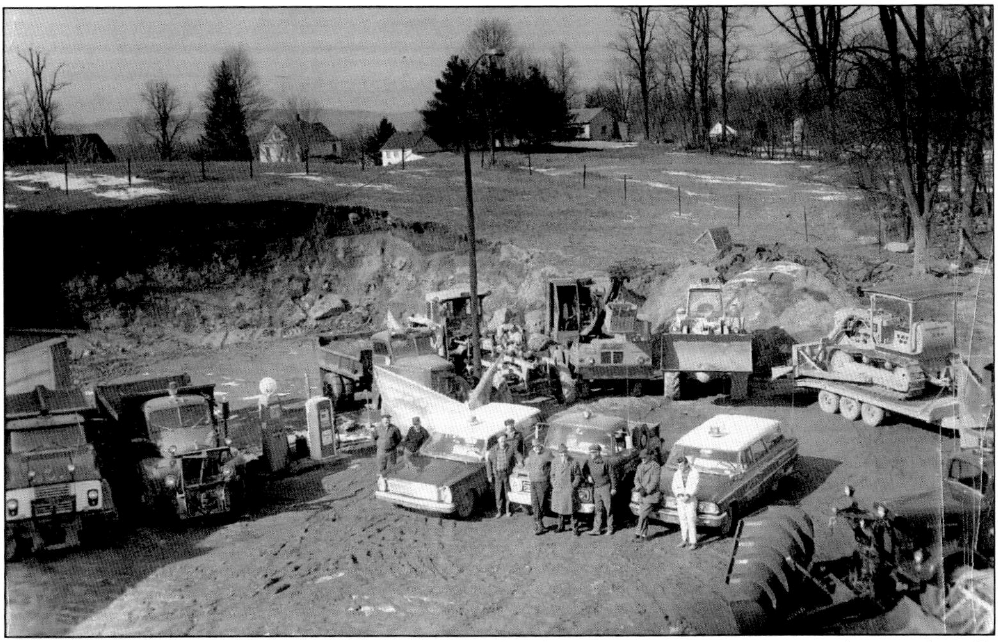

A view of the Town of Plattekill Highway and Police Departments is captured around 1965, taken from the Route 44/55 bridge. At the time, the highway department operated out of a small office located underneath the bridge. In 1973, a highway department garage and office were built on the site, as was the Plattekill Town Hall. (Courtesy of George Dougherty and the Town of Plattekill Highway Department.)

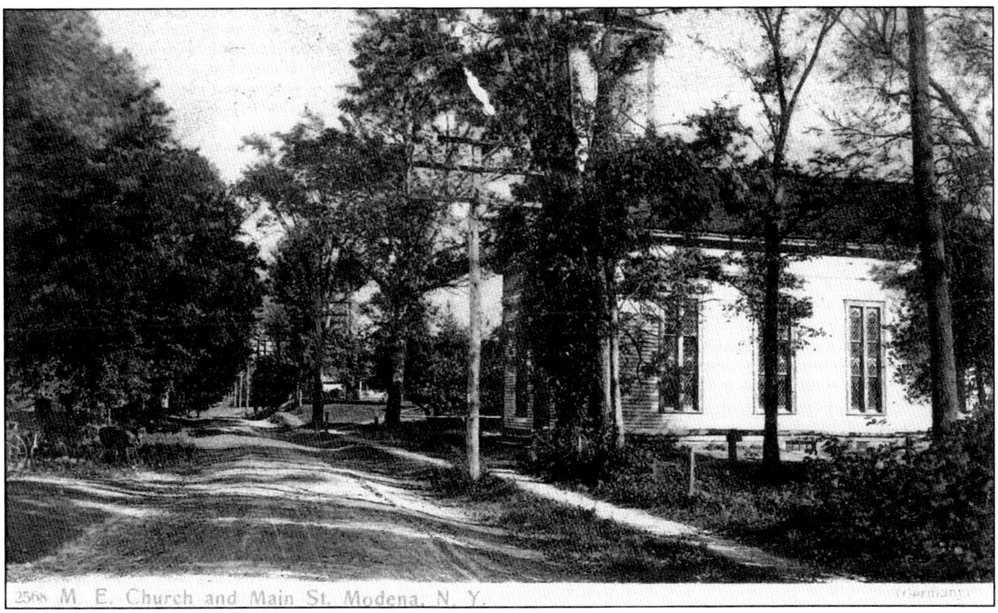

On various early postcards including this one, from about 1907, this section of road just east of the Route 32 and Route 44-55 intersection in Modena was labeled either "Maple Avenue" or "Main Street." Today this is part of State Route 44/55, and the area serves as a crossroads for the town. To the right can be seen the Modena Memorial United Methodist Church building. (Courtesy of author's collection.)

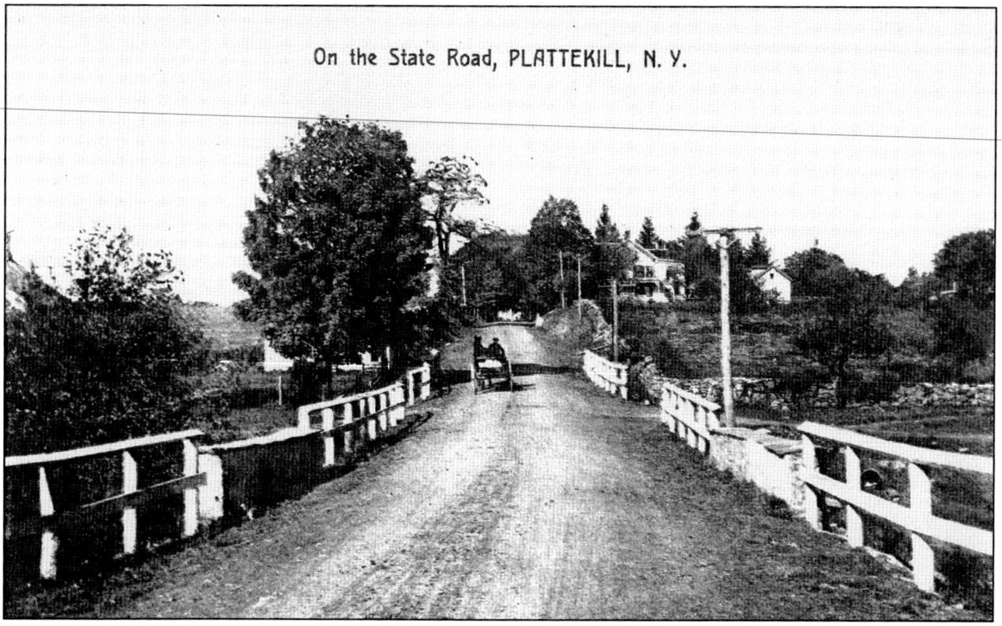

An early postcard shows the State Road in Plattekill looking north. The Garrison Boarding House can be seen to the top right. When the New York State Thruway was built in the 1950s, many roads, such as this one, were altered. The road is now known as Firehouse Road and is a dead end. Route 32 runs over the thruway on a bridge just east of this area. (Courtesy of author's collection.)

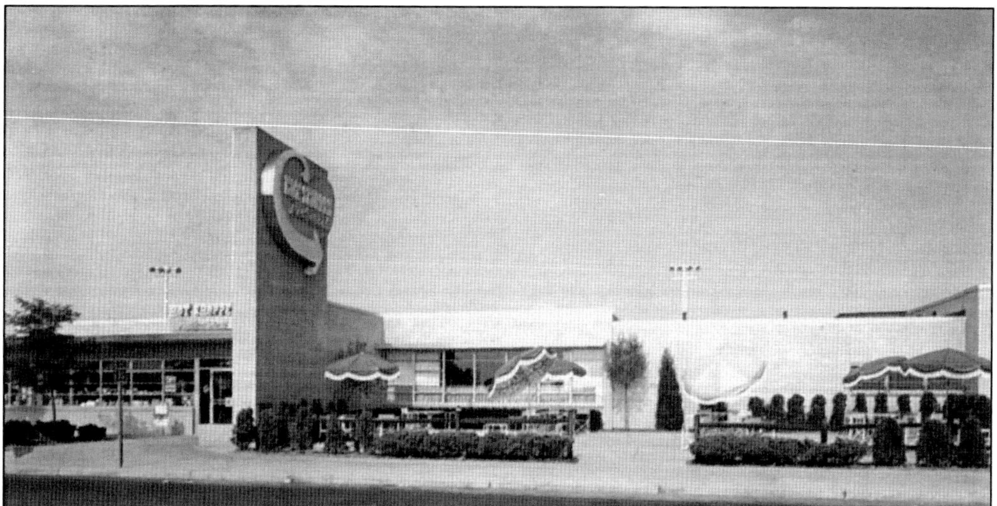

By the 1950s, the Thomas E. Dewey New York State Thruway was constructed, with a portion running through the town of Plattekill. Today, there are two "Hot Shoppes" service areas on the thruway bearing the names of Plattekill hamlets, the southbound Moderna Travel Plaza (shown here in the 1960s) and the northbound Plattekill Travel Plaza. Both service areas are actually located just south of Plattekill, in the town of Newburgh. (Courtesy of Shirley Anson.)

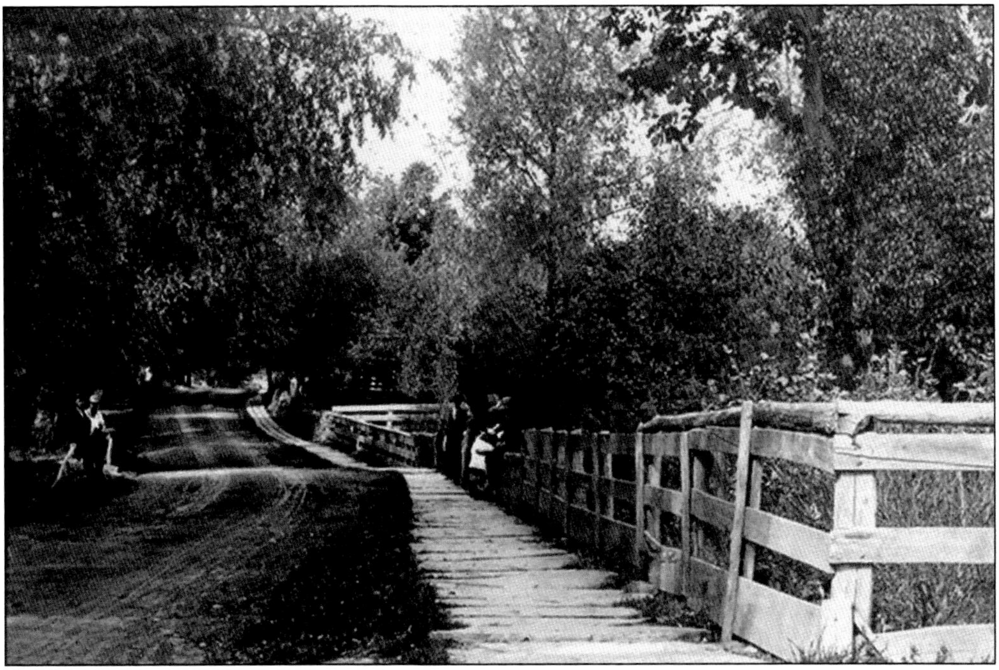

Many of the town's roads were named for early settlers, their occupations, or various natural features. Maple Avenue in Clintondale was appropriately named for the abundance of maple trees that grew along the road. This photograph, from a stereoview image taken in the 1880s, shows Maple Avenue as it appeared before many of the later stores and residences appeared. (Courtesy of Jeffrey Kraus and antiquephotographics.com.)

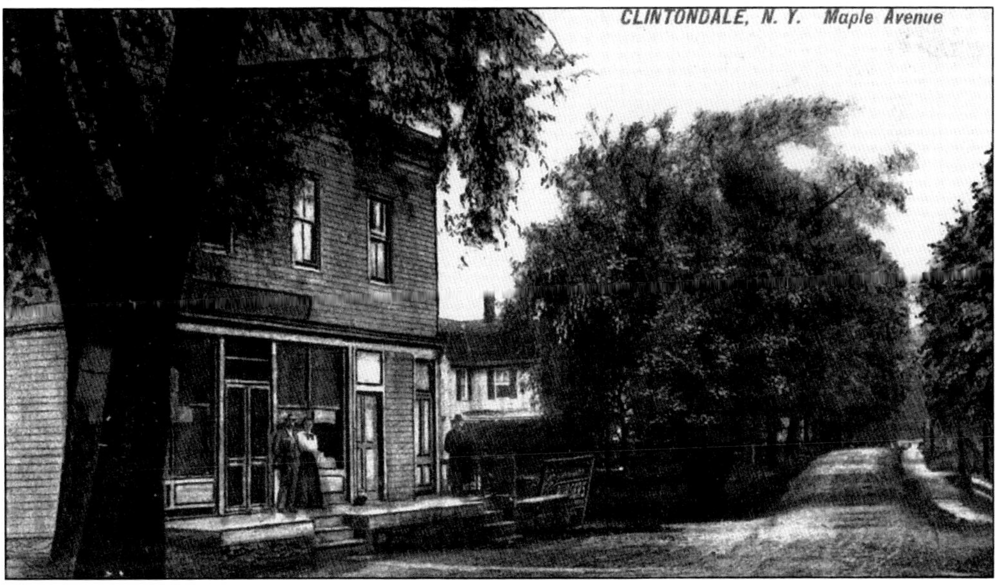

The same Maple Avenue was paved in concrete in 1925, and concrete sidewalks were installed. A 1924 article in the *New Paltz Independent* reported that the new road was a necessity, as the dirt road was in very bad condition due to heavy traffic. A public service group, known as the Clintondale Improvement Association, helped to raise money for the new sidewalks. (Courtesy of *Friends and Neighbors: A Pictorial History of the Town of Plattekill and Southwest Lloyd.*)

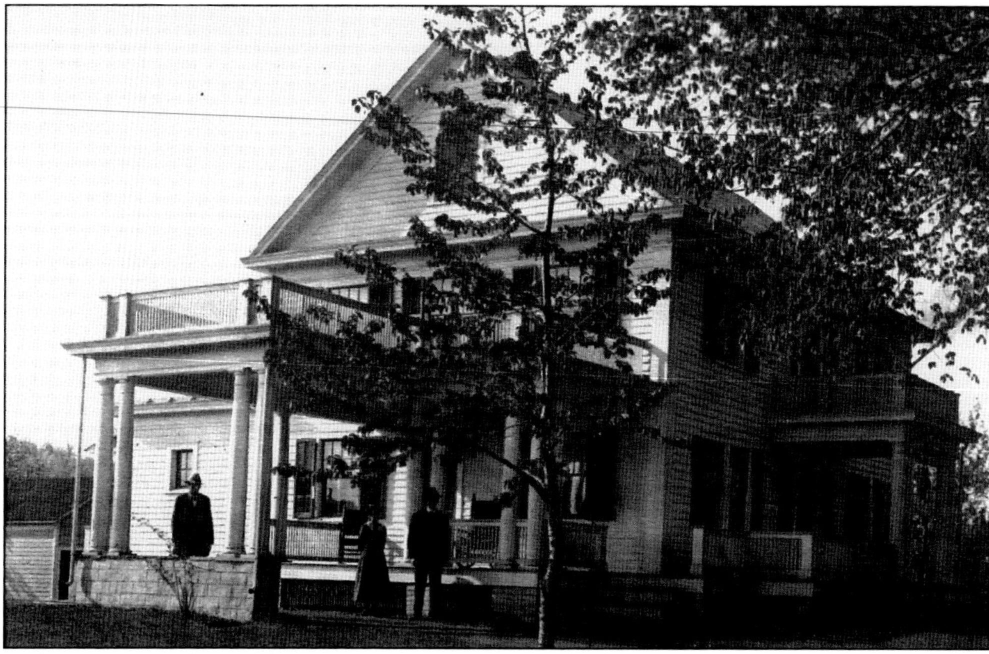

Hull Avenue in Clintondale is named for early settlers to the area. In early records, it is marked as part of the "Road to the Paltz and Baker's Store" which led from the Farmer's Turnpike (today Milton Turnpike) to Elting's and Lefevre's Corners (today Clintondale). It was eventually named after the Hull family, some of whom are pictured here at the Hull House. (Courtesy of Shirley Anson.)

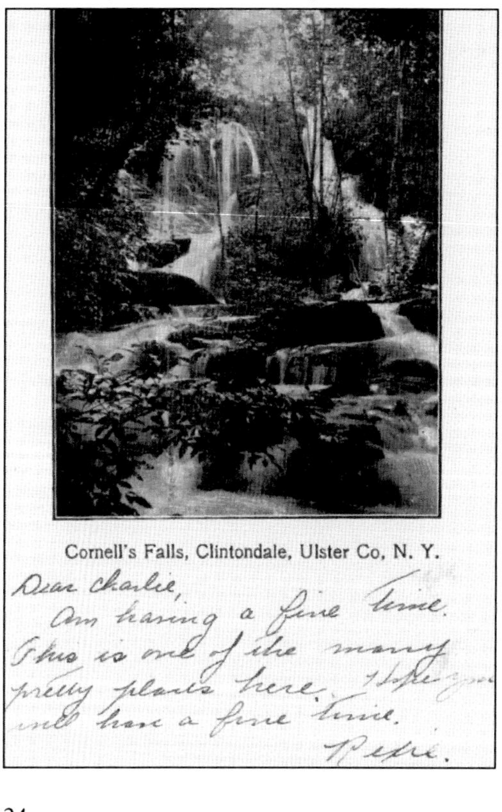

In his 1894 history of the hamlet, historian P. N. Mitchell referred to present-day Crow Hill Road in Clintondale as both "Rockwood Heights" and "Cascade Avenue" for its natural features including these falls, which are still visible at its base. The road once connected to Basket Street but today is a dead end. (Courtesy of author's collection.)

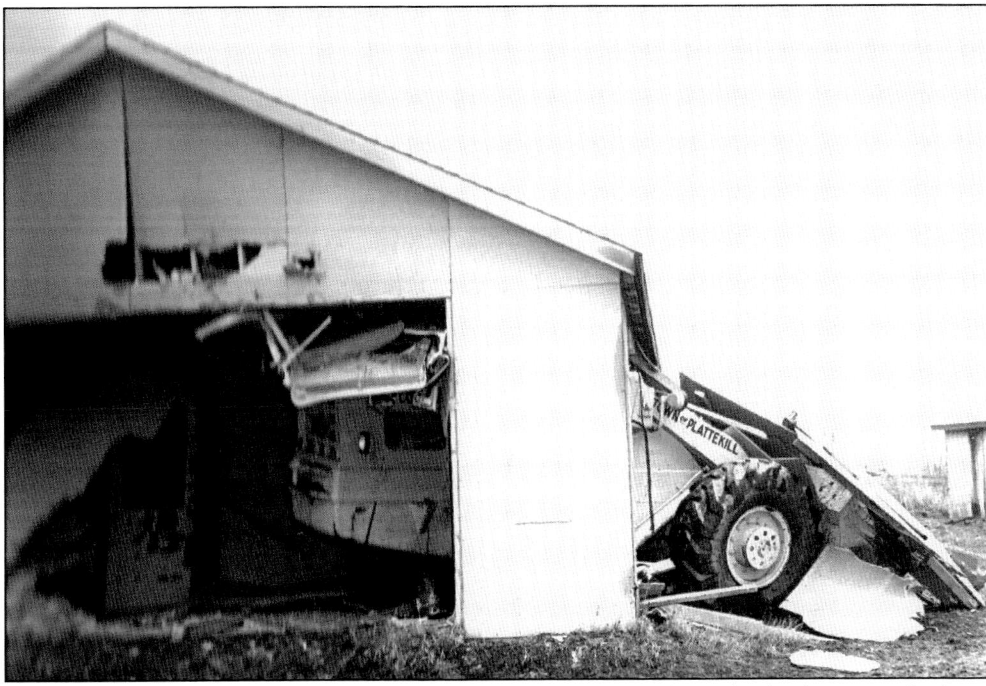

During the 1960s, the town of Plattekill made the news when the brakes on a highway department front-end loader failed, and the machine crashed into a building on the Stanley Orchards property. Driver Russell Coy of Clintondale was seriously injured in the accident. Chief Constable Lester Wager rushed Coy to St. Luke's Hospital in Newburgh in his police car, as the Modena Fire Department's new ambulance was not yet in service. The farmhouse, which sometimes housed migrant workers, was damaged. No one was living in it at the time. Coy recovered from his injuries. (Courtesy of Sonny Wager.)

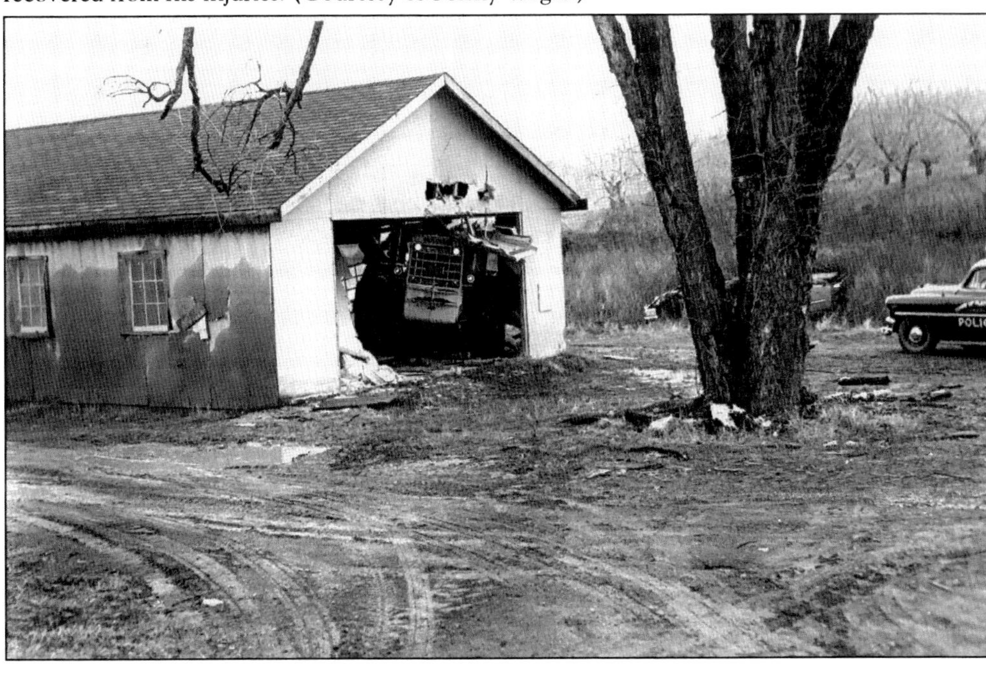

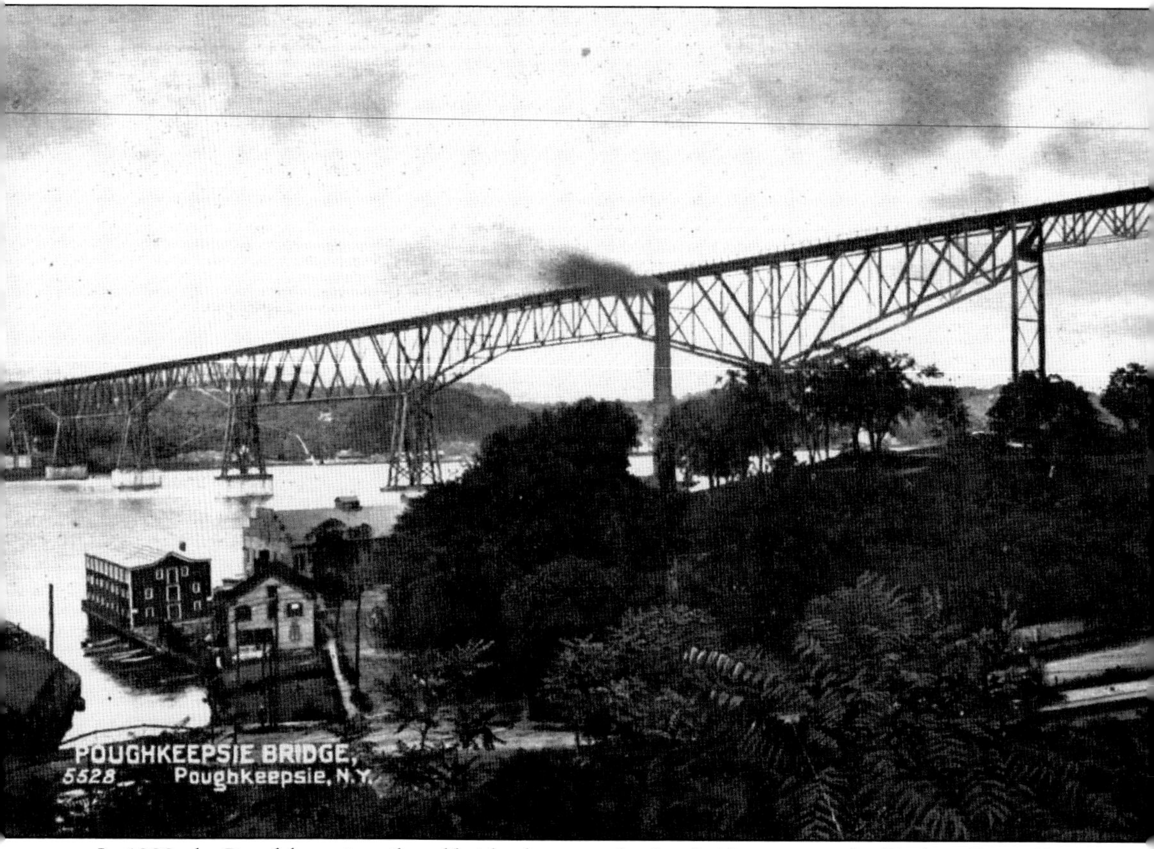

In 1888, the Poughkeepsie railroad bridge became the first bridge to span the Hudson River. Prior to its completion, according to historian Carlton Mabee, a group of 19 planners were loaded into sleighs and driven through Ulster County following potential rail routes and speaking with residents who stressed the need for such routes. The committee passed through Modena, which later became the only main depot within the town of Plattekill. In addition to freight service, the Bridge Route provided passenger service from Modena, so that residents could shop in Poughkeepsie, take a trip on a Hudson River dayliner, or change trains to visit other locales. The Clintondale station was built in the late 1880s; however the station was actually located within the town of Lloyd. After public outcry, a small platform was built at Elting Crossing (today Hurd's Road). Many businesses in Modena and eventually Clintondale grew because of the railroad, and many Plattekill men worked for the railroad, riding the local "Scoot" train to work at the Maybrook rail yards. (Courtesy of author's collection.)

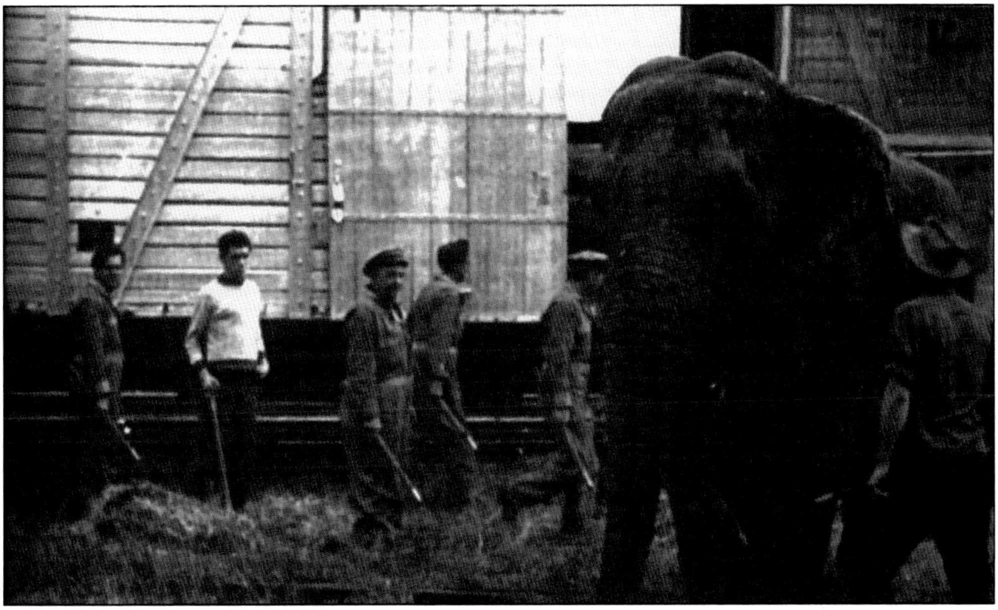

Freight trains moving through Plattekill hauled a variety of items including coal, lumber, fruit—and the occasional circus. From the late 1800s to the late 1950s, circuses large and small traveled by rail through the area on the way to Pennsylvania or Connecticut. A 1956 picture by Ralph Aiello shows one of the Barnum and Bailey elephants let out for exercise at the Maybrook rail yards. (Courtesy of Carl Aiello.)

Danbury to Campbell Hall	D	M	S	M	S	M	S	M	S	M	S	M	S	M	S	M	S
Danbury to Mallory	0.74	2	58	2	13	1	47	1	29	1	16	1	07	0	59	0	53
Mallory and Fair Grounds	1.43	5	43	4	17	3	26	2	52	2	28	2	09	1	54	1	43
Fair Grounds and Mill Plain	2.44	9	46	7	19	5	52	4	52	4	12	3	40	3	15	2	56
Mill Plain and Brewster	5.50	22	10	16	30	13	12	11	00	9	28	8	15	7	19	6	36
Brewster and Dykemans	2.38	9	31	7	08	5	43	4	46	4	06	3	34	3	10	2	51
Dykemans and Towners	3.28	13	07	10	50	7	52	6	34	5	38	4	55	4	22	3	56
Towners and West Patterson	2.39	9	34	7	10	5	44	4	47	4	07	3	35	3	11	2	52
West Patterson and Holmes	1.33	5	19	3	59	3	11	2	40	2	17	2	00	1	46	1	36
Holmes and Whaley Lake	1.90	7	36	5	42	4	34	3	48	3	16	2	51	2	32	2	17
Whaley Lake and West Pawling	2.66	10	38	7	59	6	23	5	19	4	35	3	59	3	32	3	12
West Pawling and Poughquag	2.19	8	46	6	34	5	16	4	23	3	46	3	17	2	55	2	38
Poughquag and Green Haven	2.23	8	55	6	41	5	21	4	28	3	50	3	21	2	58	2	41
Green Haven and Stormville	2.17	8	41	6	31	5	12	4	20	3	44	3	15	2	53	2	36
Stormville and Hopewell Junction	3.69	14	46	11	04	8	51	7	22	6	21	5	32	4	54	4	26
Hopewell Junction and Fishkill Plains	2.48	9	55	7	26	5	57	4	58	4	16	3	43	3	18	2	59
Fishkill Plains and Didell	1.24	4	58	3	43	2	59	2	29	2	08	1	52	1	39	1	29
Didell and Briggs	2.56	10	14	7	41	6	09	5	07	4	24	3	50	3	24	3	04
Briggs and Manchester Bridge	1.90	7	36	5	42	4	34	3	48	3	16	2	51	2	32	2	17
Manchester Bridge and S. S. 110	3.51	14	02	10	32	8	25	7	01	6	02	5	16	4	40	4	13
S. S. 110 and Poughkeepsie	1.10	4	24	3	18	2	38	2	12	1	54	1	39	1	28	1	19
Poughkeepsie and Highland	2.34	9	22	7	01	5	37	4	41	4	01	3	31	3	07	2	49
Highland and Loyd	3.48	13	55	9	86	8	21	6	58	5	59	4	73	4	38	4	10
Loyd and Clintondale	2.89	11	34	8	40	6	56	5	47	4	58	4	20	3	51	3	28
Clintondale and Elting	.86	3	26	2	35	2	04	1	43	1	29	1	17	1	09	1	02
Elting and Mowbray	1.62	6	29	4	52	3	53	3	14	2	47	2	26	2	09	1	57
Mowbray and Modena	2.01	8	02	6	02	4	49	4	01	3	27	3	01	2	40	2	25
Modena and Relyeas	2.27	9	05	6	49	5	27	4	32	3	54	3	24	3	01	2	43
Relyeas and St. Elmo	3.23	12	55	9	41	7	45	6	28	5	33	4	51	4	18	3	53
St. Elmo and East Walden	2.31	9	14	6	56	5	33	4	37	3	58	3	28	3	04	2	46
East Walden and Berea	2.59	10	22	7	46	6	13	5	11	4	27	3	53	3	27	3	06
Berea and Maybrook	3.52	14	05	10	34	8	27	7	02	6	03	5	17	4	41	4	13
Maybrook and Campbell Hall	2.85	11	24	8	33	6	50	5	42	4	54	4	16	3	47	3	25

A timetable shows time and distance between stations on the Central New England Railroad line. Mowbray Crossing was a flag and milk stop, as was Relyea Crossing, both within Plattekill. Some school children in New Hurley, Modena, and Clintondale who lived near the railroad would take the train to school in Highland, as the walk from the train to that school was closer than to other schools in Plattekill. (Courtesy of *Friends and Neighbors: A Pictorial History of the Town of Plattekill and Southwest Lloyd.*)

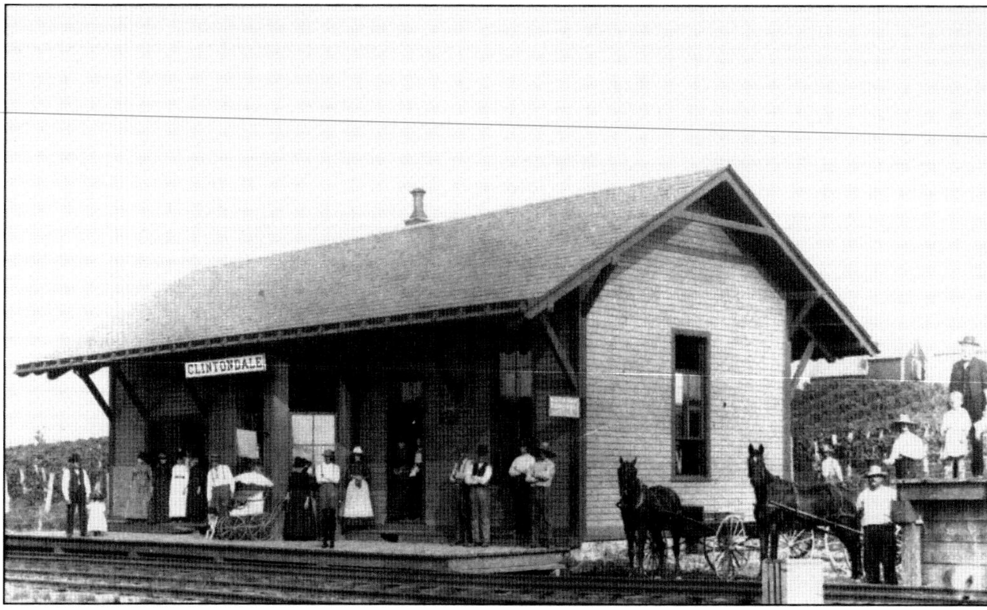

The Clintondale Station, pictured here around 1890, was actually located in the town of Lloyd, two miles away from the hamlet of Clintondale. Before Station Road was laid out on 1889, the depot was nearly inaccessible to those living nearby. The Clintondale Station building burned down in 1965. (Courtesy of *Friends and Neighbors: A Pictorial History of the Town of Plattekill and Southwest Lloyd.*)

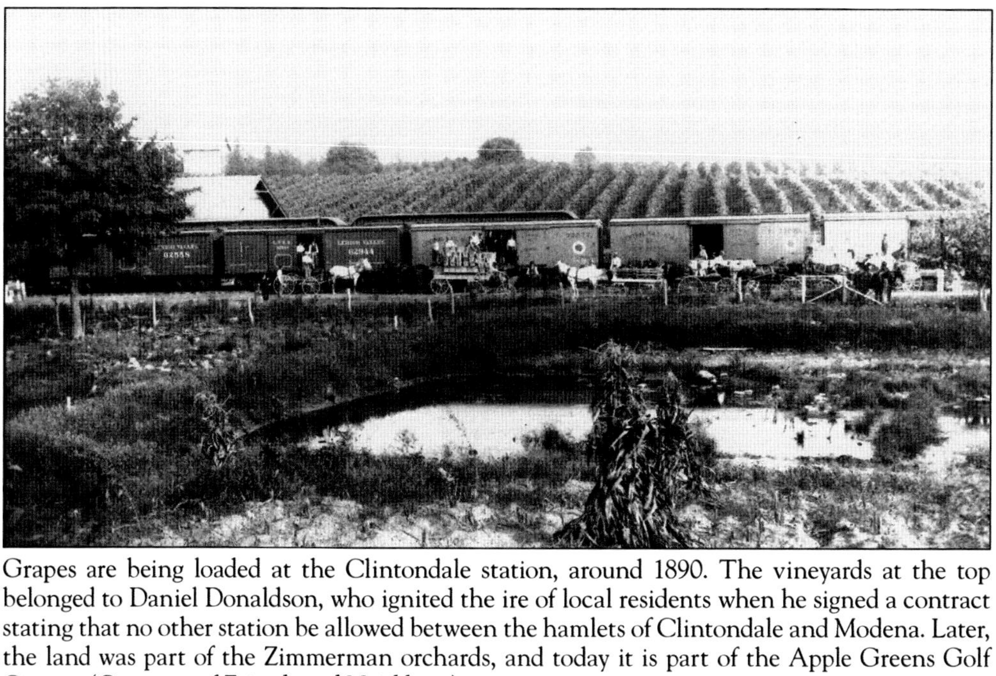

Grapes are being loaded at the Clintondale station, around 1890. The vineyards at the top belonged to Daniel Donaldson, who ignited the ire of local residents when he signed a contract stating that no other station be allowed between the hamlets of Clintondale and Modena. Later, the land was part of the Zimmerman orchards, and today it is part of the Apple Greens Golf Course. (Courtesy of *Friends and Neighbors.*)

The Modena Station was located near present-day Plate Road. The station burned down twice; first in 1890 and later in 1928. The station building was later moved to the Moran property and used as housing for migrant workers, where it burned down in the 1960s. Pictured here are Modena residents Eber Palmer (left) and Rolief Ward at the Modena station house. (Courtesy of Shirley Anson.)

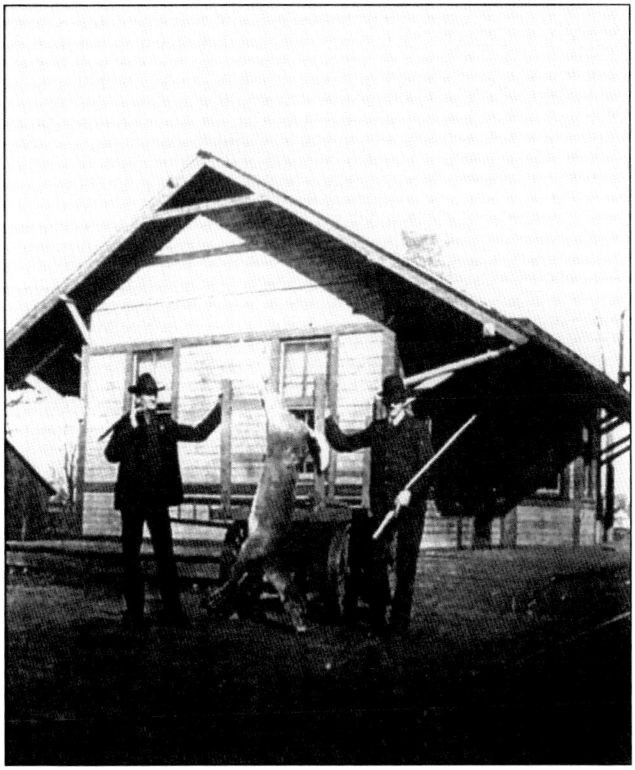

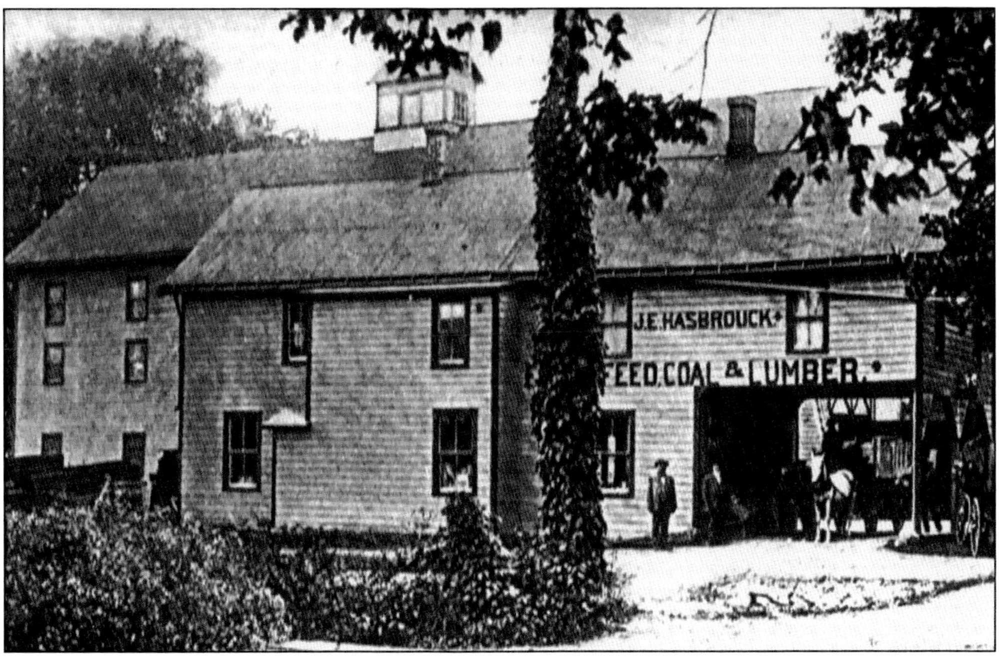

The coming of the railroad meant the arrival of new business opportunities for the town. J. E. Hasbrouck and A. P. Limeburner were both well-known businessmen who owned and operated coal, lumber, and feed yards. The Hasbrouck Feed, Coal and Lumber yards, pictured here in the early 1900s, were built around 1895. (Courtesy of the Office of the Plattekill Town Historian.)

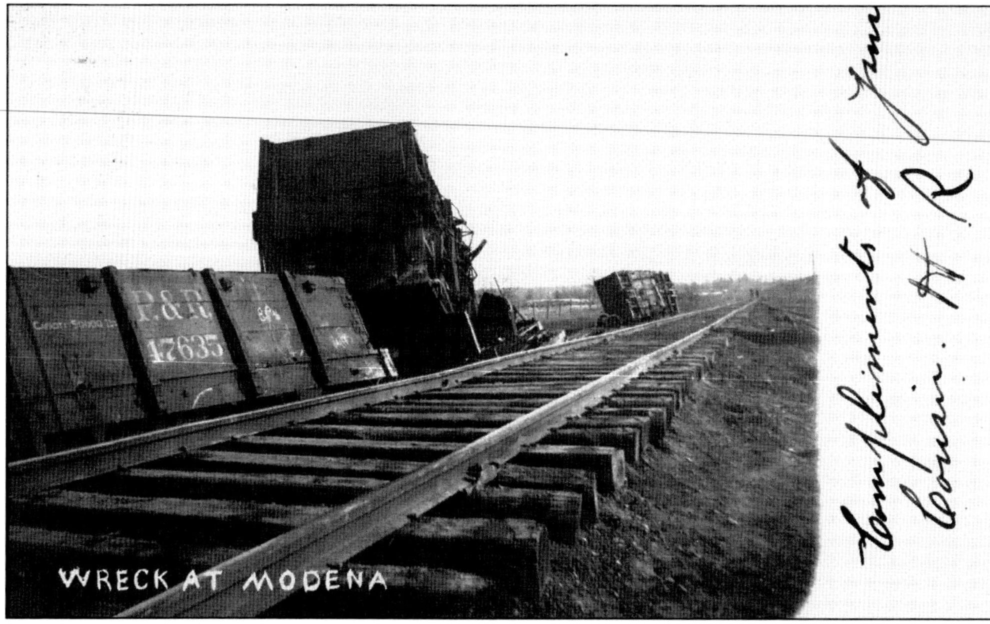

According to historian Shirley Anson, several accidents occurred in Plattekill while the rail lines were still active. In the late 1800s, someone tried to intentionally derail trains by setting rocks on the tracks while at least six people were killed crossing the tracks at various points in the town. Overpasses installed on Route 32 and Route 44/55 alleviated some of the problems. These early postcards depict at least one of the derailings that took place in Modena. Fires were also commonplace on the tracks, as sparks from the train would ignite the wooden tires and surrounding brush. (Courtesy of the Plattekill Historical Society.)

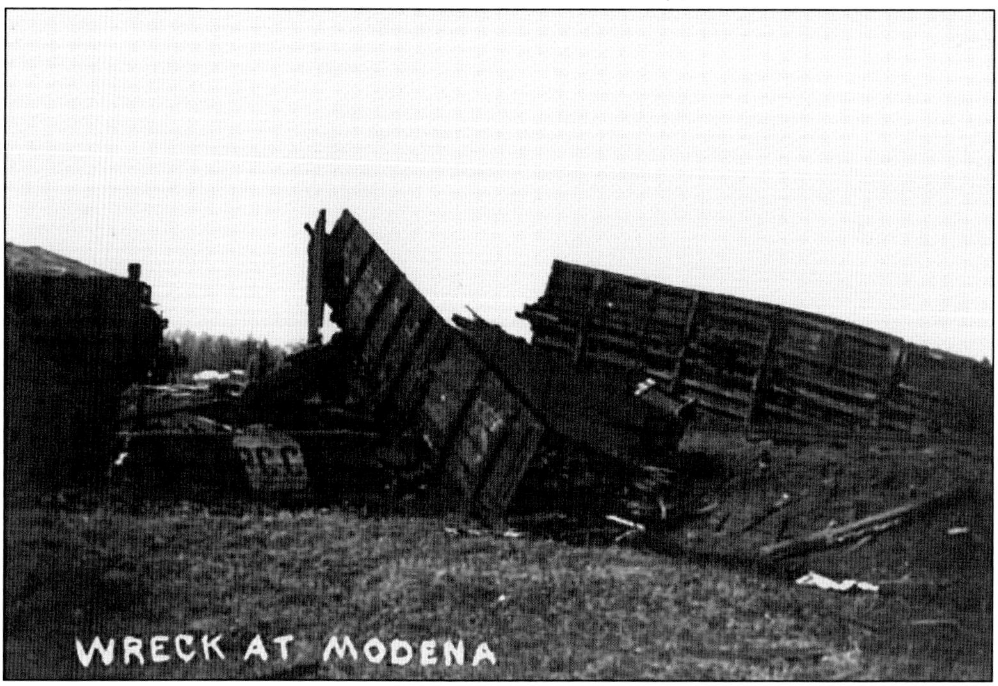

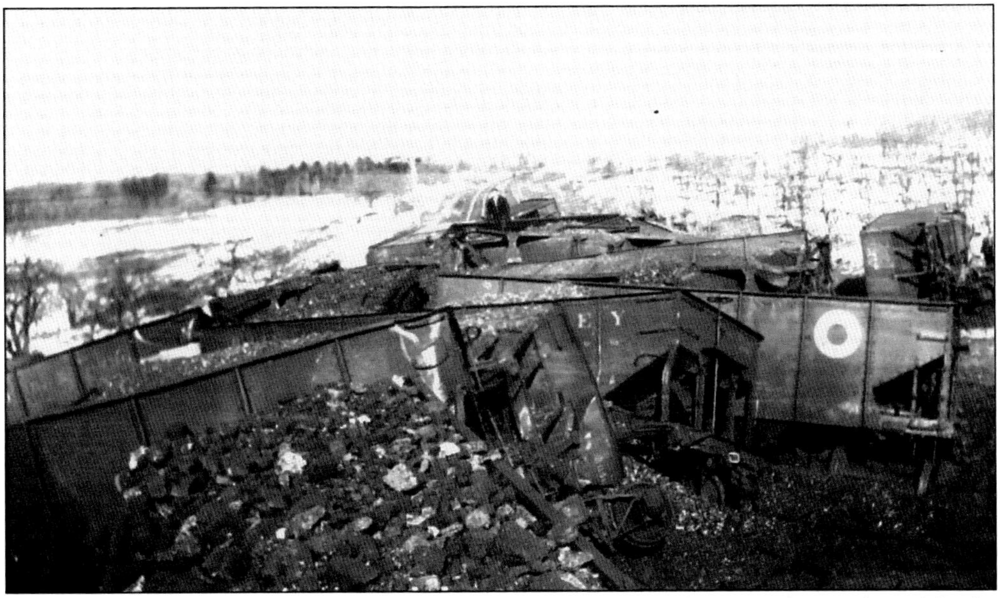

Signals installed at crossings throughout the town helped to cut down on the number of deaths caused by collisions with the trains, but train derailings continued. During the 1930s, at least three accidents occurred near the Clintondale Station, including one in 1936 that caused 10 freight cars to derail and sheared off a section of the Clintondale Station house. According to Anson, a station agent had left the building minutes before the accident took place. Reportedly he never again stood in the station house while a train was passing. The pictures here were taken sometime in the 1930s by Clintondale resident Anthony Palazzo Sr. (Courtesy of *Friends and Neighbors: A Pictorial History of the Town of Plattekill and Southwest Lloyd.*)

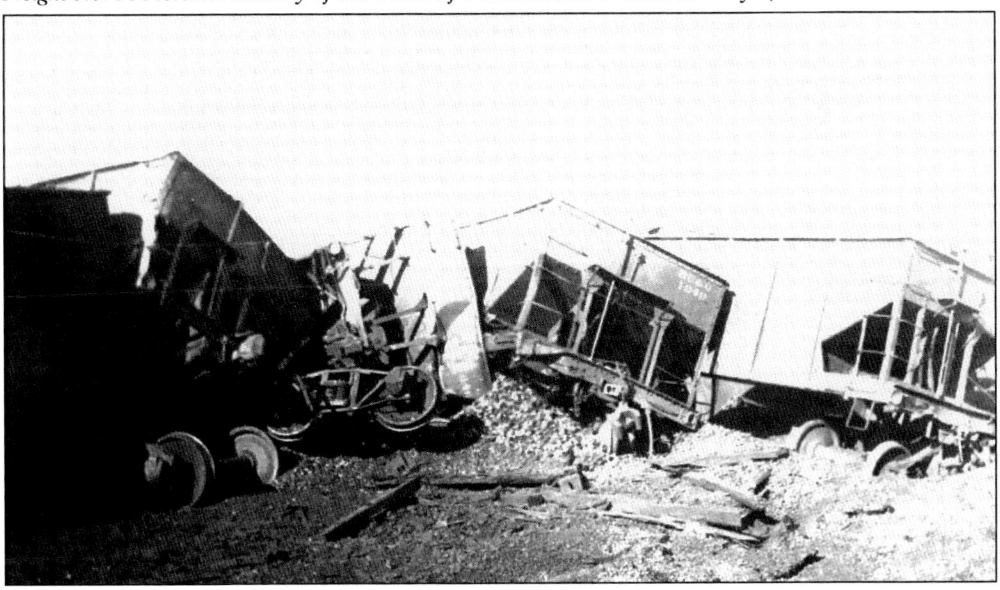

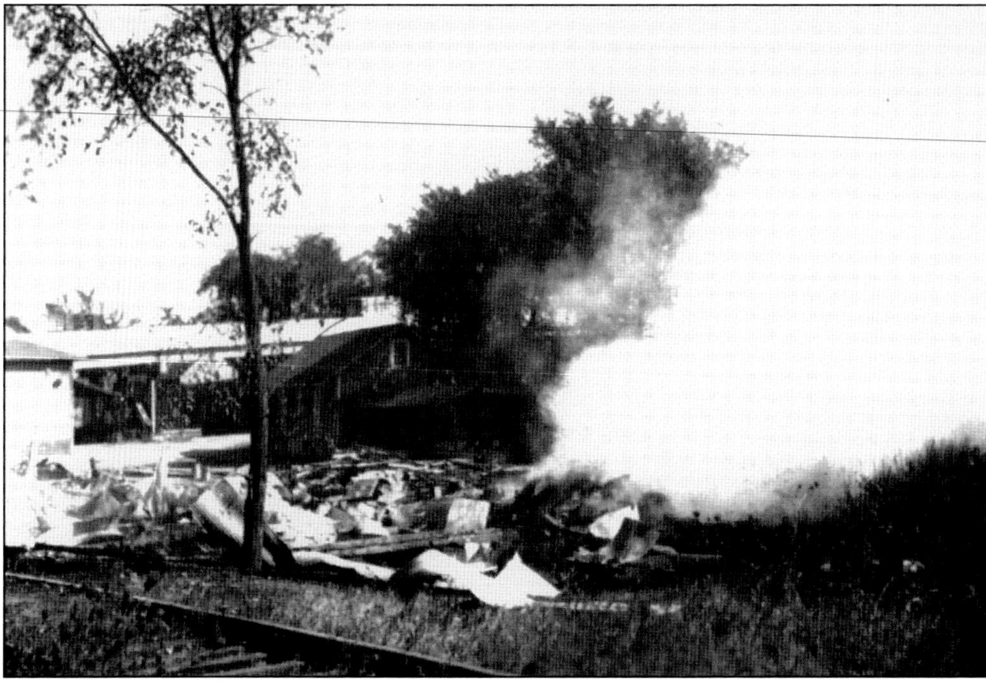

A 1948 fire burned two buildings and a lumber shed at the Hasbrouck lumberyards. The fire then spread to piles of lumber and a third building. Local newspapers at the time reported the cost of the damage to be between $15,000 and $20,000. The fire, along with others in the area during the same time frame, were believed to have been deliberately set. The railroad tracks can be seen in the foreground of both pictures, while the Route 44/55 bridge over the railroad, built in the 1930s to accommodate increasing traffic through Modena, can be seen at top. (Courtesy of the Office of the Plattekill Town Historian.)

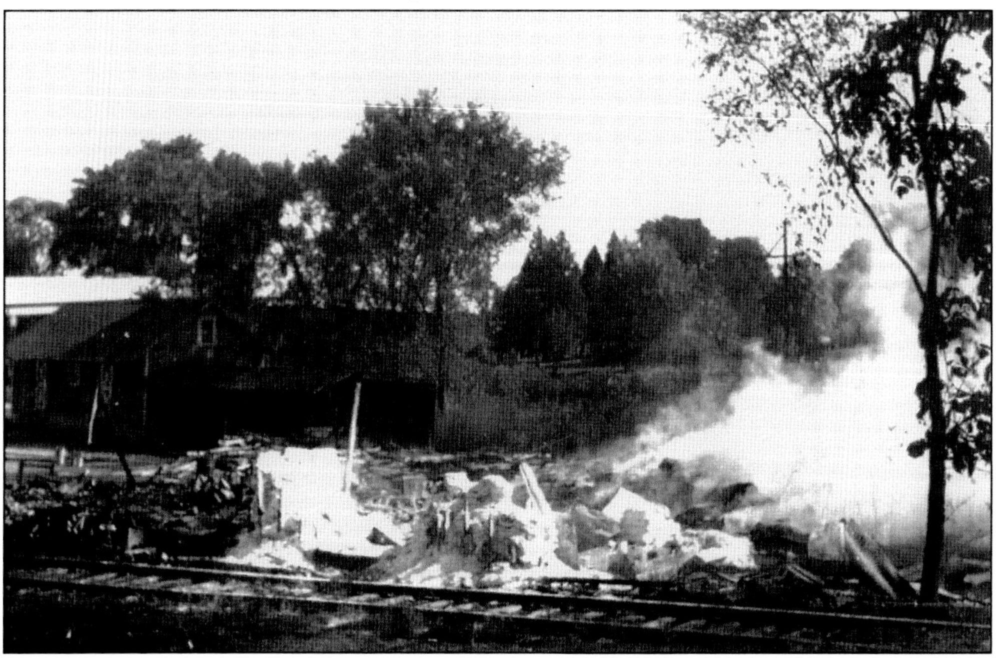

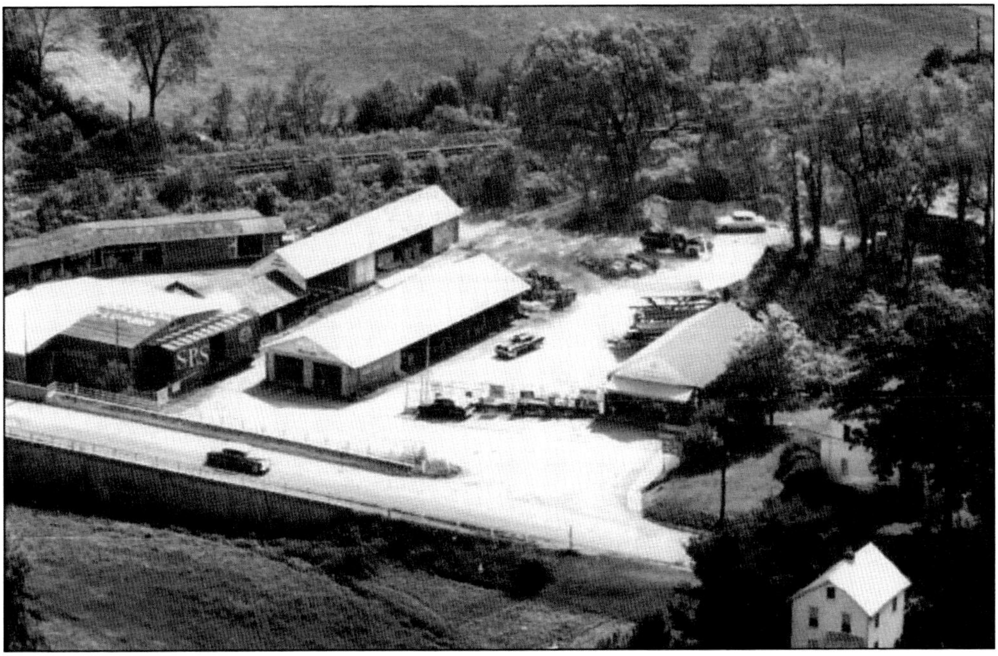

Pictured here is an aerial view of the Hasbrouck lumberyard as it appeared in the 1950s or 1960s. Portions of the yard burned in 1932 and later in 1948, with its buildings rebuilt both times. The land in the foreground is part of the Plattekill Town Hall property today. The road is Route 44/55, just east of the Route 32 intersection. (Courtesy of *Friends and Neighbors: A Pictorial History of the Town of Plattekill and Southwest Lloyd.*)

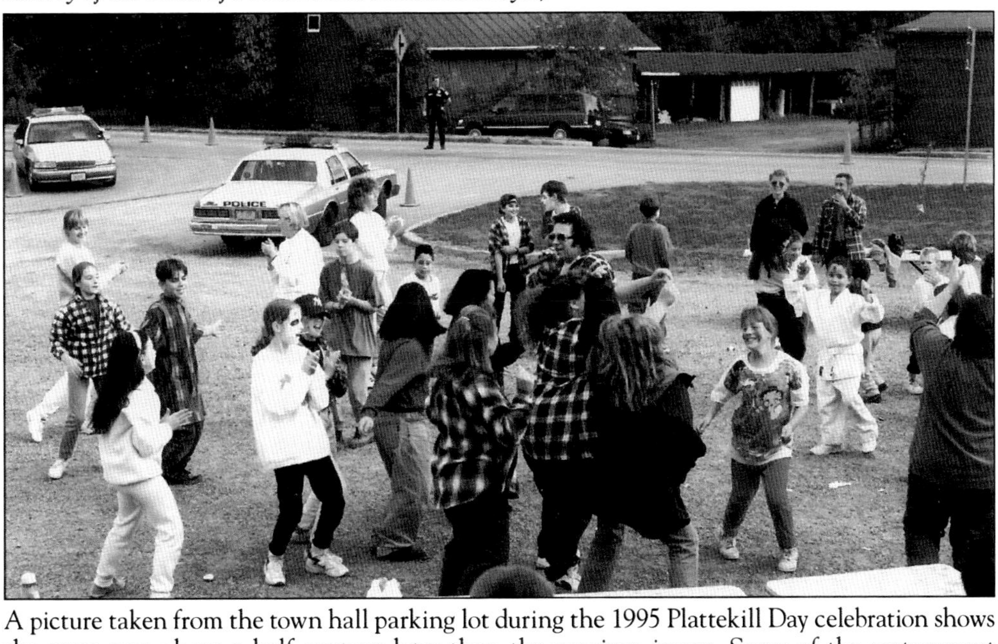

A picture taken from the town hall parking lot during the 1995 Plattekill Day celebration shows the same area about a half century later than the previous image. Some of the easternmost buildings in the former Hasbrouck lumberyard were still standing, while the Route 44/55 bridge had been taken down. Today the area where the buildings are pictured is now an access road to Route 32. (Courtesy of the Office of the Plattekill Town Historian.)

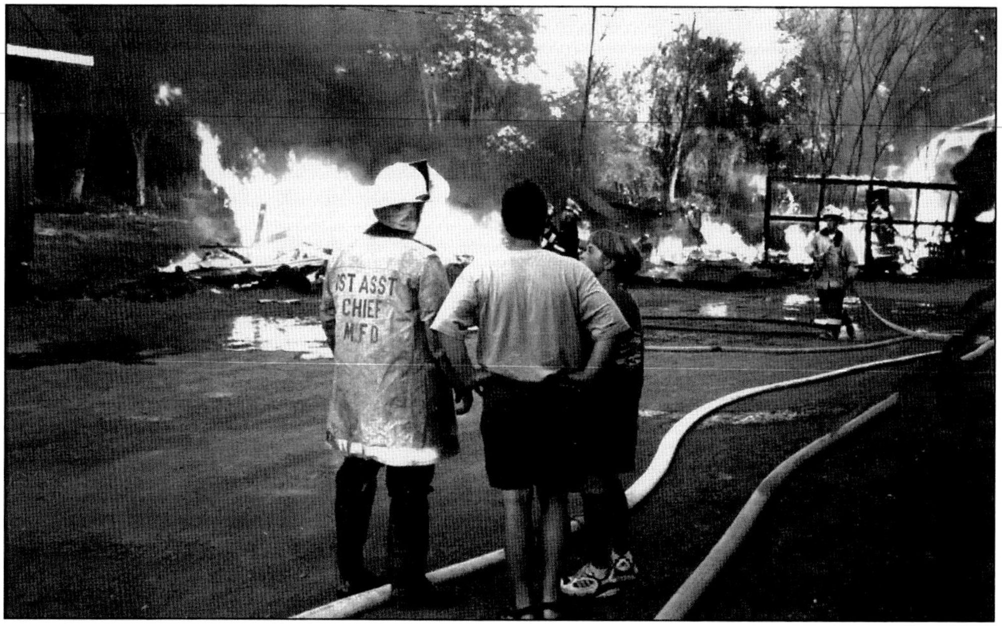

Only a few buildings from the original lumberyard are left standing today. Several of the buildings that had fallen into disrepair were burned down by the Modena Fire Department as part of a drill in 1997. Today part of the property is used as an access road for the Hannaford grocery store and Route 32 while remaining buildings house small businesses including a pizzeria and a beauty salon. (Courtesy of author's collection.)

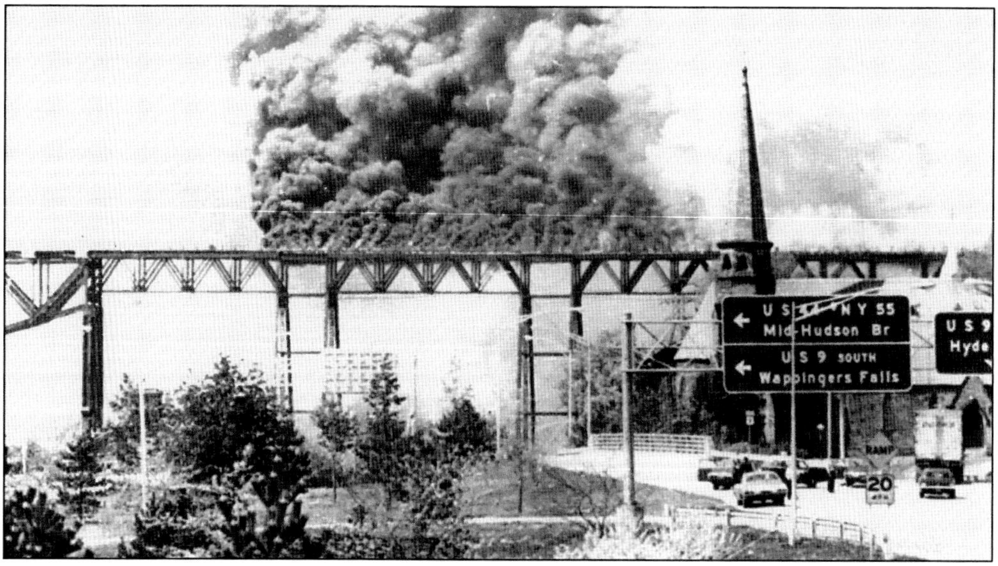

On May 8, 1974, the Poughkeepsie portion of the Poughkeepsie railroad bridge caught fire, shortly after a train crossed from the Highland side of the river. Water lines on the bridge that had not been properly maintained were of little use in helping to fight the fire, and more than 700 feet of the bridge was burned beyond repair. The first bridge to span the Hudson River became the first to be abandoned as well. With managing company Pennsylvania Central Railroad already bankrupt, the bridge was declared irreparable and rail traffic on the western side of the Hudson River reduced to local runs. (Courtesy of Shirley Anson.)

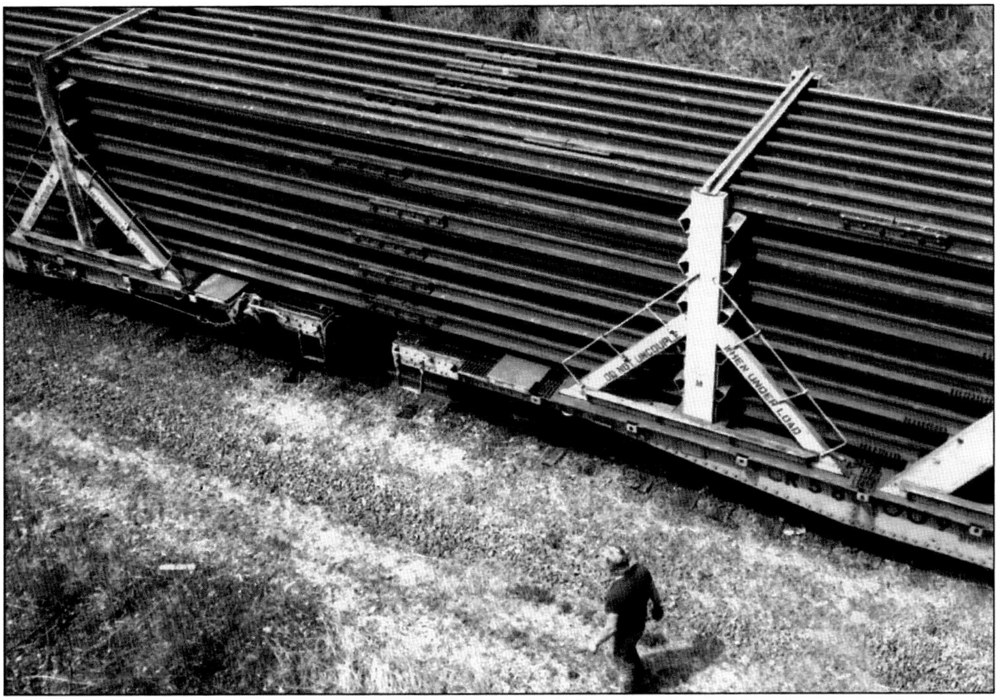

Extensive damage to the Poughkeepsie bridge reduced rail traffic to local runs in the 1970s. Trains continued to move through Plattekill to reach Central Hudson and the Pratt lumber yards in Lloyd until 1982. By 1983, the rails were removed, as shown here in pictures taken from the Route 32 bridge. The bridges on Route 44/55 and Route 32 were taken down the following year. (Photographs by Shirley Anson.)

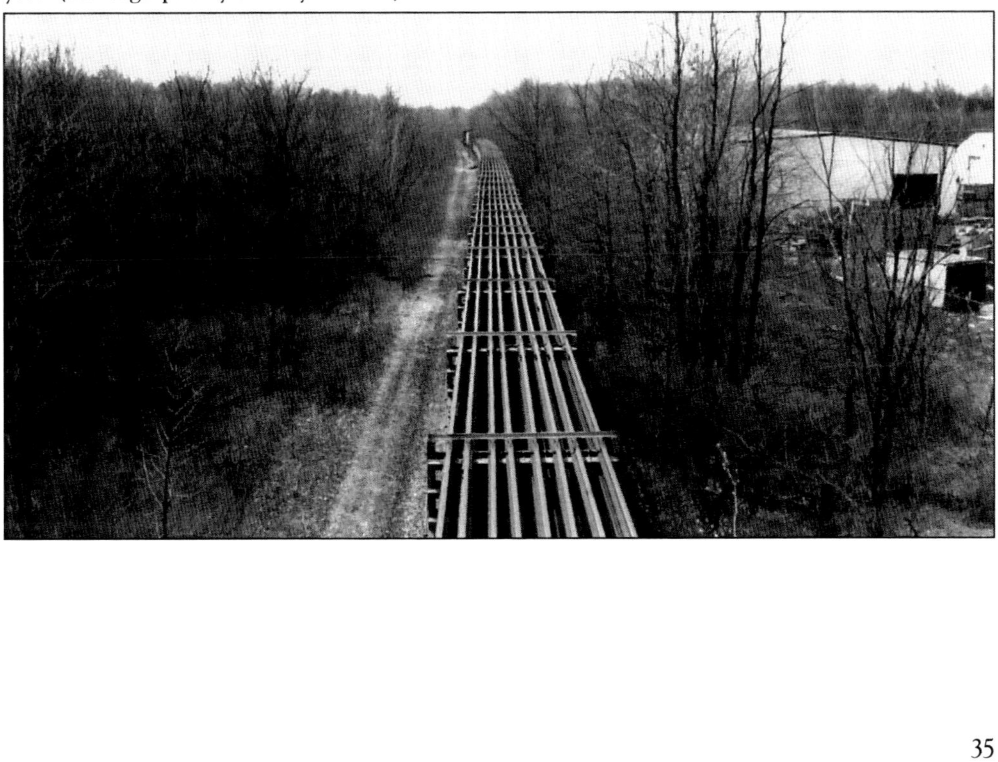

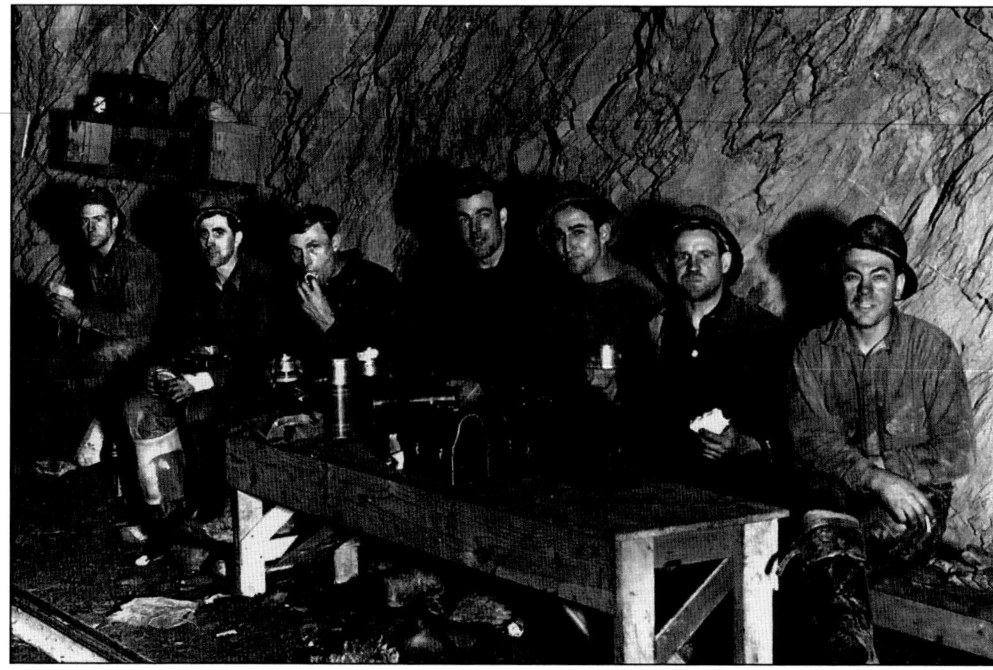

In 1937, work began on the Plattekill shaft No. 5 of the New York City aqueduct system. According to Alfred Cole of Highland, workers ate together in the shaft as they had to stay underground for the entire shift. Cole normally worked the graveyard shift (11:00 p.m. to 7:00 a.m.) and remembered these pictures being taken of workers on the daytime shift (7:00 a.m. to 3:00 p.m.). (Courtesy of Shirley Anson.)

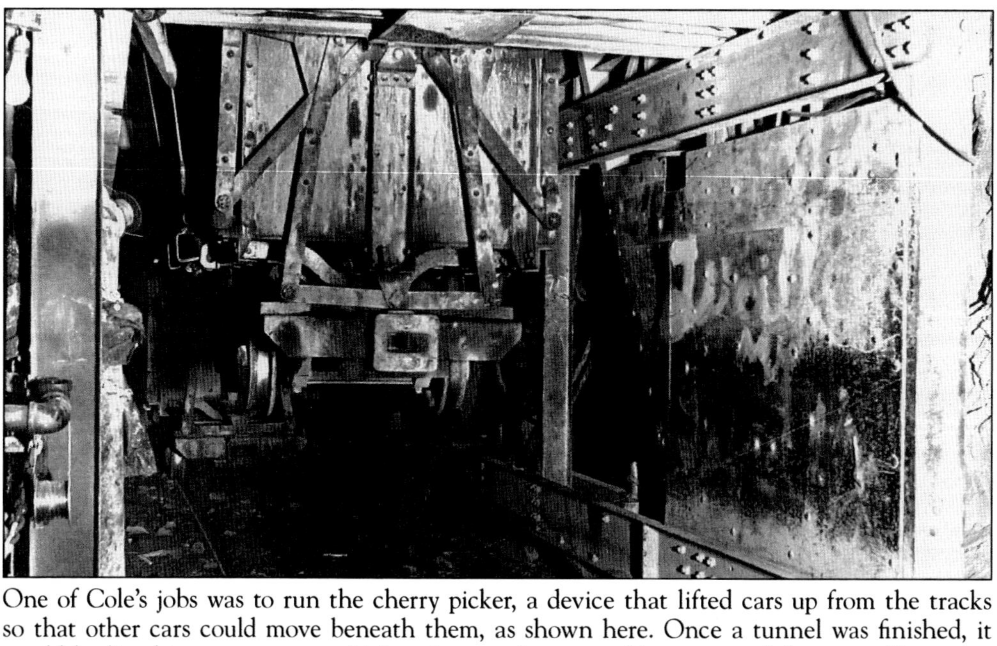

One of Cole's jobs was to run the cherry picker, a device that lifted cars up from the tracks so that other cars could move beneath them, as shown here. Once a tunnel was finished, it would be lined in concrete, at which point another one of his responsibilities would involve drilling holes through the overhead concrete to help push out any air pockets. (Courtesy of Shirley Anson.)

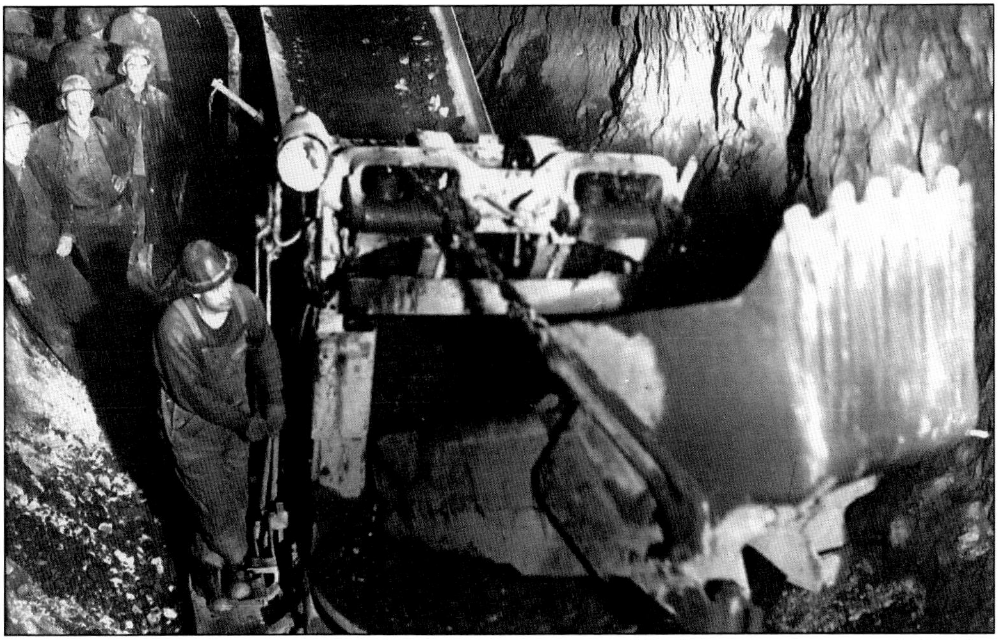

One worker operates a digging machine to remove dirt and load it onto a conveyor belt. The belt brought the soil to cars which then brought it to the surface. Workers in this section were digging from the Plattekill No. 5 shaft to the Marlborough No. 5A shaft. (Courtesy of Shirley Anson.)

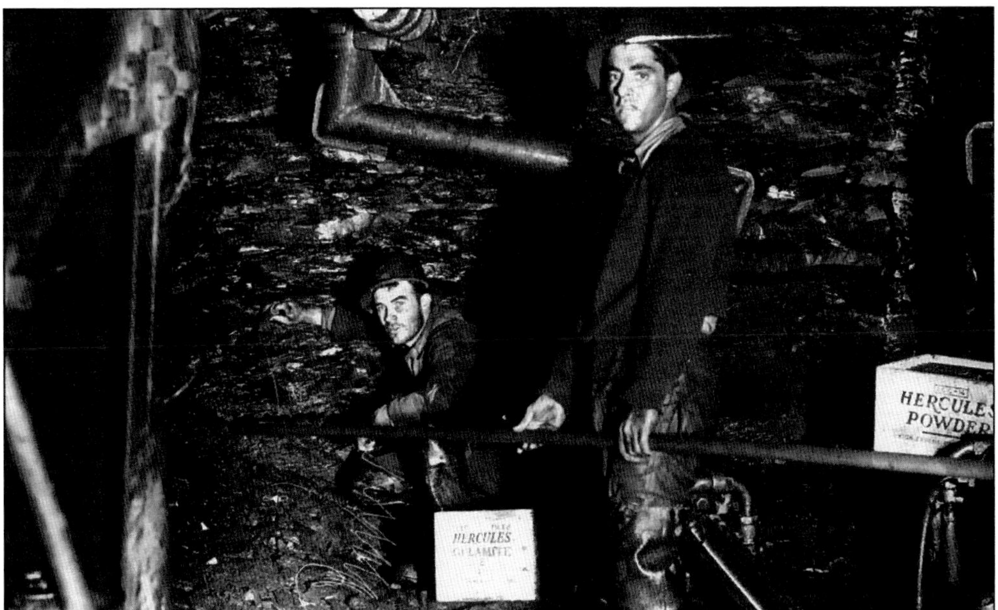

These two men are workers setting blasting caps into the holes. While the blasting occurred, the men would remain in the tunnels, about 150 feet away. Once the smoke and debris were cleared and the area was deemed safe, workers would return to the area. Despite the potential danger, Cole recalled only two job-related deaths during the time he worked on the aqueduct. (Courtesy of Shirley Anson.)

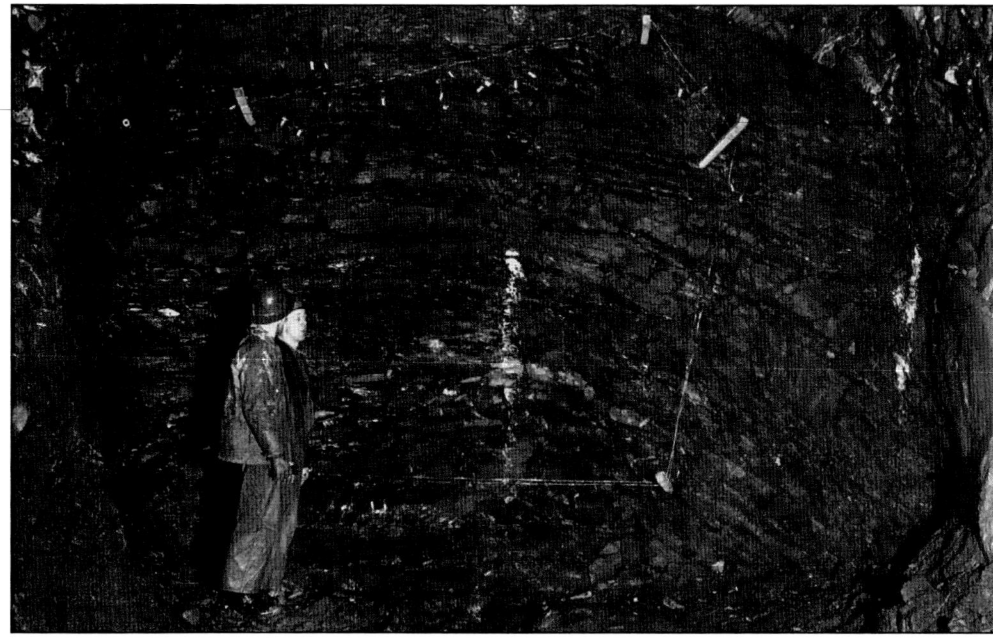

Aqueduct workers stand near wires set up in the next area to be blasted. The areas were wired on a delay, so that they would not blast simultaneously. Dust and debris from the blast were vented outside of the tunnel through an underground ventilation system. (Courtesy of Shirley Anson.)

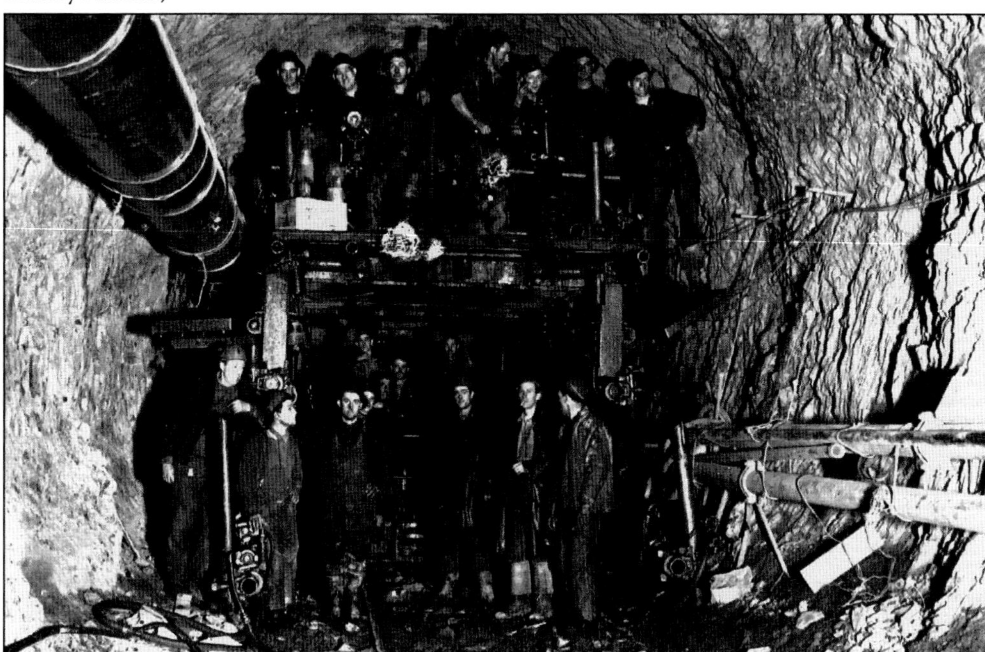

Workers pose near drilling machinery within one of the tunnels. The metal tube seen in the left of the picture had a reverse mechanism installed so that it could be used to vent smoke and dust from the tunnel or could pump in oxygen. Pipes housing water and electric service for the tunnels can be seen on the right of the picture. (Courtesy of Shirley Anson.)

Three

Religious and Educational Life

The earliest settlers in the town of Plattekill met in each other's homes for worship but by the late 1700s were looking to build permanent structures to house their churches. As early as 1767, the first formal application was made by members of the Dutch Reformed congregation to form a church in the town of Shawangunk. The high grounds near what was to become New Hurley in the town of Plattekill provided the site for a church, and by 1774, the first church was constructed. In the area of present-day Plattekill and Clintondale, members of the Plattekill Valley Friends were able to begin work on a meeting house by 1794. Since those times, Plattekill has been home to many other churches and religions. At the present, seven churches remain active in town.

The earliest schoolhouses were also the homes of early settlers. By the mid-1800s, numerous "neighborhood schools" had been built throughout the town, and by the 1880s, Plattekill had at least 10 public schools, many of them one- or two-room schoolhouses. The centralization of the Wallkill and Highland School Districts in the 1940s effectively closed most of the neighborhood schools and the Modena School was the only neighborhood school to remain open after centralization. Today, the former Ardonia School building still stands and serves as the Plattekill Police Department office while the former Modena School is used today as the Plattekill Library and the Plattekill Senior Center. The rest of the early schools are long gone, having been either torn down or remodeled as private residences.

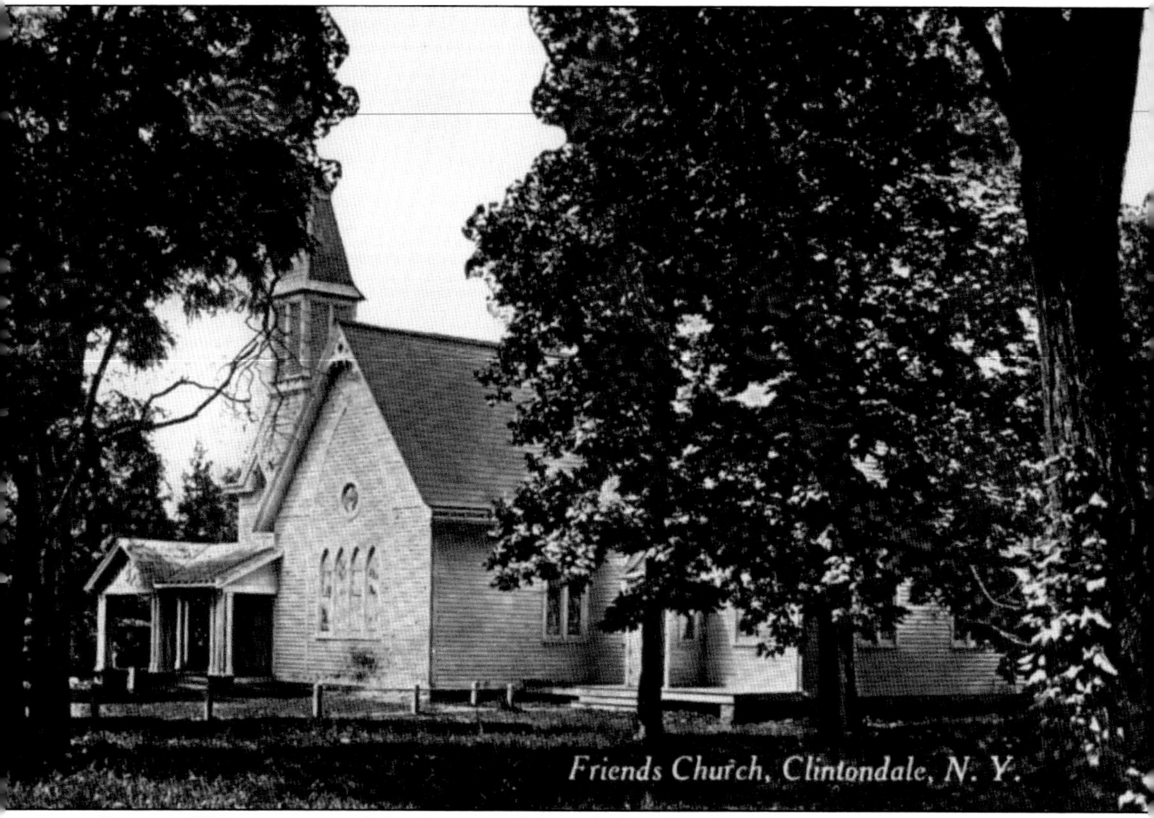

Prior to 1790, meetings of the Society of Friends (Quakers) were held in private homes in the area that is present-day Clintondale. The first Quaker meetinghouse in Clintondale was built in 1811, along what is today Crescent Avenue. Prior to that time, meetings were held in Plattekill or at homes in Clintondale. The post and beam structure, along with the property upon which it was erected, cost about $300. The original building was moved across the street in 1889 when the new meetinghouse was built (pictured here in a postcard view) and used as a funeral home, a Temperance Hall, a private residence, and then stood empty for many years. In 1983, members of the Clintondale Friends Church helped to move the structure back to the church grounds, to a site near the original. A 100-year anniversary celebration of the new meetinghouse was held in 1989, at which time the original meetinghouse was dedicated. (Courtesy of Shirley Anson.)

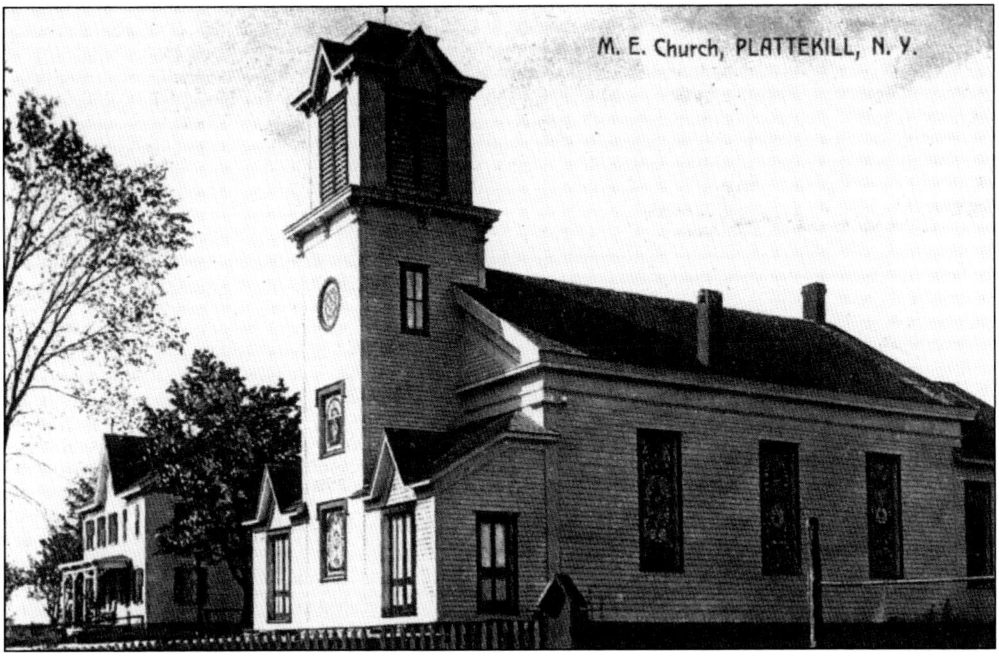

At one point, the town of Plattekill was home to four different Methodist churches, in Clintondale, Ardonia, Plattekill, and Modena. Pictured here is a postcard of the Plattekill Methodist Episcopal Church, which was built in 1840 (above). To the left of the church is the parsonage. The church stood near the Plattekill Community Grounds Cemetery but was torn down in 1969 when the churches in Plattekill, Clintondale, and Modena merged. At right is a program from a 1933 Christmas music festival held at the church. Many of the family names noted on the program are still found in Plattekill today. Today only the Modena Memorial United Methodist church remains an active congregation. (Courtesy of Shirley Anson.)

Christmas Music Festival

of the

Plattekill M. E. Church Choir

assisted by

Mme. Caryl Bensel, Dramatic Soprano

Friday Evening, December 29th, 1933

at 8:15 at the Church, Plattekill, N. Y.

CHOIR

SOPRANO

Miss Susie Fosler
Miss Dorothy Fowler
Mrs. Herbert W. Hahn
Mrs. V. B. Wager
Miss Viola Loertscher
Miss Alice Stoneberg
Miss Ethel B. Lozier

ALTO

Mrs. Arthur Diener
Miss Elizabeth T. Fosler
Mrs. Dorothy M. Sullivan
Miss Gertrude Topping

TENOR

Mr. Arthur H. Fosler
Mr. L. C. Ratcliff
Mr. Chas. Stoneberg

BASS

Mr. Myron E. Fosler
Rev. Herbert W. Hahn
Mr. S. J. White
Mr. Milton F. Van Duzer

ACCOMPANISTS

Miss Marion R. Harris
Mrs. Herbert W. Hahn

Conductor, Mr. Joseph Bensel

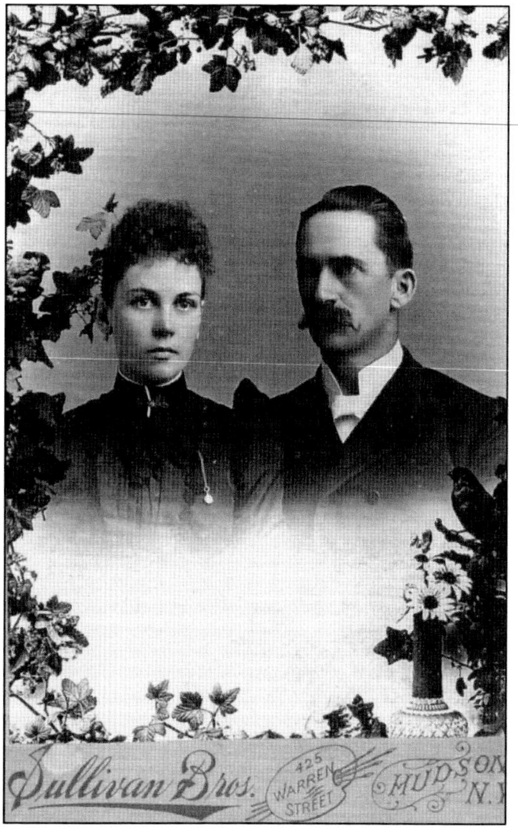

The Reverend Joel Henry Lincoln was the pastor of both the Plattekill Methodist Episcopal Church and the Rossville Church in the town of Newburgh. Lincoln was born in 1858 in the town of Chester, Orange County, and died in 1952 in Kingston. This picture, from around 1909, is of Lincoln and his wife, Carrie. (Courtesy of Shirley Anson.)

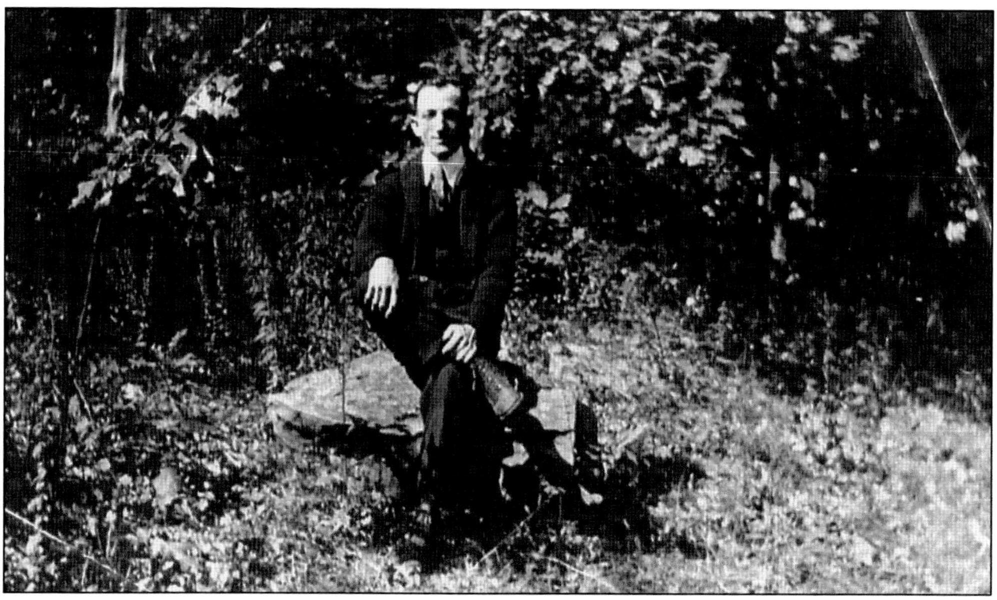

Herman Otto Nagle was the minister of the Plattekill Methodist Episcopal Church from April 1923 to April 1925. While he was the pastor, Nagle's son, Wilbur Frederick Nagle, was born. This picture of Herman was taken around 1923 on the church grounds in Plattekill. (Courtesy of Shirley Anson.)

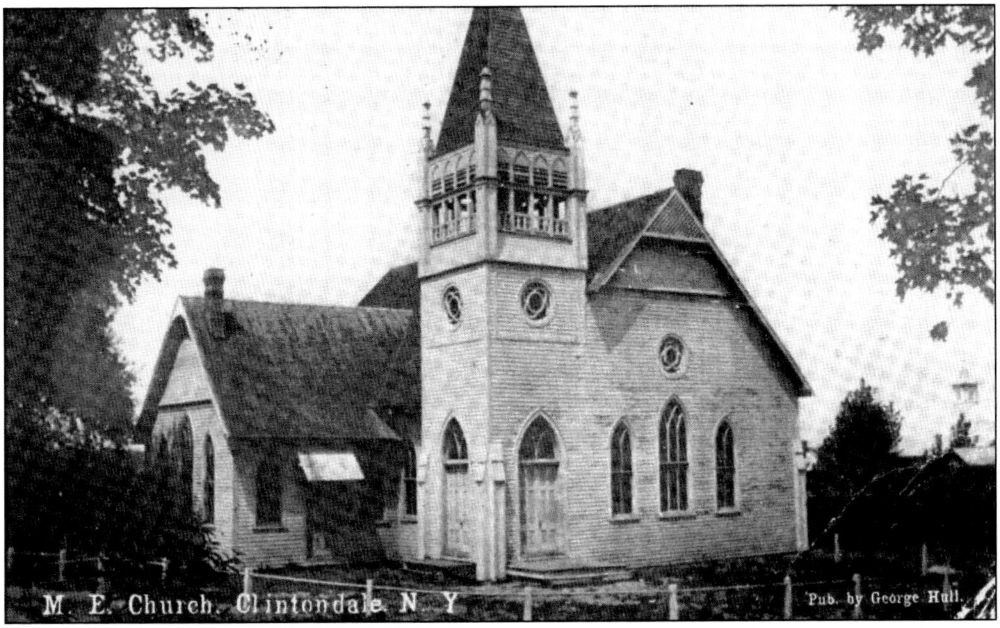

The Clintondale Methodist Episcopal Church, pictured here around 1909, was built in 1894 at the corner of Route 44/55 and Maple Avenue. Originally Clintondale residents attended church at the East Plattekill Methodist Church in Ardonia. Later services were held at a chapel on Maple Avenue. In 1872, the Methodist Church building in Lattintown was dismantled and rebuilt in Clintondale. A new church was built in 1894. (Courtesy of Shirley Anson.)

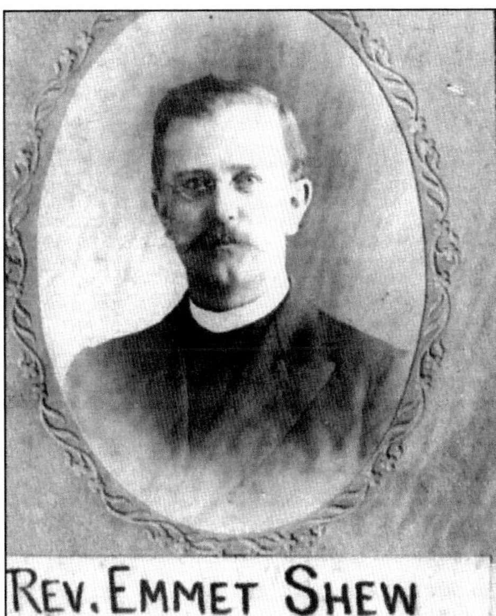

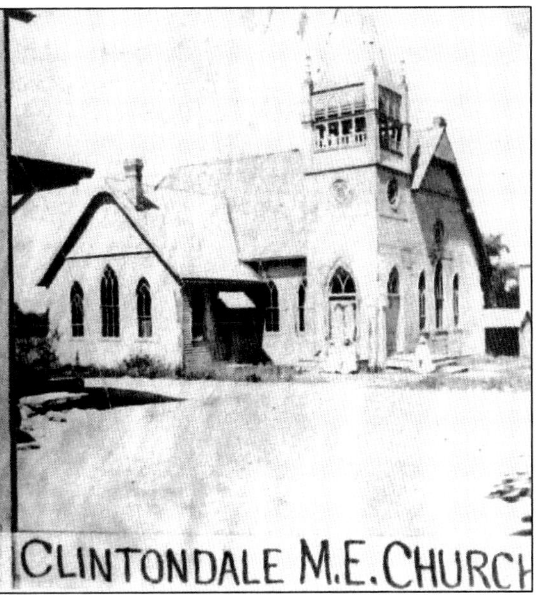

Rev. Emmit Shew served the Clintondale Methodist Episcopal Church from 1902 to 1905. The church's first minister was S. G. Keyser, who served from 1872 to 1873. In their 1959 history, Jerome and Elizabeth Hurd, and Ralph and Alice Van Siclen report that since the church's beginnings, "there have been the participation by its ministers in christenings, weddings, funerals; the ministering to the sick and sorrowing; counseling to the troubled." (Courtesy of Shirley Anson.)

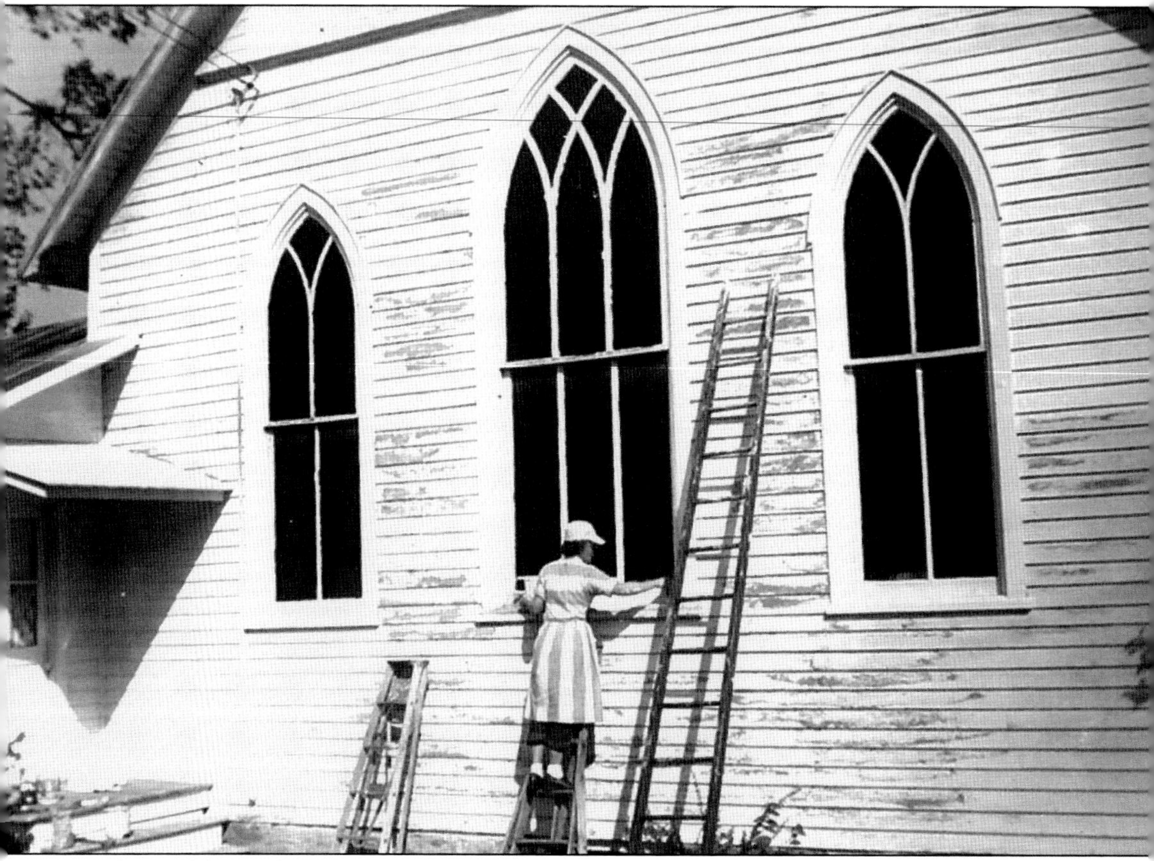

Clintondale resident Kay Lyons is pictured painting the Clintondale Methodist Episcopal Church sometime in the 1940s. From its beginnings, the church was supported by community effort. Clintondale teacher P. N. Mitchell wrote and sold copies of his 1894 *History of the Village of Clintondale* to raise funds for the building of the church, while area quilters sold quilt squares to pay the mortgage on the building. (Courtesy of Plattekill Historical Society.)

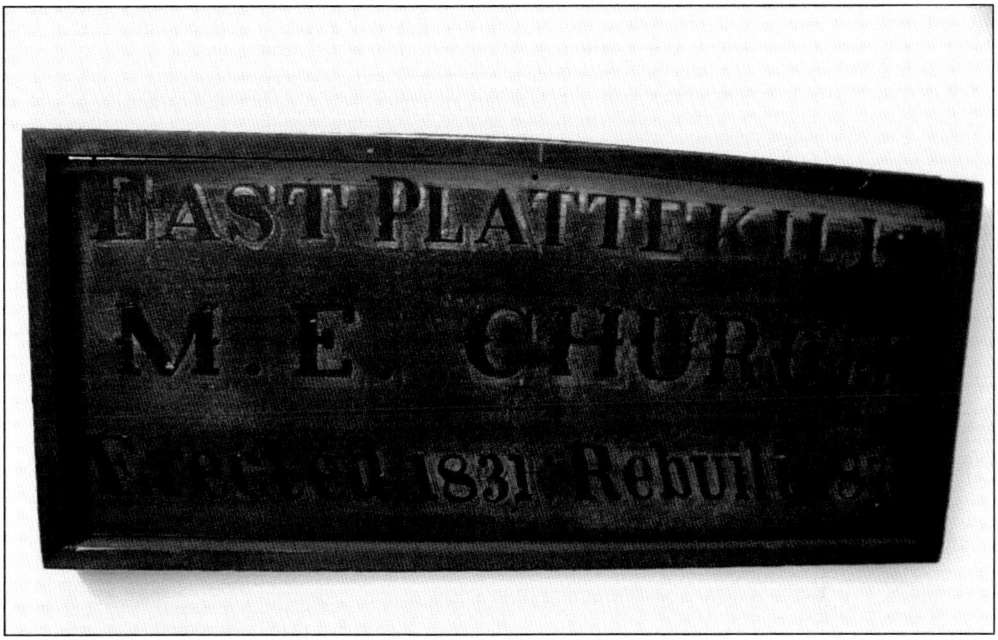

The East Plattekill Methodist Episcopal Church along Milton Turnpike in Ardonia was built in 1829. When it closed its doors for the last time in 1908, the steeple was removed, the church bell was relocated to the Rossville Church in Newburgh, and the building renovated into a private residence. Pictured here is a sign from the original church discovered in the attic of the building. (Courtesy of Sue Coy Doyle.)

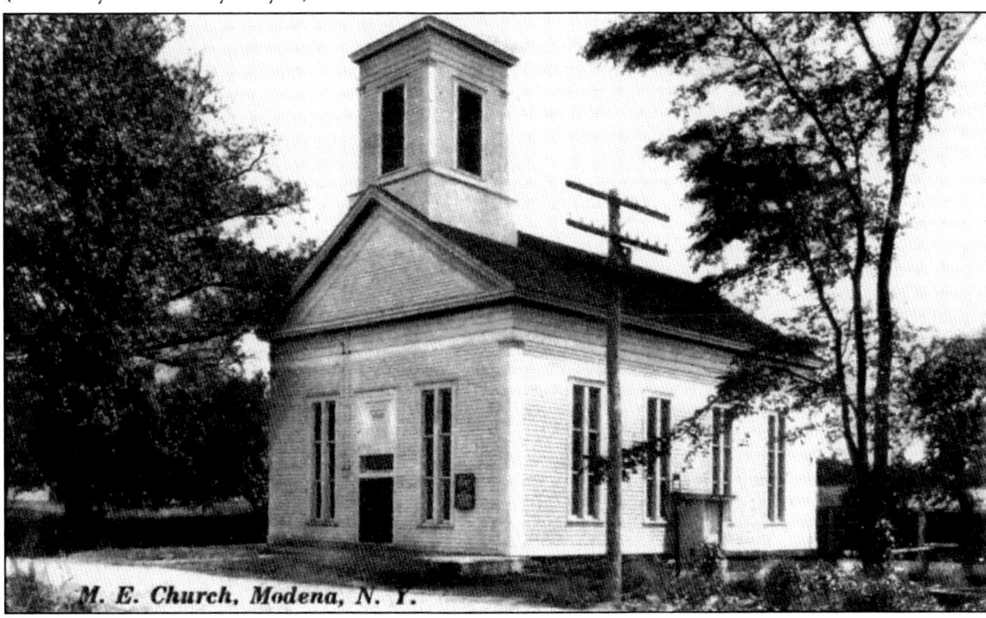

Pictured here is the Modena Memorial United Methodist Church, built in 1855. The first Methodist church in Modena was built in 1826 and was replaced by this structure in 1855. When the Methodist churches in Plattekill merged in 1969, this church became the only remaining Methodist church within the town. In 2005, the church celebrated its 150-year anniversary with a special camp meeting anniversary service. (Courtesy of Shirley Anson.)

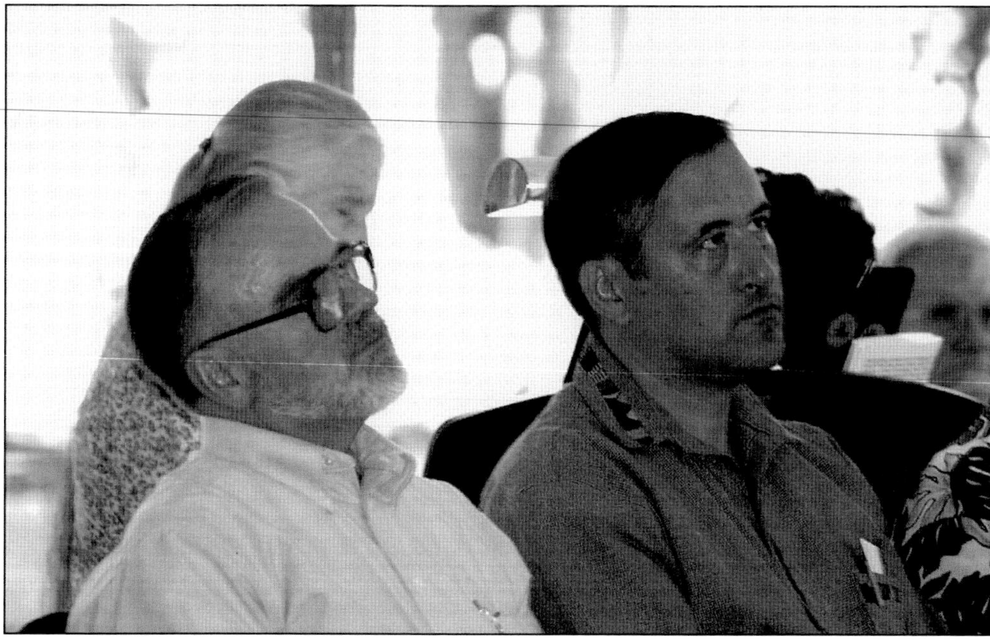

Rev. Dan Whitley (left) of the Clintondale Friends Church and Rev. David Mantz of the Modena Memorial United Methodist Church are pictured here at the 150-year anniversary camp meeting service held on Sunday, November 6, 2005. A daylong anniversary celebration included guest speakers, musical and dance performances, and a special service in the style of an old-time camp meeting. (Photograph by Elizabeth Werlau, reprinted from the *Southern Ulster Times*.)

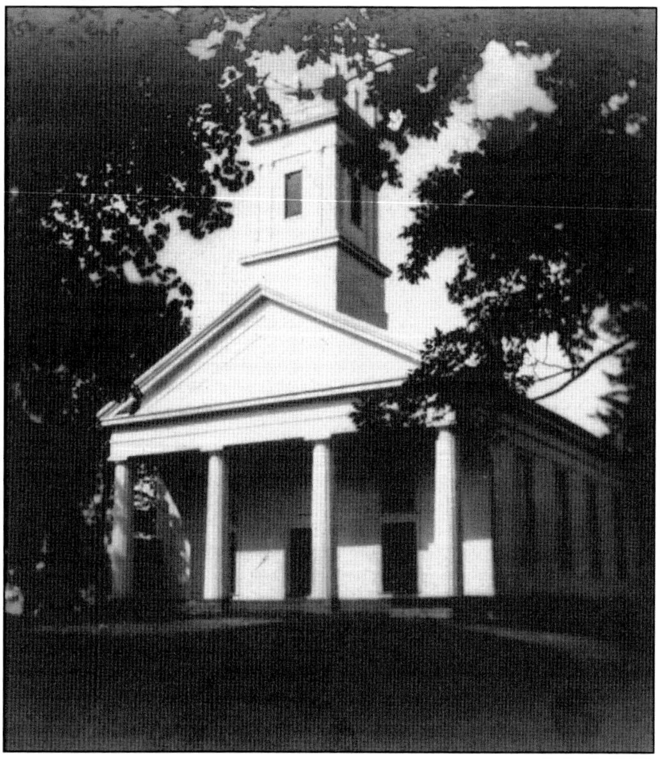

Land for the New Hurley Reformed Church (pictured here) was purchased from Denne Relyea on December 21, 1773, for five shillings. A rough building was erected on the site by 1774. The parsonage property was purchased in 1828 from Jabez Munson for $1,125. The current church and parsonage were built in 1835, while the church hall was built in the 1950s by Clintondale contractor Lawrence Morse. (Courtesy of Shirley Anson.)

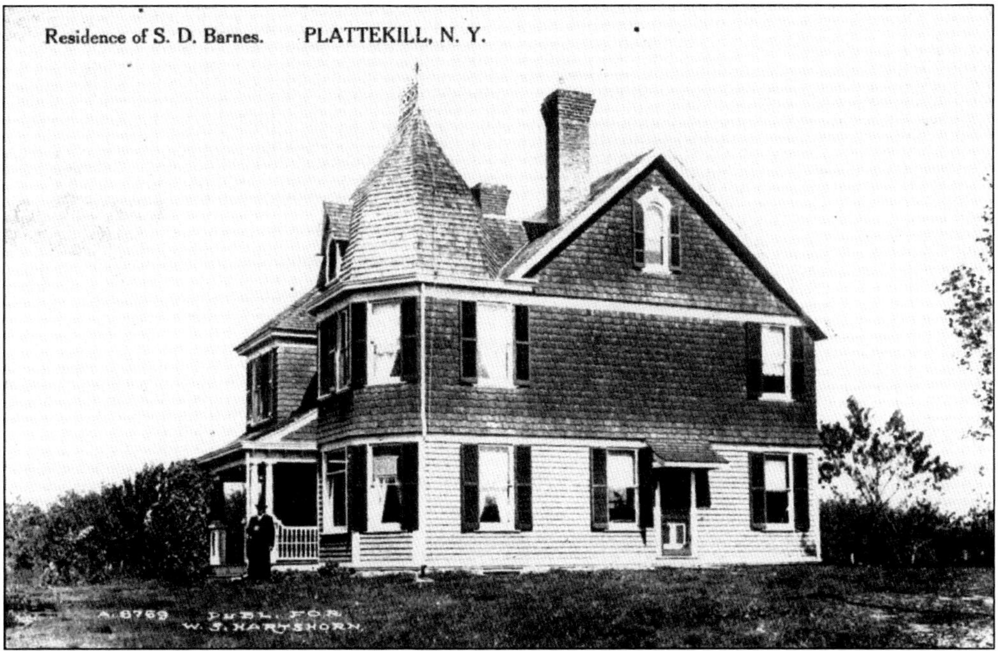

The Barnes residence, pictured here on a postcard from the 1930s, became the rectory of the Our Lady of Fatima Catholic Church, the first permanent Catholic church in Plattekill. In the early 1940s, masses were said in Plattekill by the Reverend George B. Fagan of New Paltz, who would conduct services at various locales, including Simon's Inn on Unionville Road and in a local packing house. (Courtesy of author's collection.)

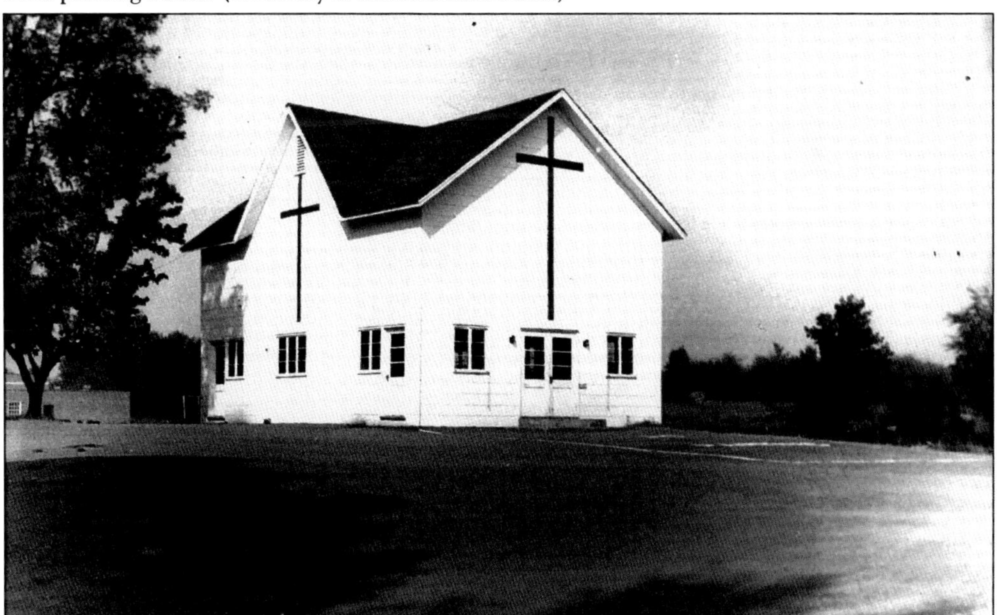

In February 1949, Plattekill residents Patrick Fleming, Charles Martino, Albert Moran, and Francis Murphy took loans against their own property to purchase Doris Deiner's house and barn so that Plattekill would have a permanent Catholic church. The stable of the barn became the original church, shown here, which has since been expanded. (Courtesy of Micki Obermeyer.)

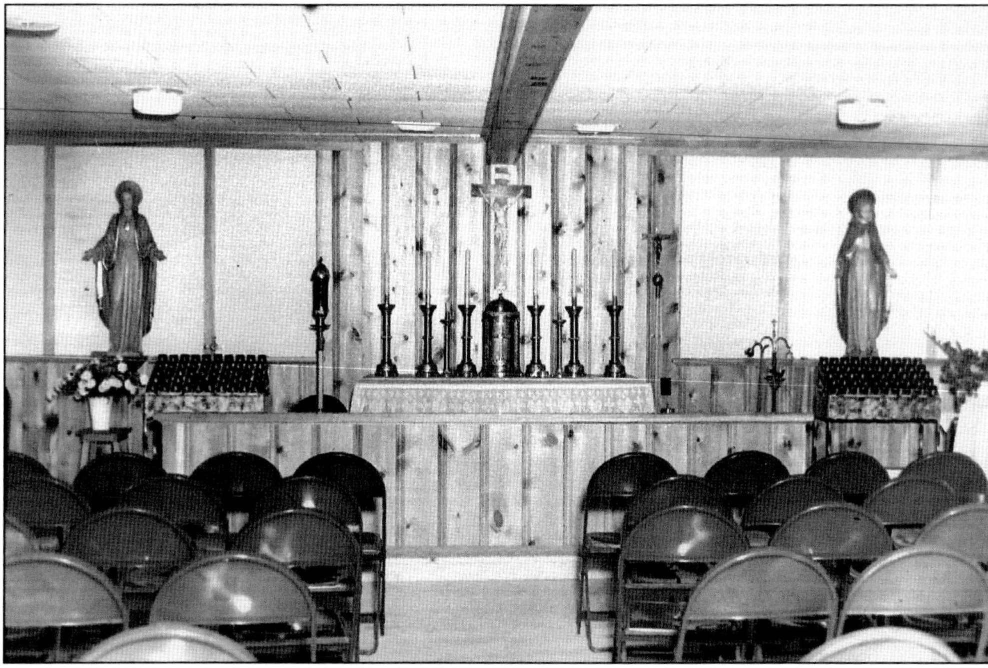

While the former barn was being converted into a church, mass was held in the house on the property. When finished, the stable became the alter of the new church, shown here. The first mass in the former barn was said on July 1, 1950, by the Reverend John Mahoney of New Paltz. (Courtesy of Micki Obermeyer.)

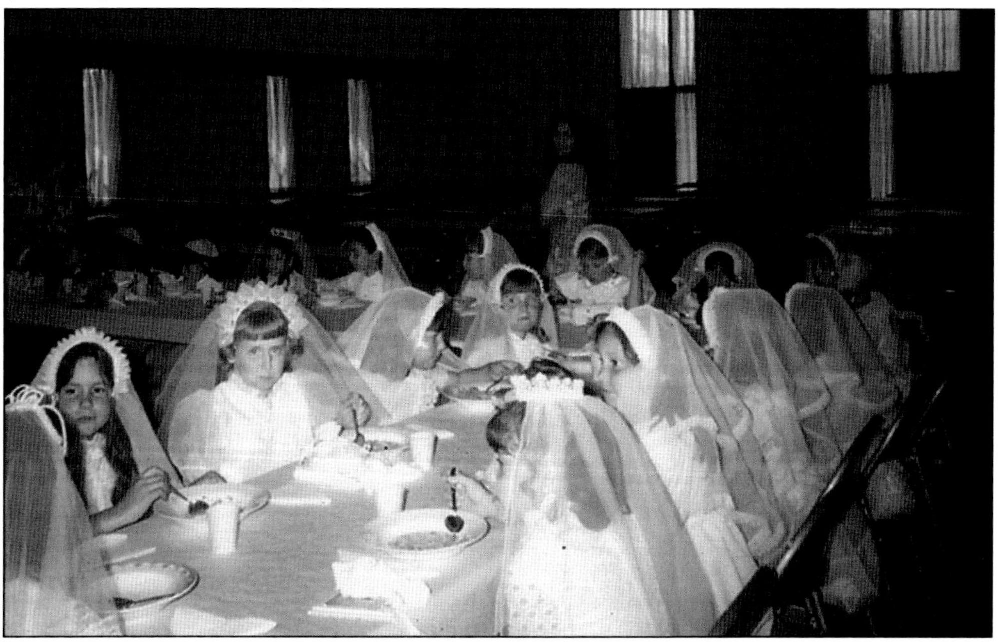

Members of a first communion class wait in the Our Lady of Fatima Catholic Church parish hall during May 1971. The hall was officially dedicated in June 1971. The first communion recorded at the church took place in 1960, while the first as a parish was held in 1976. (Courtesy of Daniel and Carol Feldt.)

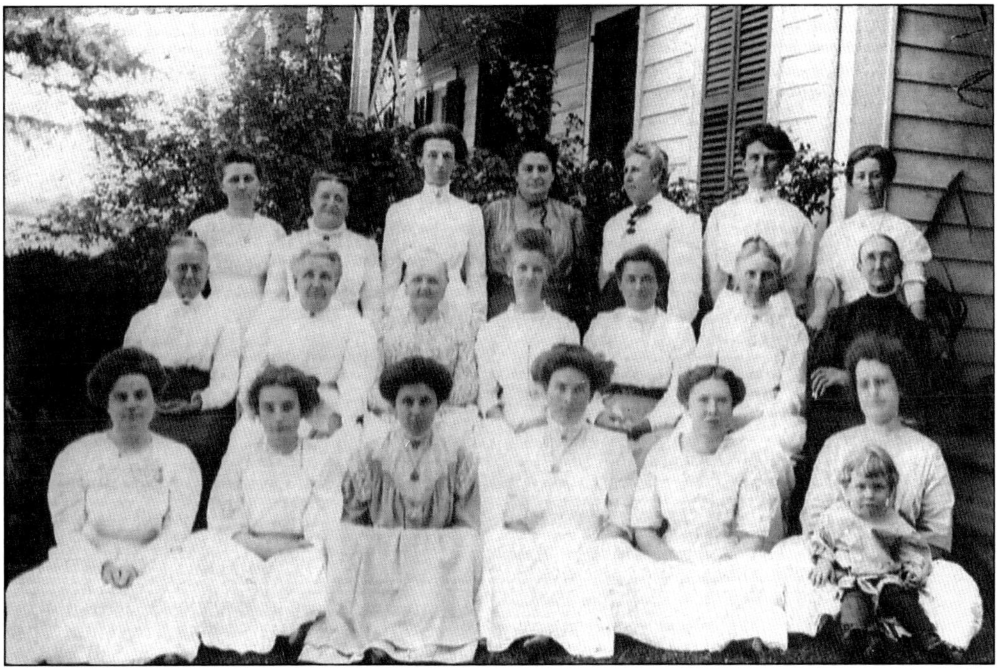

A Plattekill Women's Christian Temperance Union (WCTU) meeting was captured in this c. 1909 photograph taken at the George Nabor residence. The town had at least two active WCTU groups, one in the hamlet of Plattekill and one in Clintondale. The George Nabor property was located along Plattekill-Ardonia Road. (Courtesy of *Friends and Neighbors: A Pictorial History of the Town of Plattekill and Southwest Lloyd.*)

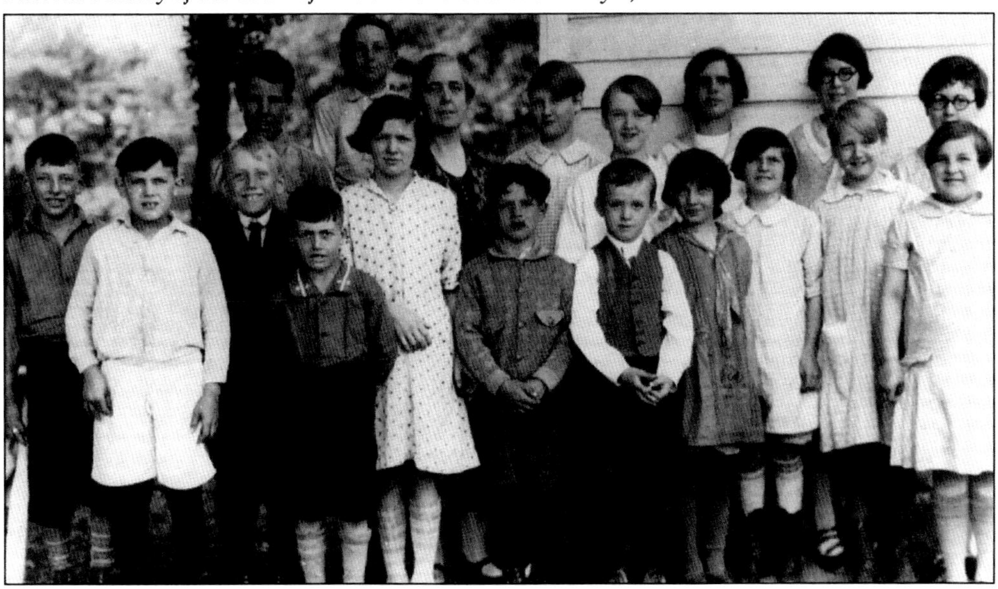

The Sylva School, located near New Hurley Road in Plattekill, was one of Plattekill's many neighborhood schools. It was also called Caper Hill School at one time. The school closed in 1943 when the Wallkill School District became centralized. Children from the Loertscher and Moran families are pictured here around 1930, as well as teacher Mrs. Benedict. The building pictured here no longer stands. (Courtesy of the Moran family.)

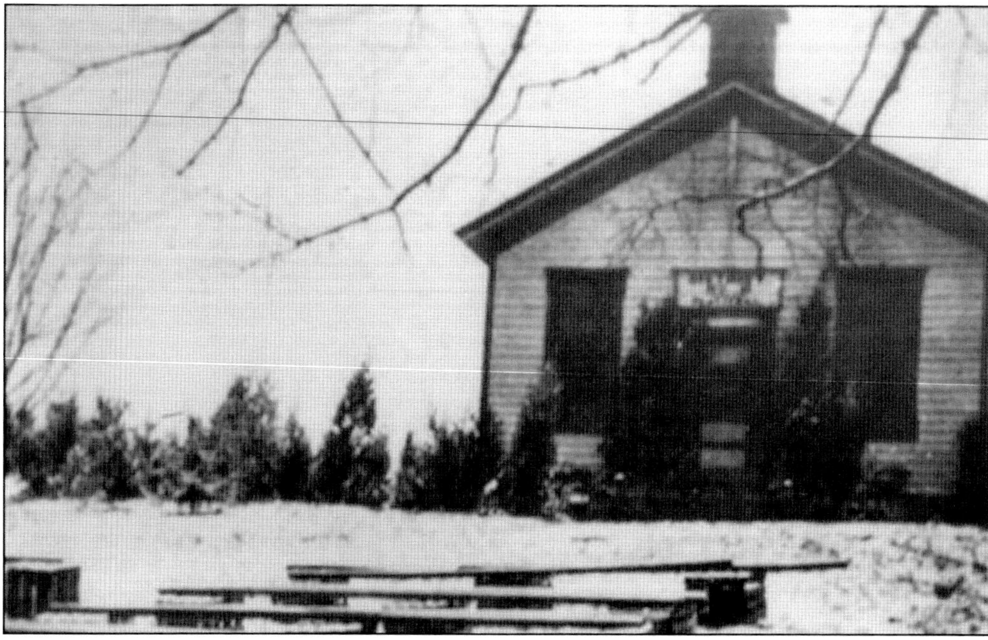

The Gerow Neighborhood School, shown here around 1940, was another school closed after centralization. The school was located along Plattekill-Ardonia Road; it has since been remodeled for use as a private residence. Gerow Neighborhood School teacher Ralph Lefevre later became editor of the *New Paltz Independent*, a weekly newspaper. The school was closed in 1942 due to centralization. (Courtesy of *Friends and Neighbors: A Pictorial History of the Town of Plattekill and Southwest Lloyd*.)

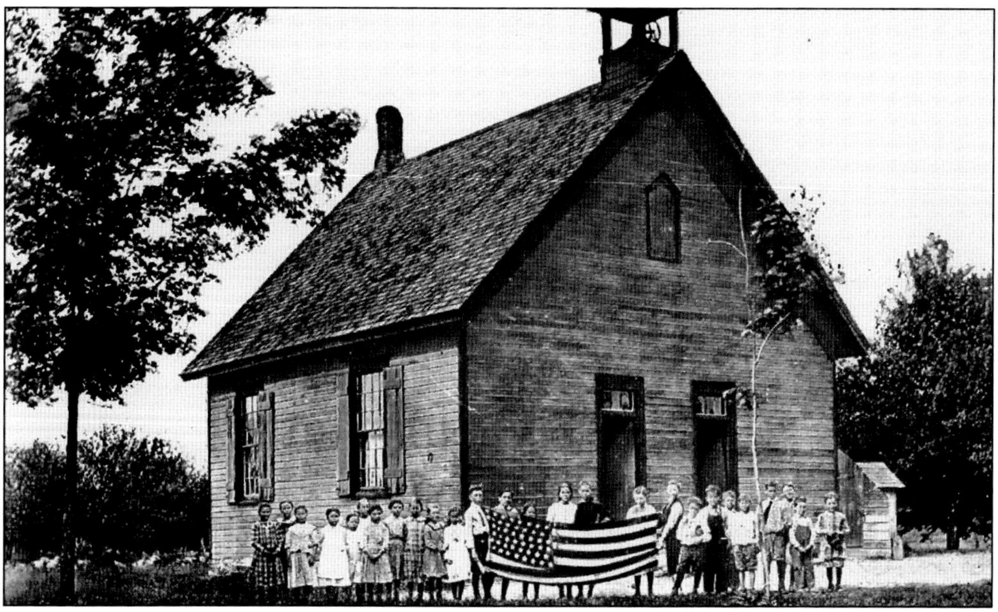

The original Ardonia School building, located at the intersection of Milton Turnpike and Coy Road, burned down in 1872 and was rebuilt. The building is used as the Plattekill Police Department headquarters today. A postcard view shows the school as it looked around 1916. (Courtesy of Shirley Anson.)

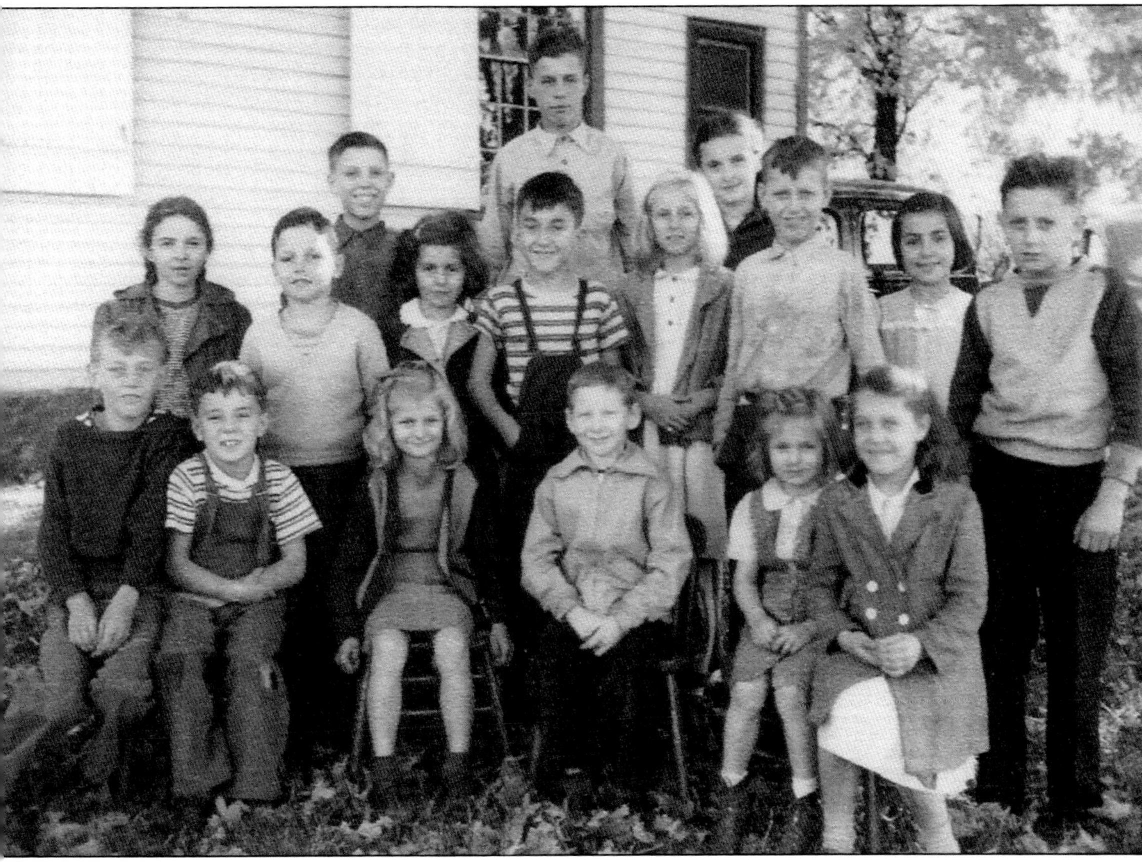

Students from an Ardonia School class, around 1947, are pictured here. They include, from left to right, (first row) Bob Riley, Johnny Bartlett, Betty Ronk, Dale Gerard, Eleanor Ronk, and Lucille Eichler; (second row) Annette Palmer, Fred Riley, Eleanor Fishella, Craig Bartlett, Marie Ronk, Myron Tompkins, Maryanne Vatulla, and Oliver T. Byrnes; (third row) Richard Tompkins, Victor Tompkins, and Marlene Palmer. Teacher Mrs. Wheelan is not present. The Ardonia School was one of the town's last one-room schoolhouses. After the school closed in 1956, the building was used as the Plattekill Town Hall from 1958 until 1973. Although the school bell is long gone, the building today looks much as it did in the late 1800s when the first students attended school here. (Courtesy of Shirley Anson.)

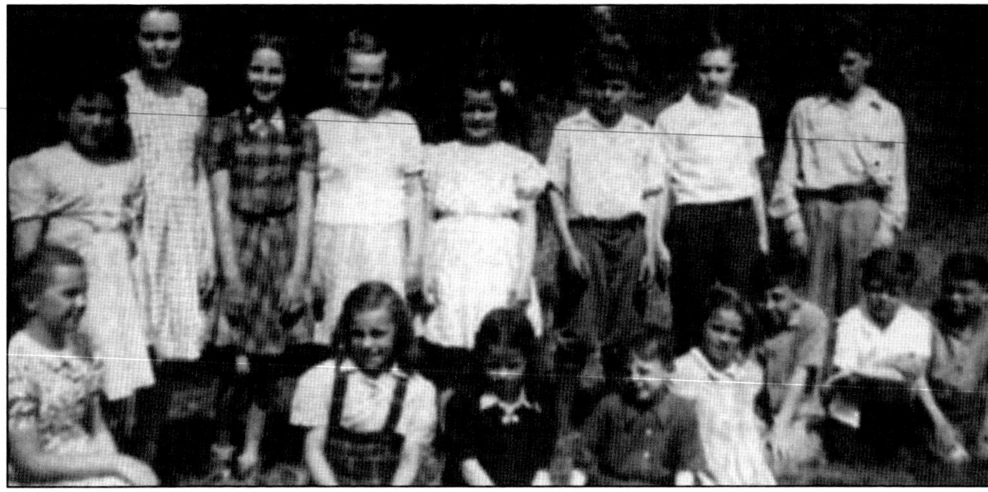

The New Hurley school was actually located in the town of Gardiner, near Denniston Road and Route 208, as reflected on this 1896 Christmas program. Teacher Byron J. Terwilliger later compiled the history *Old Gravestones of Ulster County, New York*, along with J. Wilson Poucher, M.D. During the late 1800s and early 1900s, some students in the area attended school in Highland because the train made it easier to reach that school. The original New Hurley schoolhouse was torn down as a result of construction for the New York City aqueduct system and rebuilt in 1909 within the town of Plattekill. The school closed in 1944, the same year this photograph of New Hurley students was taken. (Courtesy of Shirley Anson.)

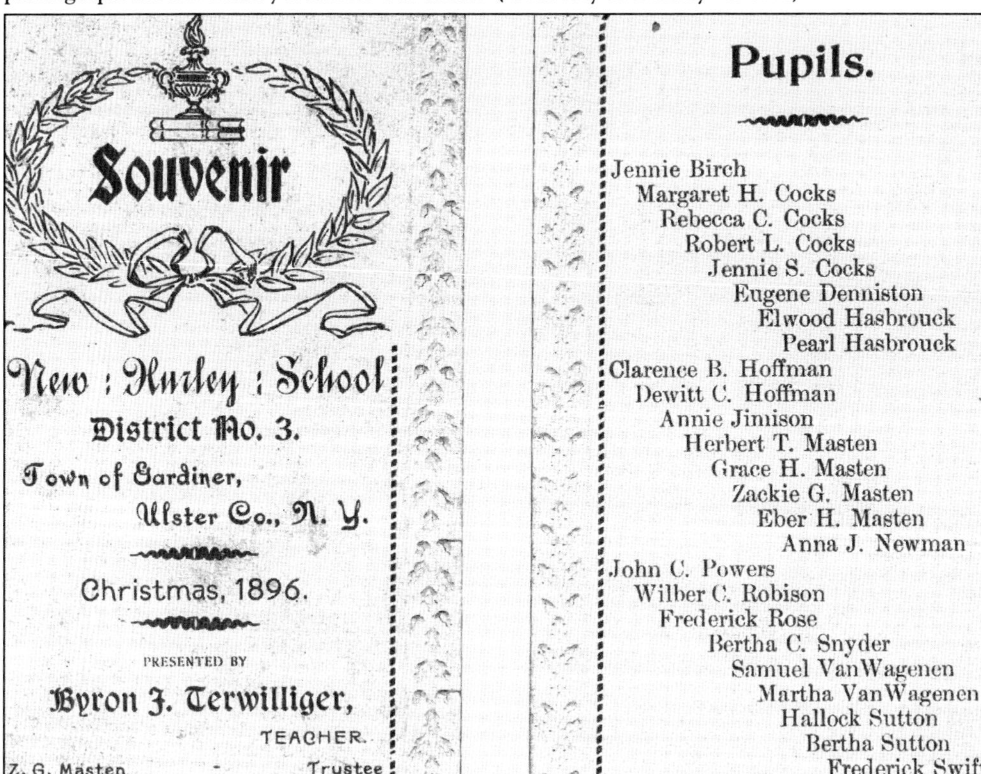

Souvenir

New : Hurley : School
District No. 3.
Town of Gardiner,
Ulster Co., N. Y.

Christmas, 1896.

PRESENTED BY
Byron J. Terwilliger,
TEACHER.

Z. G. Masten - Trustee

Pupils.

Jennie Birch
Margaret H. Cocks
Rebecca C. Cocks
Robert L. Cocks
Jennie S. Cocks
Eugene Denniston
Elwood Hasbrouck
Pearl Hasbrouck
Clarence B. Hoffman
Dewitt C. Hoffman
Annie Jimison
Herbert T. Masten
Grace H. Masten
Zackie G. Masten
Eber H. Masten
Anna J. Newman
John C. Powers
Wilber C. Robison
Frederick Rose
Bertha C. Snyder
Samuel VanWagenen
Martha VanWagenen
Hallock Sutton
Bertha Sutton
Frederick Swift

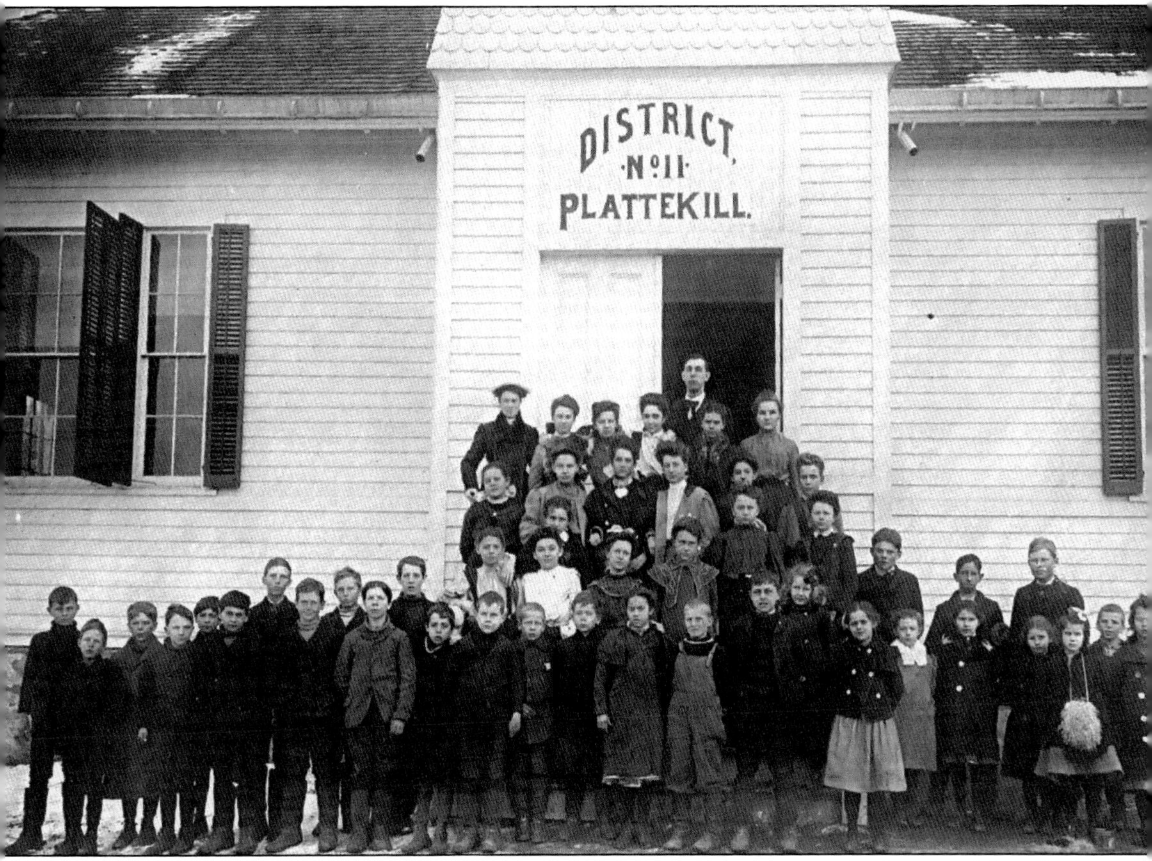

In the early 1800s, Clintondale children were either taught in the home or by Society of Friends teachers in the Quaker meetinghouse on Crescent Avenue. Two early Clintondale schoolhouses, one built in 1821 and another in 1847, were located within the town of Lloyd. The Clintondale School shown here, built in 1897, was located on South Street near the intersection of Maple Avenue and Hurds Road. The building, including heating and seating, was built for around $2,100 and was created as the District No. 11, Town of Plattekill School. The building housed two classrooms, where in addition to basic subjects the curriculum included bookkeeping, civil government, political economy, physics, algebra, geometry, rhetoric, and Latin. The school closed in 1958 due to the centralization of the Highland School district. The building had a short stint as a community center before it burned in the 1960s. It is pictured here around 1910. (Courtesy of Elizabeth Hurd.)

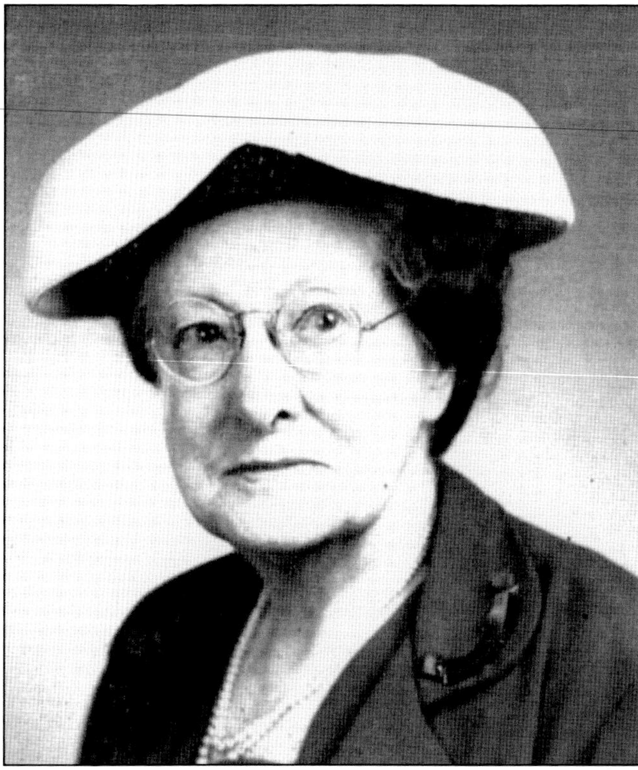

Teacher Isadora Livingston, (pictured here) taught at the Clintondale School from 1897 to 1949 and was a trustee clerk for two decades. A retirement party for Livingston was held in the Clintondale Grange Hall. For many years, Livingston also ran an ice cream parlor in Clintondale during the summers. (Courtesy of Elizabeth Hurd.)

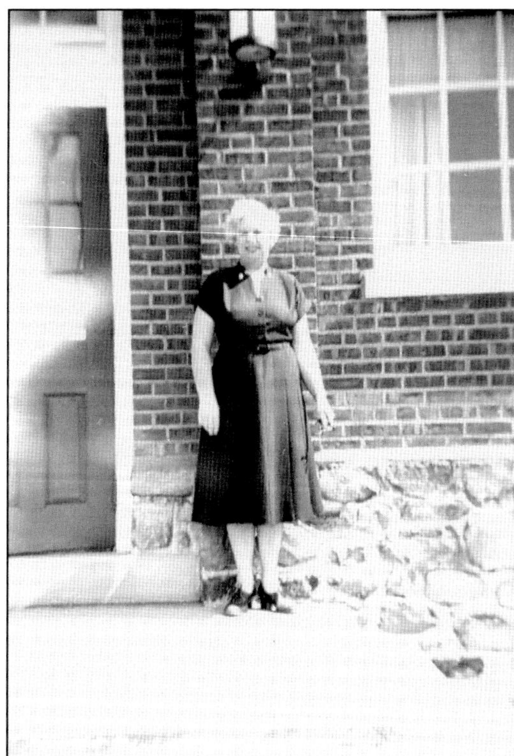

Another well-known teacher was Margaret Cook Fosler, who taught at the Modena School and at the Plattekill Elementary School before becoming the first principal of the Plattekill Elementary School. At the Modena School, she taught grades one through four in one classroom, while children in grades five through eight were taught in the other room. (Courtesy of author's collection.)

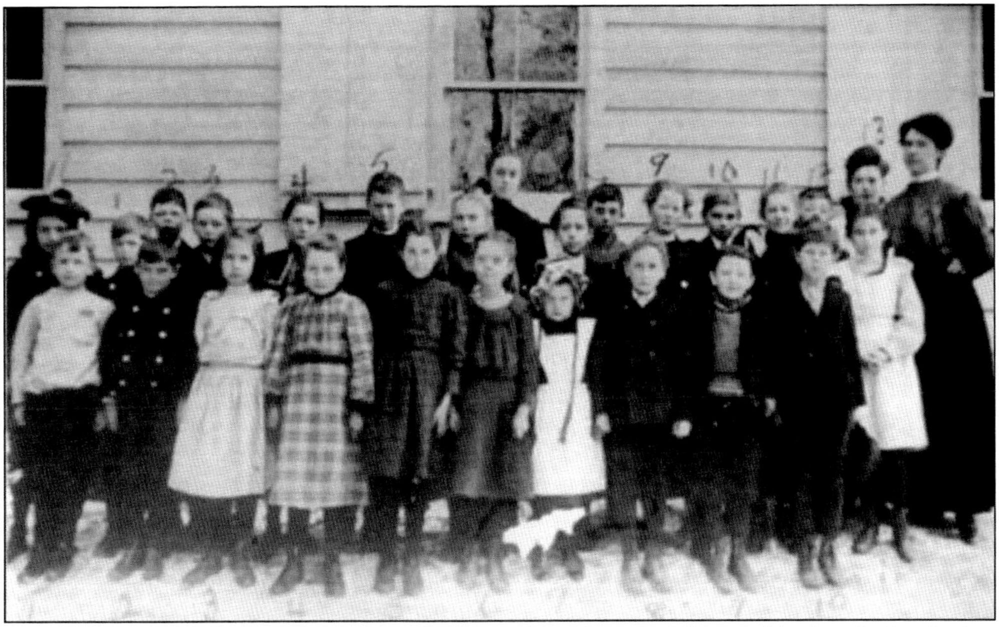

The Modena School, shown here around 1938, is the only one of the neighborhood schools that remained open after the centralization of the Wallkill School District. The two-room school located along Route 32 across from the Modena railroad station was built in 1927 by Charles and Floyd Wells. (Courtesy of *Friends and Neighbors: A Pictorial History of the Town of Plattekill and Southwest Lloyd.*)

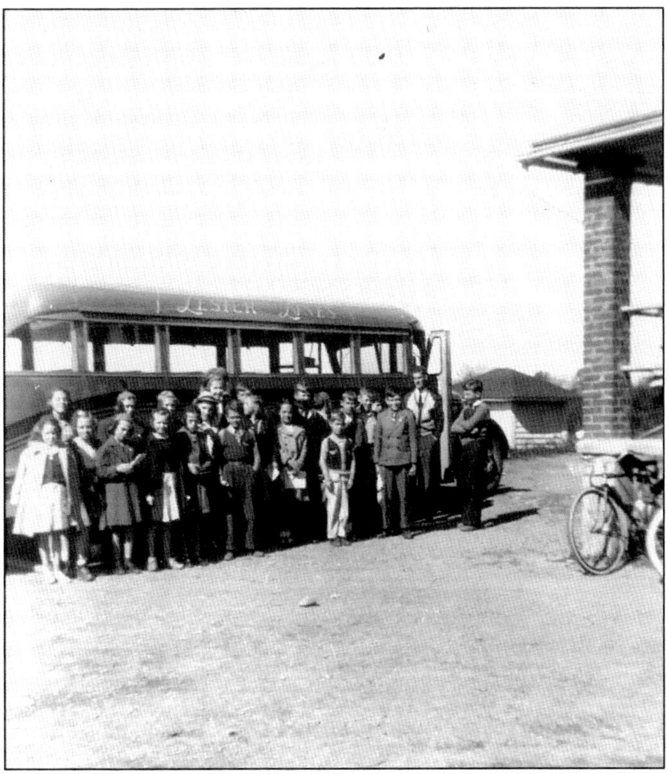

Modena School students line up for a field trip to the historic Huguenot homes in New Paltz, about 1935. Modena resident Russ Coy, a former student at the Modena School, can recall at least one trip where students rode the train from Newburgh to either Highland or Milton and said, "for children growing up in the Depression, a trip like that was a big deal." (Courtesy of Russ Coy.)

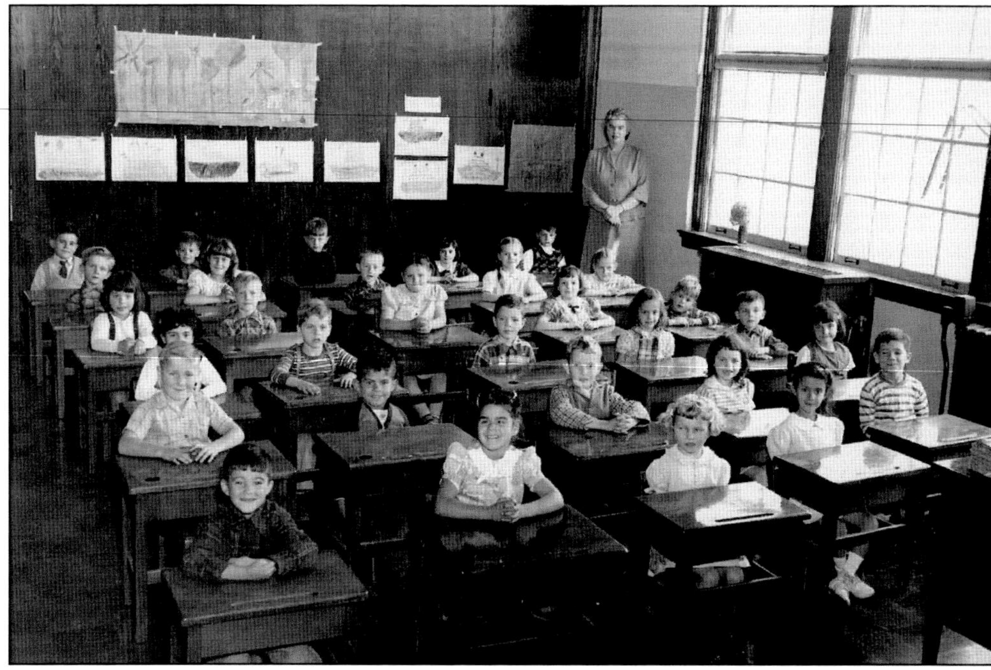

Following centralization, the Plattekill Elementary School became the primary school for most of the town. The Wallkill Central District was organized in 1938 and Plattekill Elementary School opened in 1942. An addition was completed in 1955 that consisted of two primary classrooms, a kindergarten room, an all-purpose room, kitchen, health office, and storage rooms. Pictured here is a first grade class around 1949, along with teacher Margaret Fosler. (Courtesy of author's collection.)

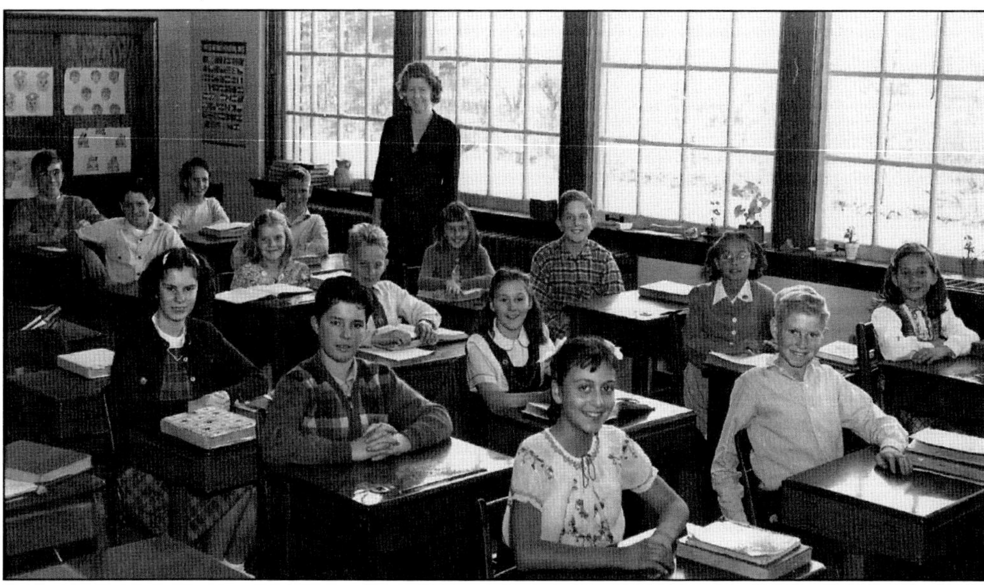

The students in the sixth grade class pictured here at the Plattekill Elementary School around 1947 would have been the oldest students in the building. Today the building still houses kindergarten through sixth grade students. Also pictured is teacher Katherine Thompson, who taught sixth grade classes for many years. (Courtesy of author's collection.)

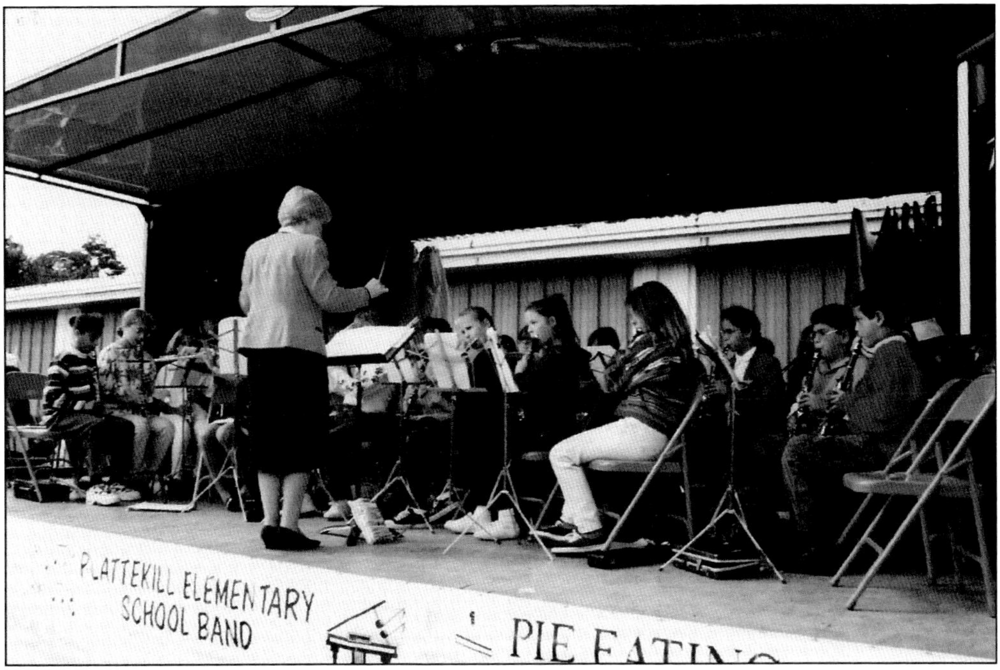

Students in the Plattekill Elementary School band are a featured highlight of Plattekill Day in 1995, under the direction of band teacher Nancy Gazek. Fourth, fifth and sixth grade students participate in the school's music program, which includes chorus, band, and string instruction. (Courtesy of the Office of Plattekill Town Historian.)

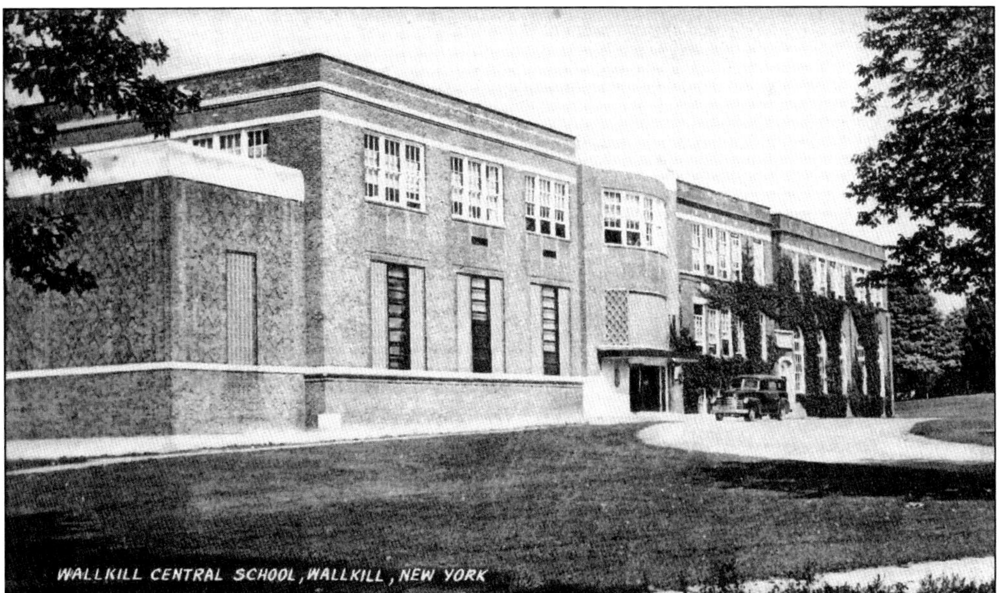

By the 1940s, the era of the neighborhood schools had just about ended, with most students in the town of Plattekill being bussed to school in either the Wallkill or Highland school districts. The new Wallkill Junior Senior High School, which housed students in grades 7 through 12, is pictured here in a postcard from the 1940s. (Courtesy of author's collection.)

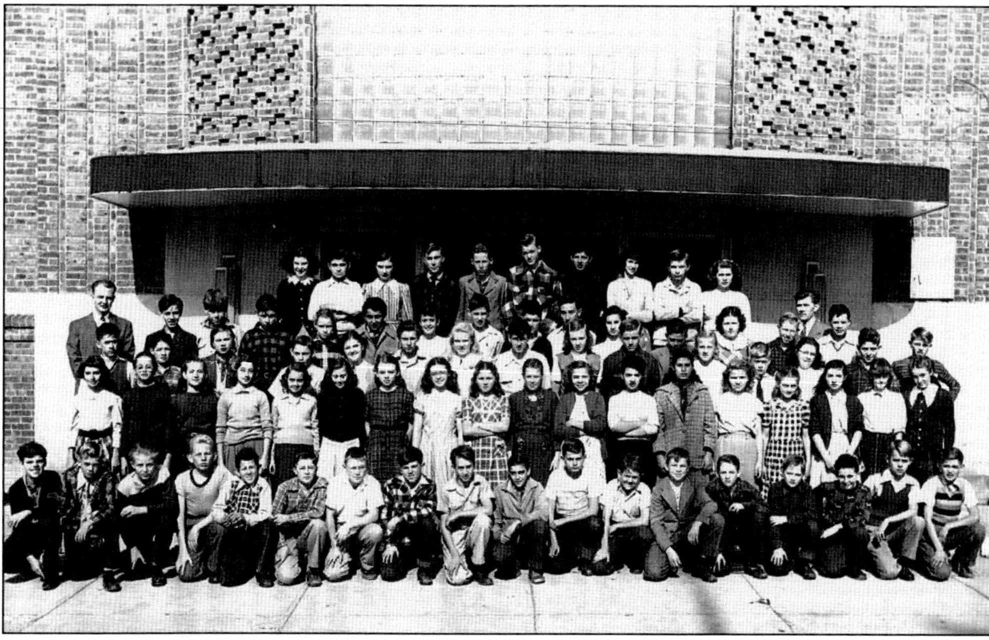

A seventh grade class in 1949 poses for their class picture in front of the Wallkill Junior Senior High School with teachers Clare Ostrander (left) and Kenneth Hasbrouck (right). Hasbrouck was a well-known historian who authored numerous books on Ulster County towns and was responsible for rescuing several 18th-century stone houses in New Paltz that have become part of the Historic Huguenot Street Museum. (Courtesy of author's collection.)

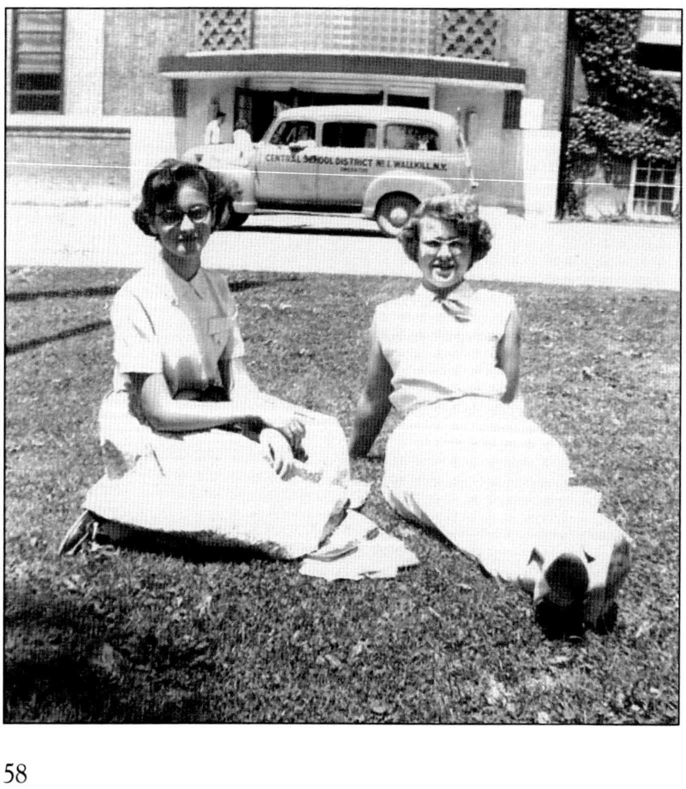

Classmates Joan (Feldt) Werlau and Joan (Ahlers) Ammeraal of the Wallkill High School class of 1954 sit on the front lawn of the Wallkill Junior Senior High School. Today the building is the John G. Borden Middle School and houses grades 7 and 8, while a separate high school building on Robinson Drive houses grades 9 through 12. (Courtesy of author's collection.)

Four

Agriculture and Commerce

In his *History of Ulster County, New York*, Nathaniel B. Sylvester referred to Plattekill's agricultural nature by pointing out that "ordinary farm products are raised in abundance and the raising of grapes and other fruits constitutes a leading industrial feature of the town." Grape production was prevalent in the 1800s, while apples are the leading crop grown in present-day Plattekill. While grapes and apples dominated, Plattekill town historian Micki Obermeyer said that most farmers raised a variety of items, including cattle, poultry, fruit, and vegetables in order to make a living. Many family farms that had relied on the sale of dairy products were put out of business with the advent of pasteurization, as the new machinery needed was cost prohibitive. Farming did give rise to many businesses that were agricultural in nature. Businesses such as blacksmith shops, cooperages, and feed stores sprung up to serve Plattekill's farmers. During Prohibition, cider mills bloomed as the demand for the legal drink increased.

General stores were quite common throughout the town and often did double-duty as post offices or telegraph and telephone offices for the area. At one point in its history, the tiny hamlet of Clintondale boasted five general stores. Other businesses throughout the town ranged from mills, creameries, and millineries to tin shops and undertaking. When the town hall building was erected in the centrally located hamlet of Modena in 1973, Modena became the unofficial business center of the town.

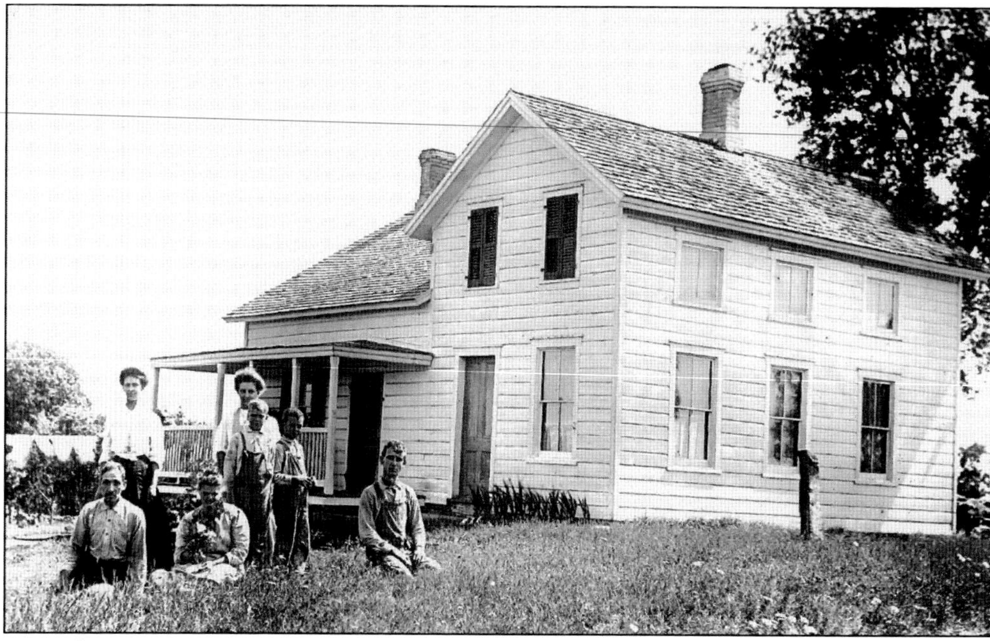

An early 1900s postcard shows a scene at the Jacob Fosler farm on Fosler road in Plattekill. The family, like many others in the area at the time, raised fruit, vegetables, cattle, and poultry that were sold locally and that supplied many of the Plattekill boarding houses and villas. (Courtesy of Micki Obermeyer.)

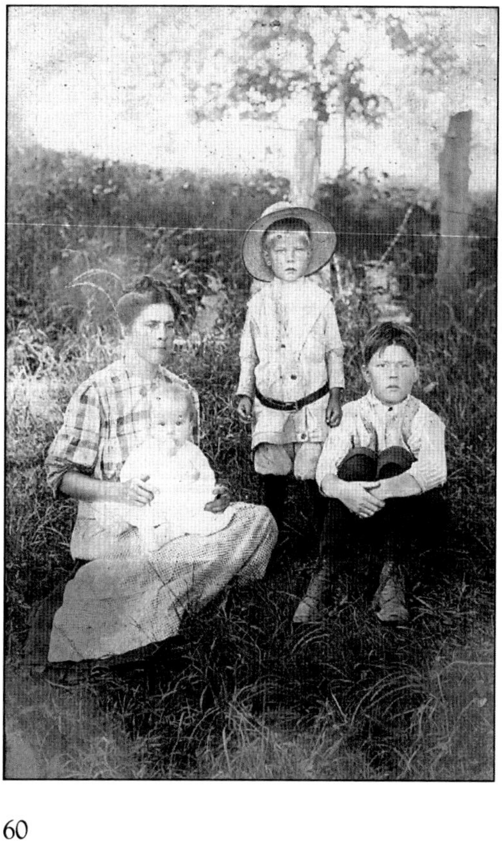

Many laborers moved from farm to farm in the local area following work. Modena resident Richard Coy worked on various farms in the area, including the Hasbrouck farms, shown here. Pictured are Coy's wife, Dora Smith Coy, and son John Leonard Coy (right), around 1902, along with two unidentified children. (Courtesy of Russ Coy.)

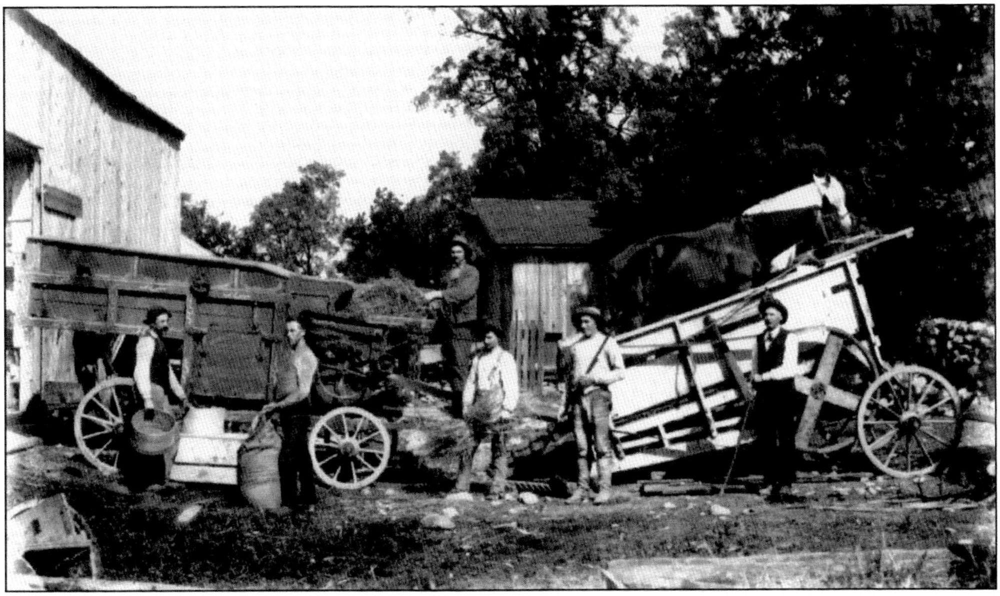

A Modena threshing crew is pictured here around 1885. Plattekill was made up of many small farms, worked by families and hired hands. Neighboring farmers would share the cost of hiring crews. The workers here, from left to right, are identified as Samuel Paltridge, Matt Ronk, John Lucy, Thomas Borland, John Cumisky, and Shaurt Terwilliger. (Courtesy of *Friends and Neighbors: A Pictorial History of the Town of Plattekill and Southwest Lloyd*.)

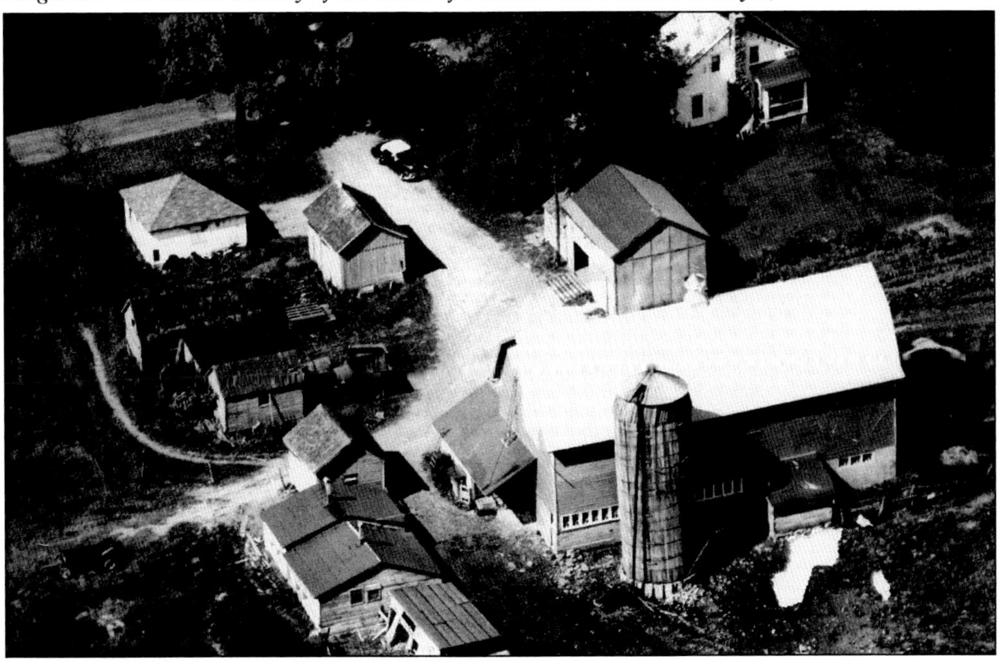

The Hoetzler dairy farm on Forest Road is pictured in an aerial view from around 1950. Plattekill historian Micki Obermeyer points out that while there were several larger farms such as this one within the town, farms of this size were not the norm. Most farmers raised just enough to support their families and to sell enough locally to be able to cover expenses. (Courtesy of Bruce Loertscher.)

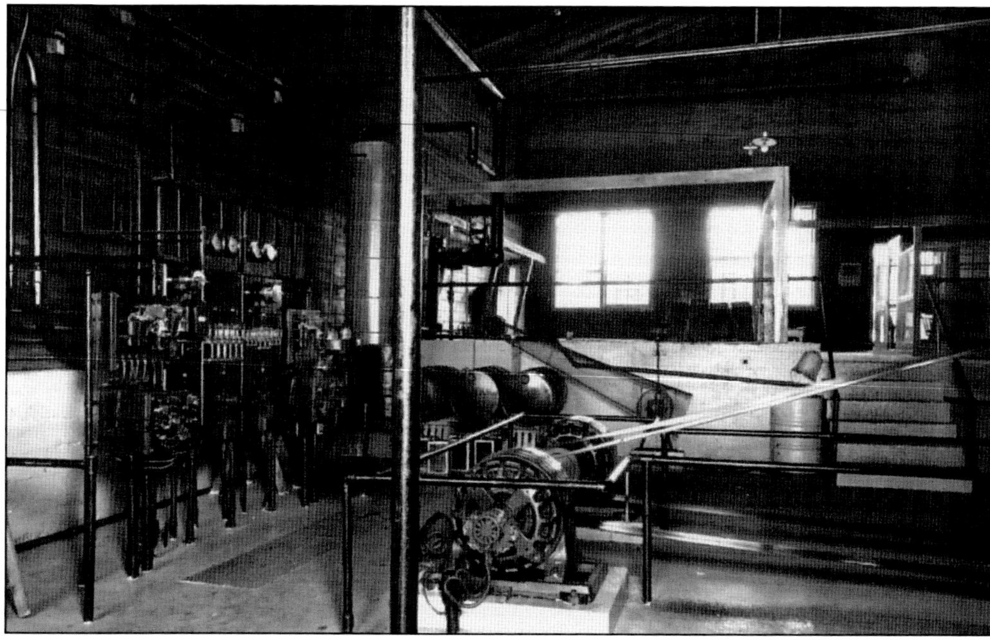

An interior view of the fruit warehouse on Station Road in Clintondale is shown here. The building, originally built in 1900, housed various businesses over the years, including the Clintondale Fruit Growers Co-Op and Hudson Valley Apple Products. The warehouse burned down on March 24, 1988. Eleven area fire departments aided the Clintondale Fire Department with controlling the fire, which burned for days. (Courtesy of *Friends and Neighbors: A Pictorial History of the Town of Plattekill and Southwest Lloyd.*)

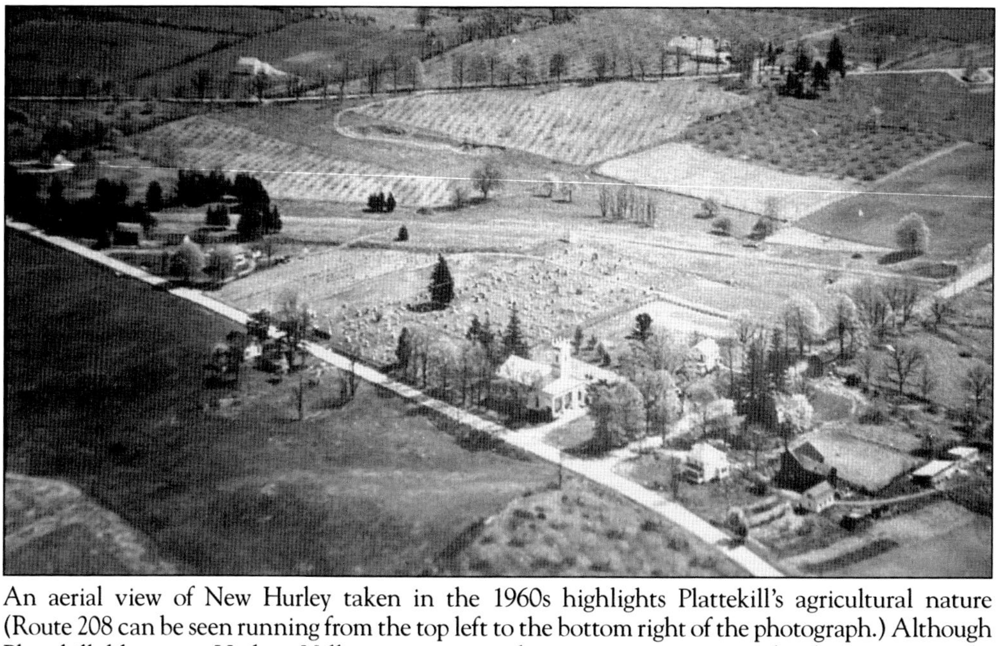

An aerial view of New Hurley taken in the 1960s highlights Plattekill's agricultural nature (Route 208 can be seen running from the top left to the bottom right of the photograph.) Although Plattekill, like many Hudson Valley communities, has seen an increase in development recently, much of the town remains undeveloped and many farms and orchards are still active. (Courtesy of *Friends and Neighbors: A Pictorial History of the Town of Plattekill and Southwest Lloyd.*)

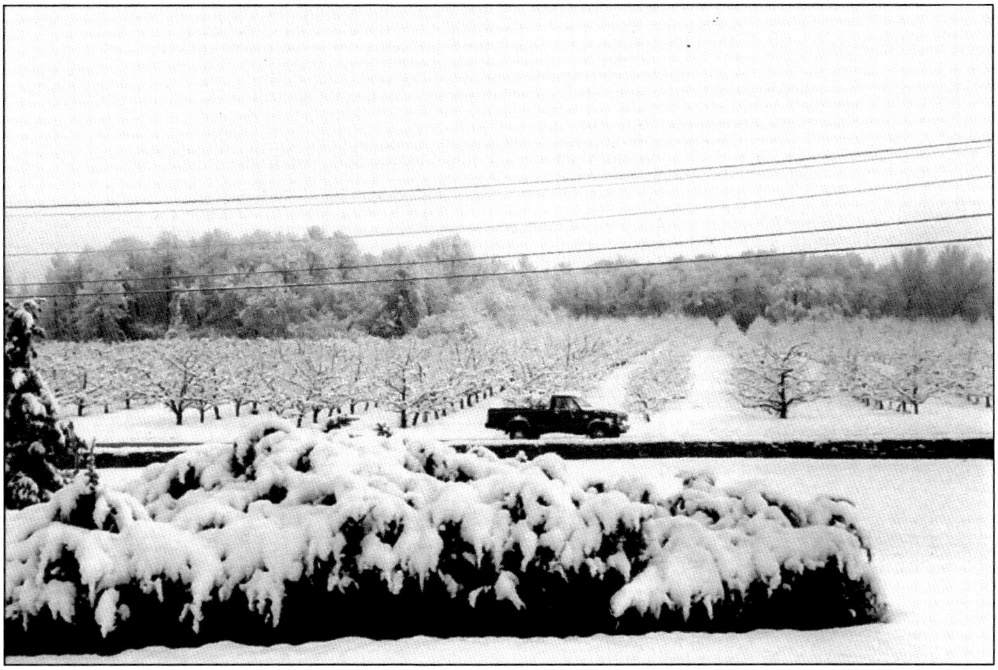

A photograph taken in 1988 along Hurd's Road in Clintondale (on the town of Lloyd border) shows the continued rural nature of the region. While apple orchards account for the majority of crops grown in the town, several family-run farms throughout Plattekill and the surrounding communities also sell Christmas trees, pumpkins, and hay. (Courtesy of Elizabeth Hurd.)

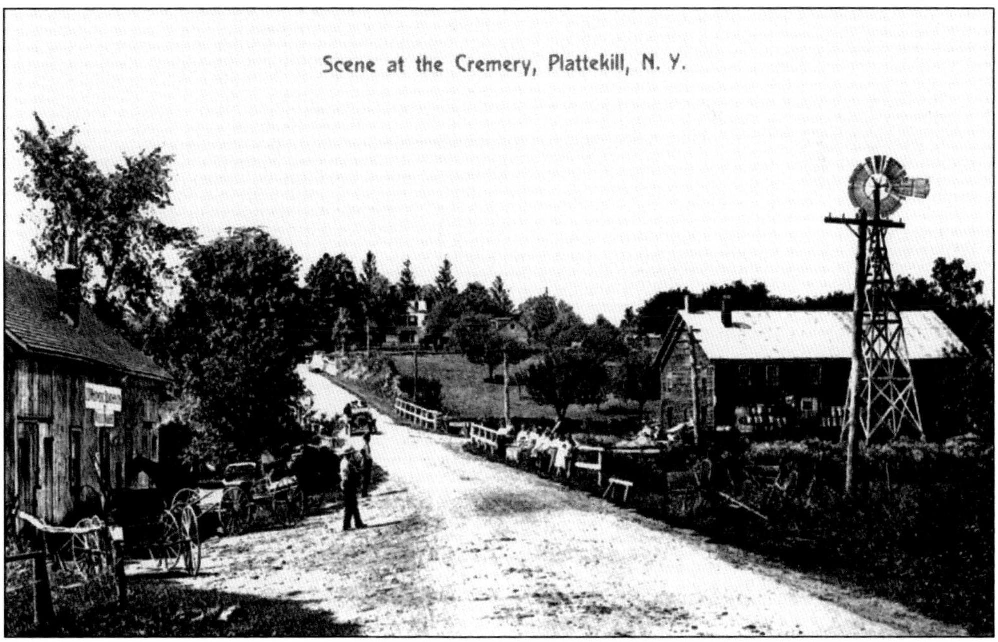

In the early 1900s, milk from area farms was processed at the Hudson Valley Dairy Company or "Valley Creamery" on State Road in Plattekill. The creamery is seen here on the right in an early 1900s postcard. The road pictured is State Road, now Firehouse Road. (Courtesy of Shirley Anson.)

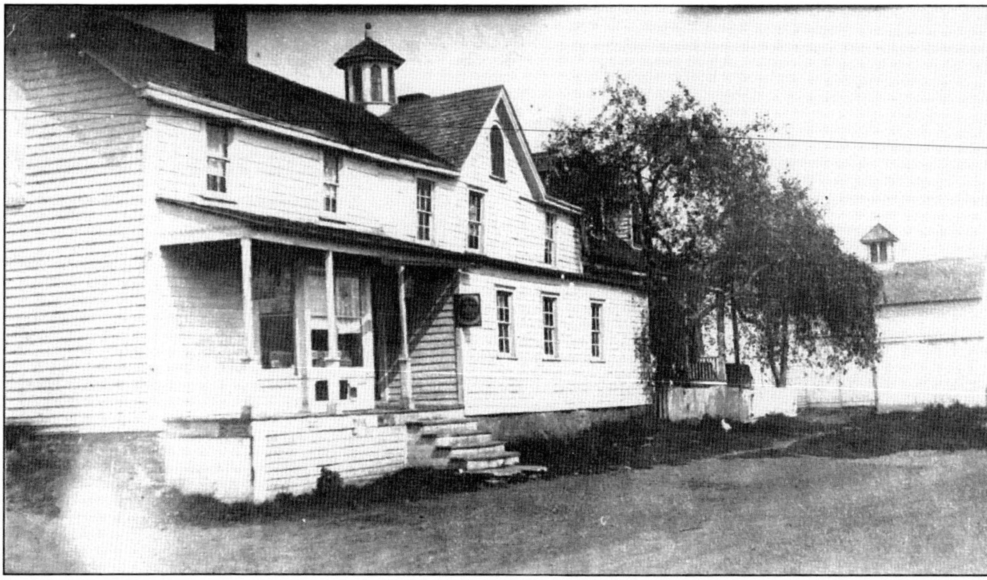

One of the earlier stores in the town of Plattekill was the William Fowler Store, shown here in photographs from the late 1800s. Fowler leased the store from his father-in-law, Daniel Martin. In the 1890s, the store served as the Plattekill Post Office, with William H. Fowler serving as postmaster from August 1897 to July 1902, and Mary E. Fowler serving as postmaster from July 1902 to September 1905. The picture below shows the interior of the Fowler store, which reportedly sold everything from dry goods and meats to clothing and shoes. During its busiest times, the store employed at least two clerks. The young man, second from right, is identified as "Harold Tinney, who ran Sylvan Orchards." (Courtesy of Shirley Anson.)

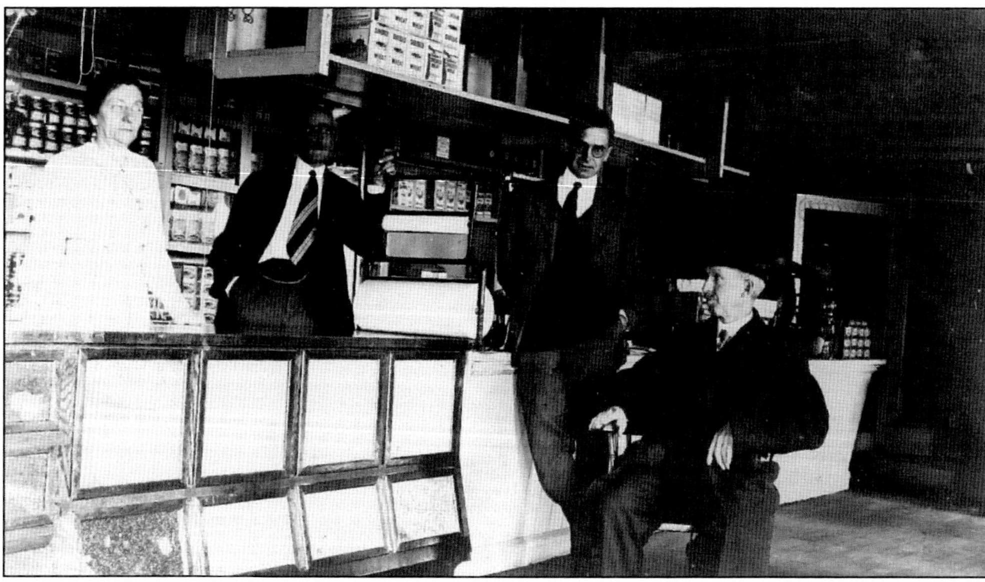

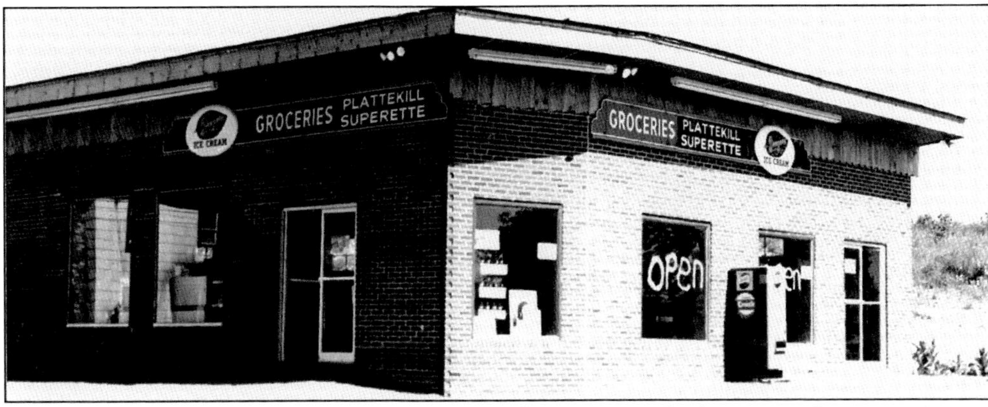

Two pictures from the 1950s show O'Jay's Plattekill Superette, which sat near the county line on Route 32, just south of the Our Lady of Fatima Catholic Church. While the hamlet was home to numerous general stores throughout the years, Plattekill town historian Micki Obermeyer describes O'Jay's Plattekill Superette as "Plattekill's first supermarket," as it had a wide variety of items for sale. When the business closed, the building was used briefly as a villa and then later torn down. Today the site is used as a gravel bank. (Courtesy of Micki Obermeyer.)

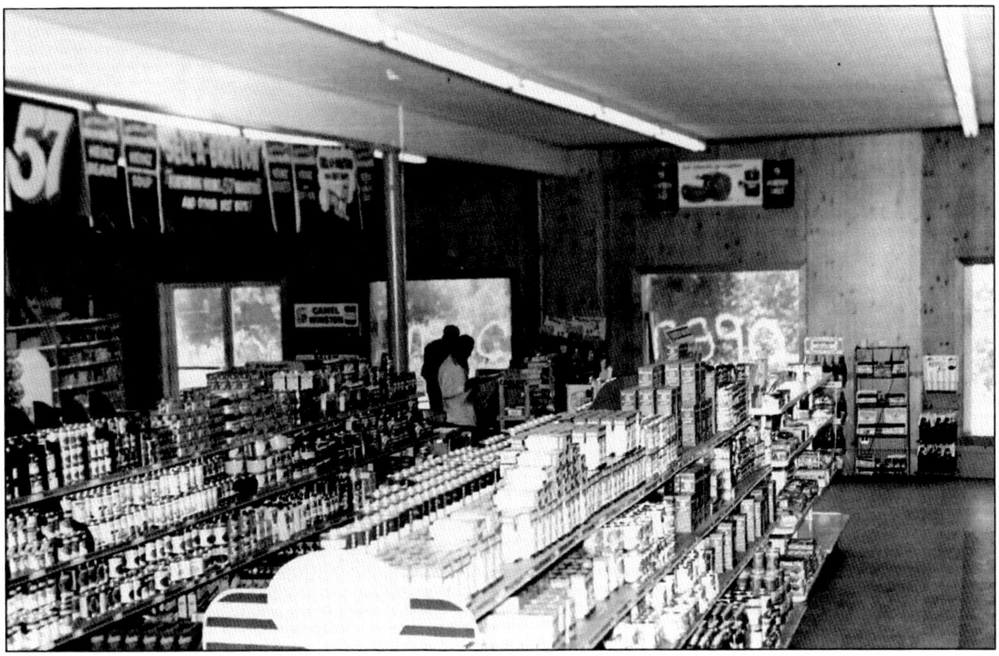

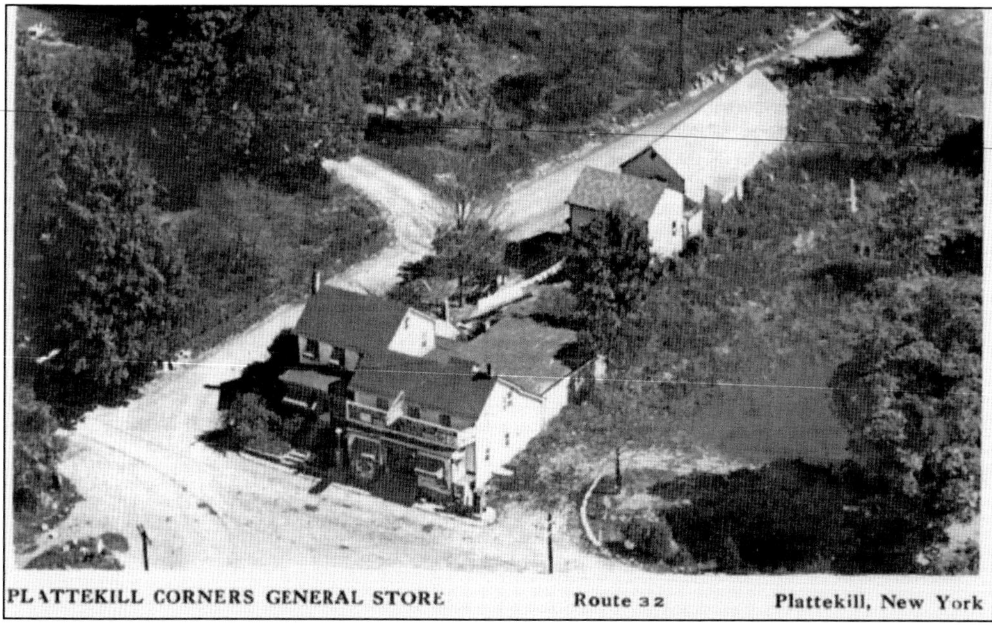

An aerial view shows the George Sisti Plattekill Corners General Store at the intersection of Route 32, Plattekill-Ardonia Road, and Huckleberry Turnpike. The back of the postcard reads, "this store, the oldest in the vicinity, was used as a toll gate for passage to West Marlboro Mountain." Today the building in the front still serves as the Plattekill General Store, while the post office sits nearby. (Courtesy of Shirley Anson.)

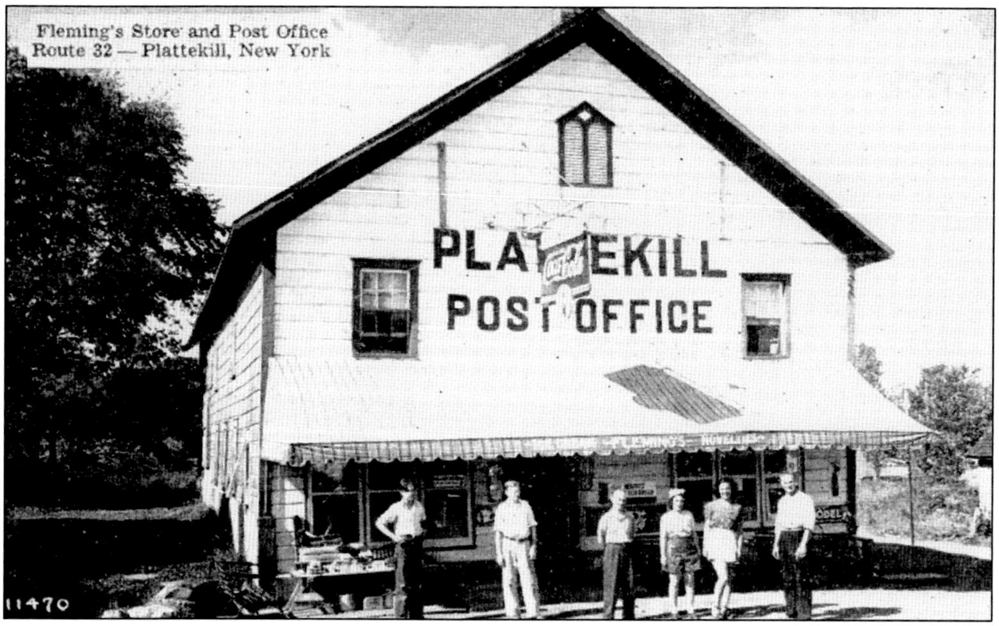

In 1937, the job of postmaster was posted for $666 annually. Patrick Fleming took over as acting postmaster in 1944 and was officially appointed in February 1945. He retired from the post in 1961. Shown here on a c. 1951 postcard is Fleming's Store and Post Office, located on old Route 32 in Plattekill (today this area would be Firehouse Road). (Courtesy of author's collection.)

A c. 1880 stereoview shows Oliver Church's residence in Modena. Church, born in 1835, owned more than 135 acres of land in Modena. He was also a landlord and owner of a wagon maker's shop, a blacksmith shop, and a butcher shop. His father, Samuel Church, owned numerous Modena businesses as well, leading one local paper to suggest in the 1870s that the hamlet be renamed "Church's Corners." (Courtesy of author's collection.)

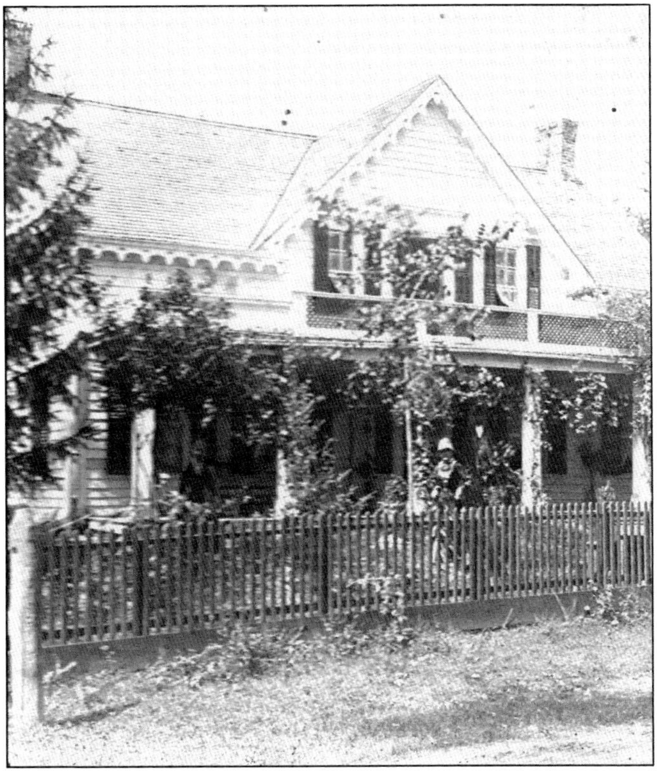

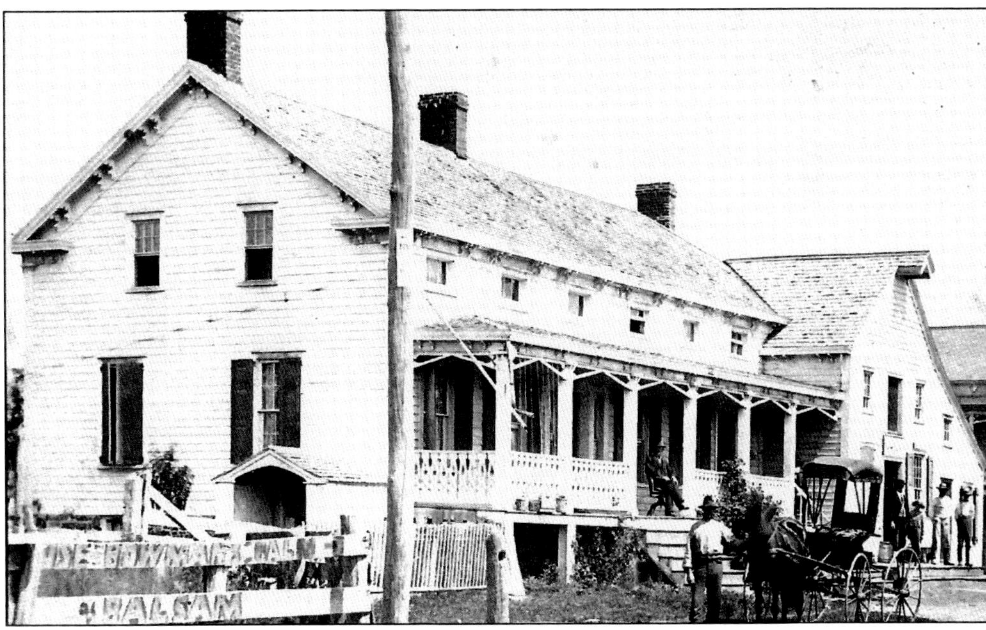

A c. 1880 stereoview shows the residence of Dr. Eber H. Heston at the four corners in Modena. (Later, the building became D. B. Grimm's store.) In the rear of the picture can be seen the Modena Hotel. Heston was a druggist and physician who practiced in Modena, Gardiner, Clintondale, and Poughkeepsie. While in Clintondale in 1896, he opened the hamlet's first drug store in the Wanzer building. (Courtesy of author's collection.)

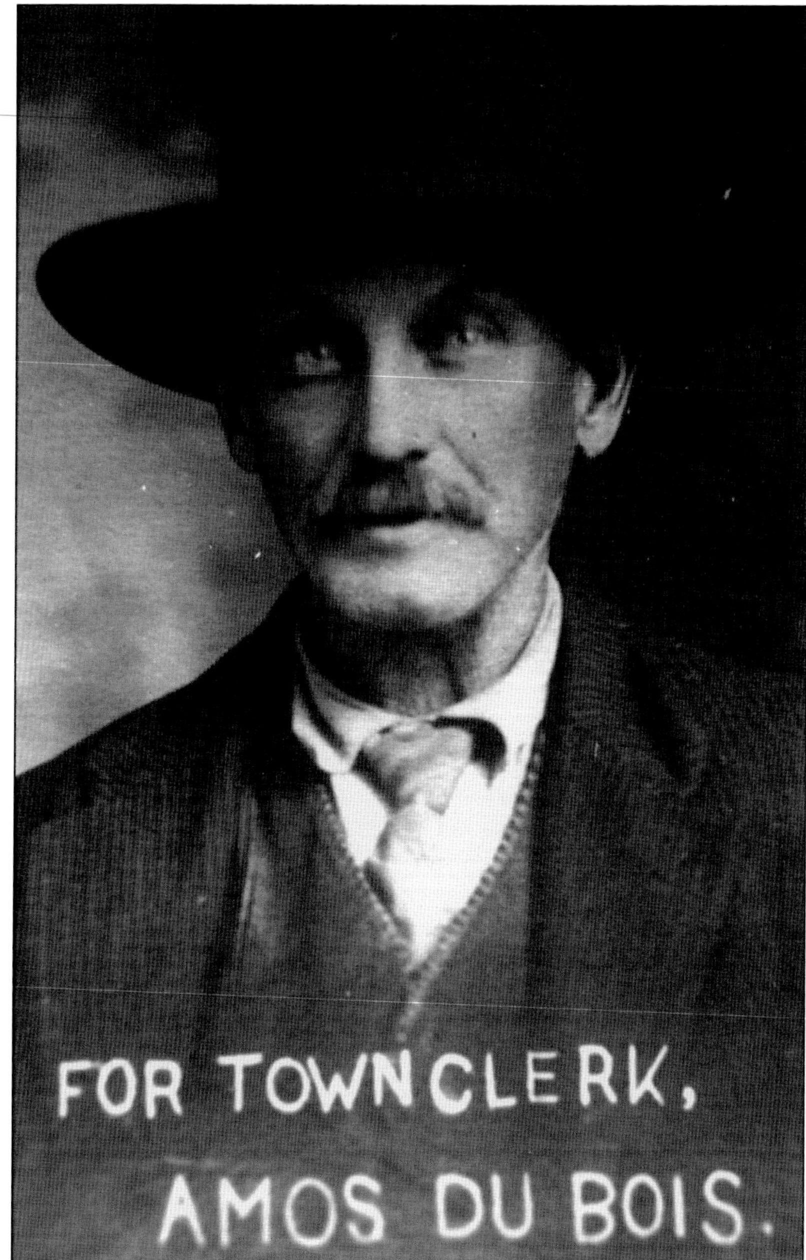

Amos DuBois was another well-known businessman in Modena. In the 1880s, DuBois was the postmaster as well as a harness maker. In addition, he ran a stage from Modena to Poughkeepsie regularly on Monday, Thursday, and Saturday. The stage carried not only passengers, but lambs, calves, and other livestock. The early 1900s were not kind to DuBois. In the winter of 1903, he suffered injuries after a heavy wind blew off the top of his store; in the fall of 1904, he became unable to run his stage after an accident in which he was thrown from a wagon whose wheels then ran over his feet. He is pictured here in on an election campaign card, about 1900. DuBois served as the town's clerk from 1900 to 1905 and from 1908 to 1913. (Courtesy of *Friends and Neighbors: A Pictorial History of the Town of Plattekill and Southwest Lloyd.*)

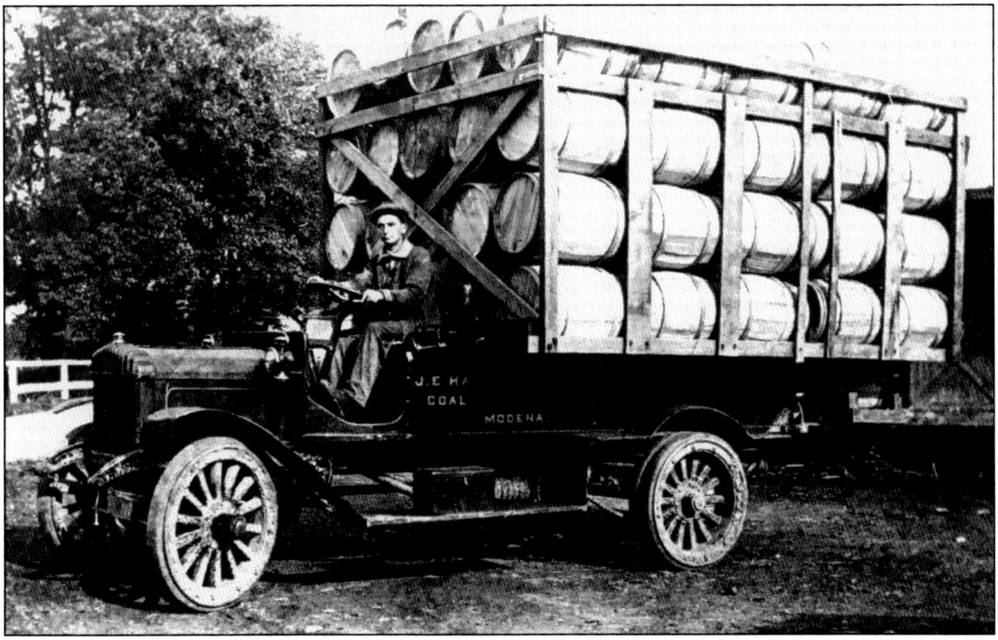

J. E. Hasbrouck owned numerous Modena businesses including a cooperage. Shown here around 1922 is Albert Terwilliger driving a vehicle loaded with apple barrels made at the J. E. Hasbrouck Cooperage. In 1923, the *New Paltz Independent* reported, "The truck of J.E. Hasbrouck Co. can be seen every day on the road delivering apple barrels." (Courtesy of the Office of the Plattekill Town Historian.)

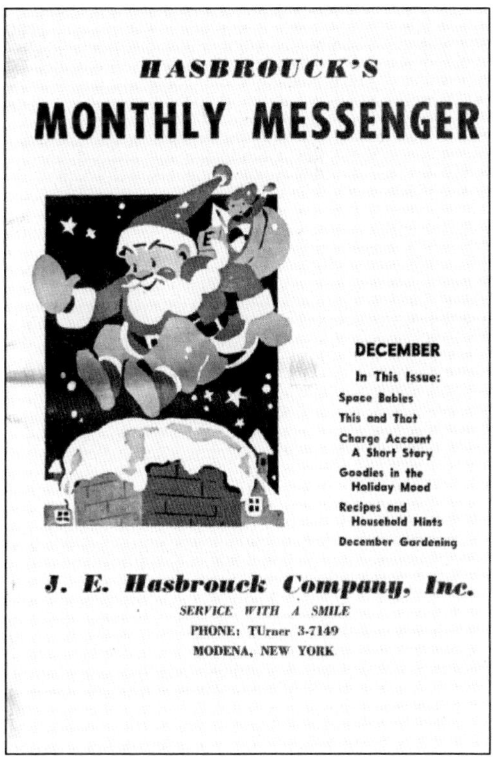

During the 1940s and early 1950s, the Hasbrouck family, owners of several Modena businesses including the Hasbrouck Feed, Coal and Lumber Company, would publish the *Monthly Messenger*, a magazine filled with recipes, gardening tips, and holiday decorating suggestions, as well as advertisements for local businesses. (Courtesy of the Office of the Plattekill Town Historian.)

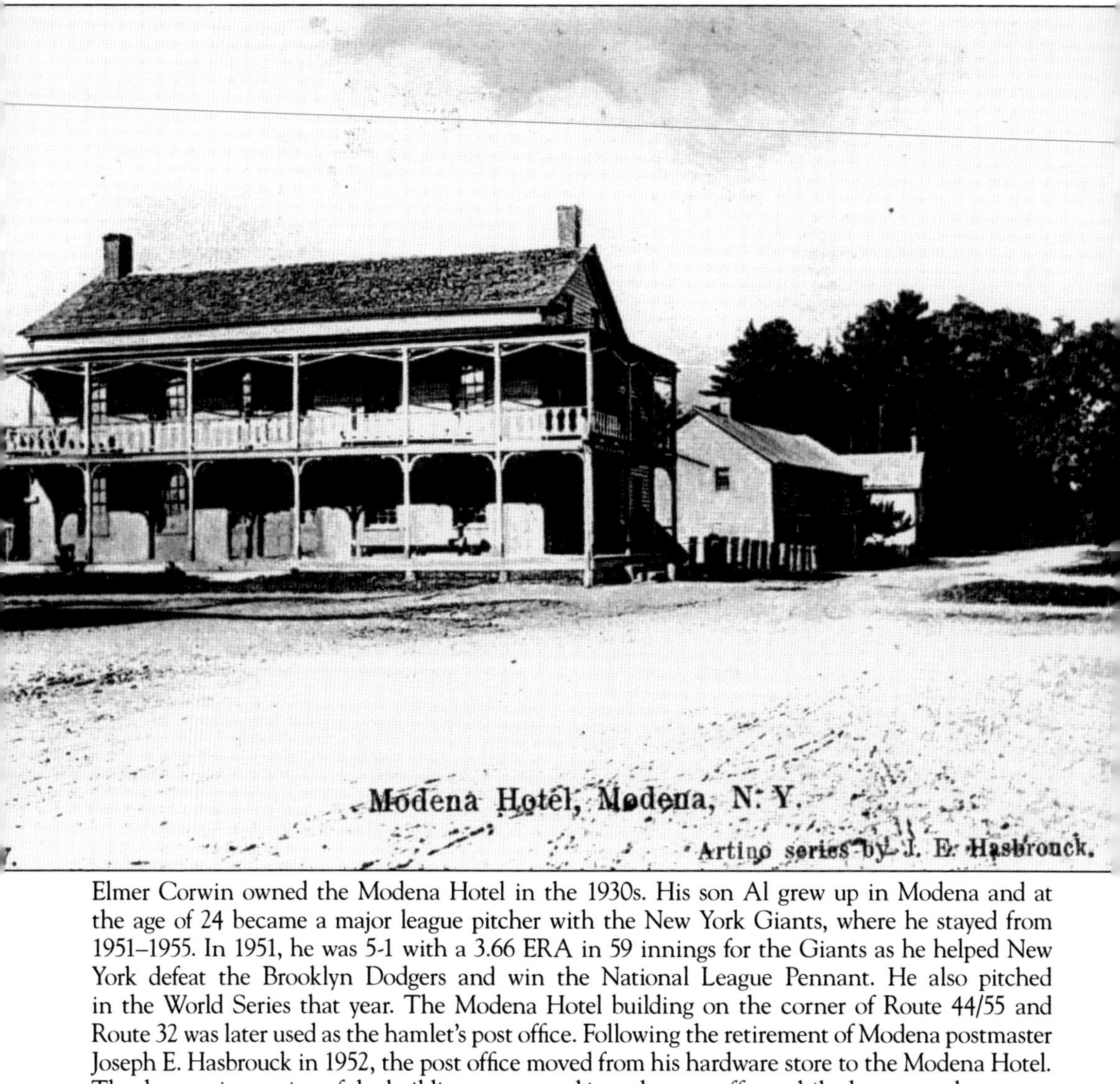

Elmer Corwin owned the Modena Hotel in the 1930s. His son Al grew up in Modena and at the age of 24 became a major league pitcher with the New York Giants, where he stayed from 1951–1955. In 1951, he was 5-1 with a 3.66 ERA in 59 innings for the Giants as he helped New York defeat the Brooklyn Dodgers and win the National League Pennant. He also pitched in the World Series that year. The Modena Hotel building on the corner of Route 44/55 and Route 32 was later used as the hamlet's post office. Following the retirement of Modena postmaster Joseph E. Hasbrouck in 1952, the post office moved from his hardware store to the Modena Hotel. The downstairs portion of the building was turned into the post office, while the rooms above were remodeled into apartments. (Courtesy of the Office of the Plattekill Town Historian.)

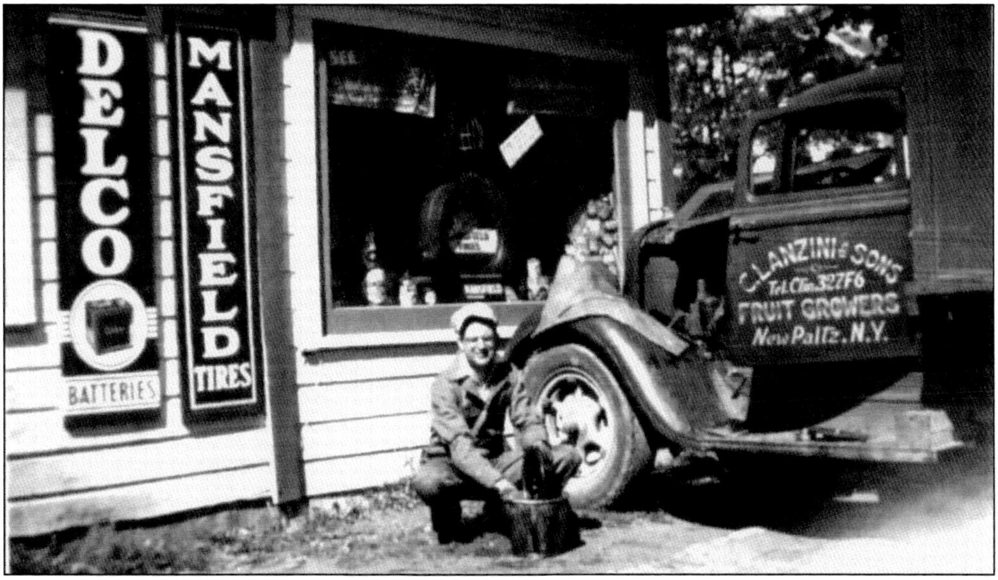

Shown here is John Denton of Modena working on a vehicle at his garage. The family-run Denton's Garage and Gulf Gas sat just south of the four corners in Modena. The garage remains today, although the gas pumps are long gone. (Courtesy of Shirley Anson.)

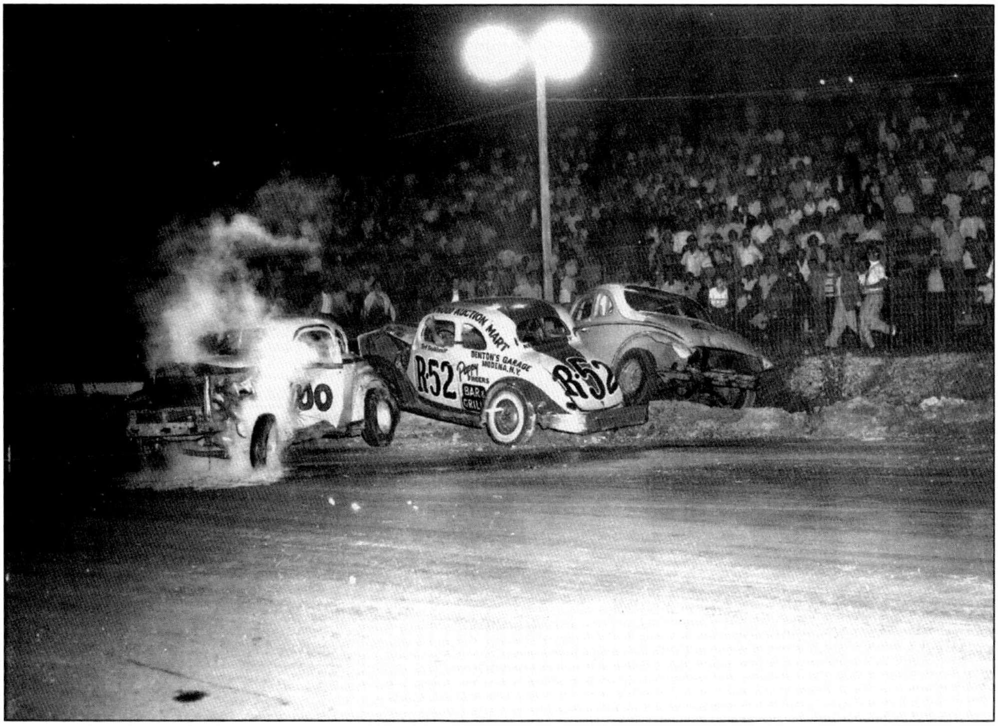

Denton, along with friends and family, would work on stock cars for the George Freer Auto Auction in Newburgh. Denton's nephew Lester "Sonny" Wager remembers staying at the garage until the early morning hours to work on the race cars. George Freer's cars R52 and R52 Jr. are shown here racing in Middletown during the 1940s. Car R52 advertises Denton's garage along its side. (Courtesy of Shirley Anson.)

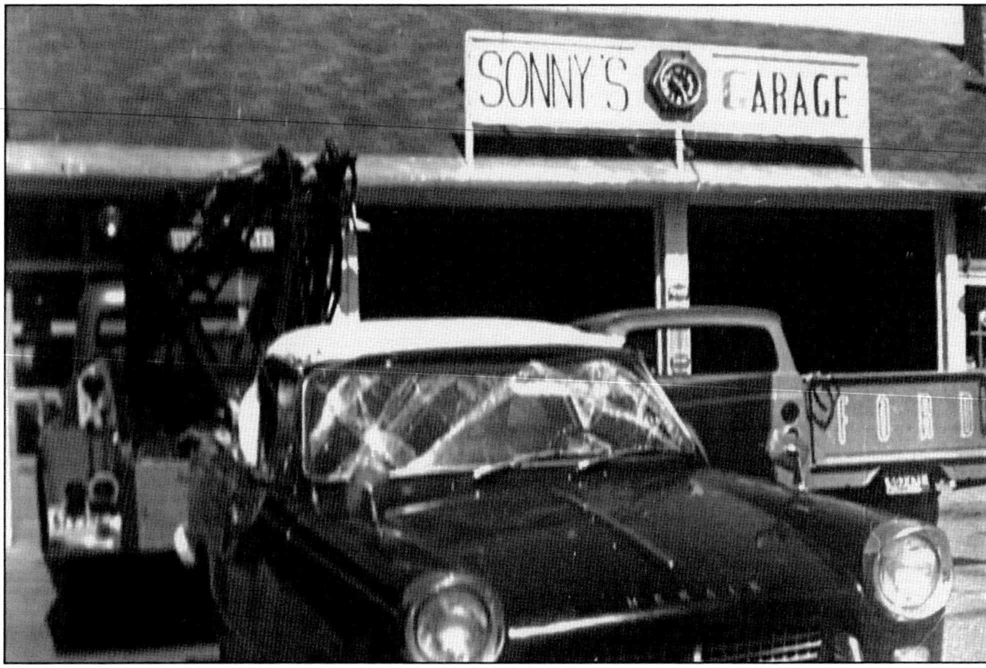

In the 1950s, John Denton's nephew Lester "Sonny" Wager purchased the garage and gas station from his uncle. Wager still owns Sonny's Garage, which he has run along with his family for more than 50 years. For more than 20 of those years, he also served as Plattekill's head constable. (Courtesy of Sonny Wager.)

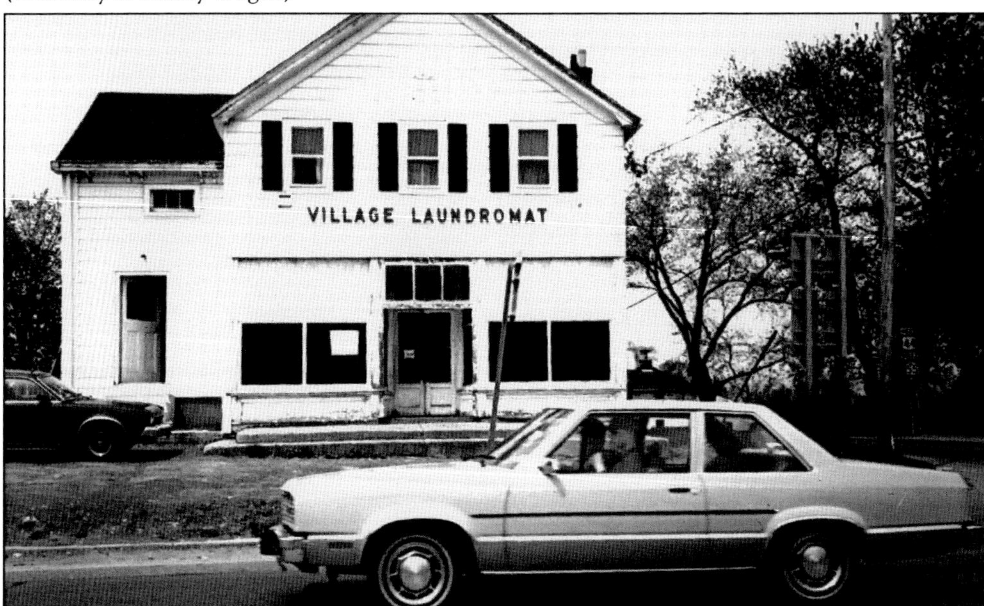

For many years, the southwest corner of the intersection in Modena was home to the D.B. Grimm store. The Grimm building was later apartments, and then a laundromat (shown here) owned by Sonny Wager during the 1970s. Today the building is once again used as apartments. (Courtesy of the Office of the Plattekill Historian.)

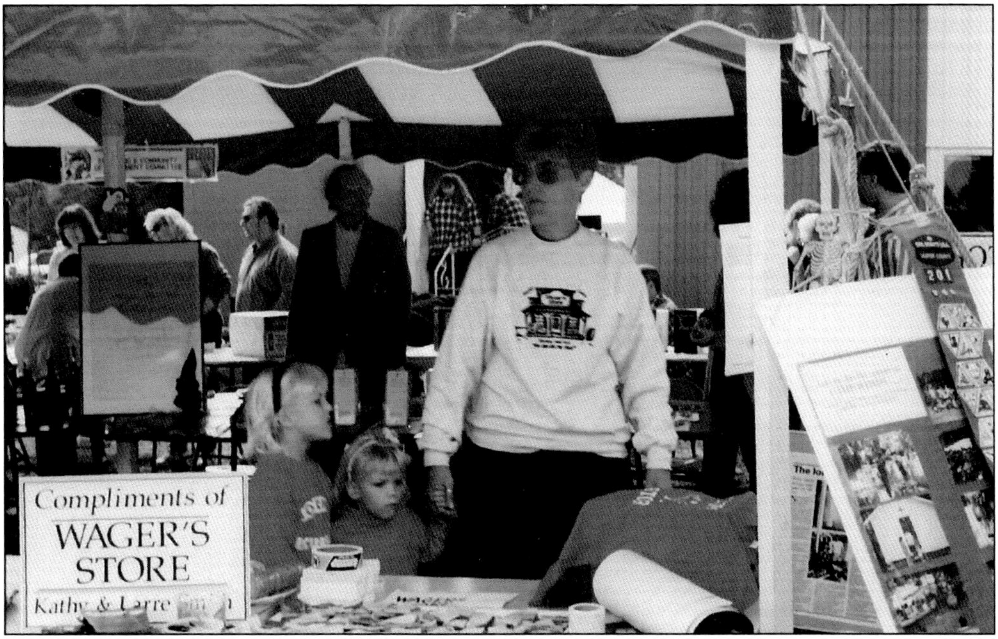

Modena was home to only one grocery store for many years—Wager's store on Route 32, run by Lester A. Wager Sr. and his wife, Belle, and later by Lester's daughter Kathy Wager Smith (pictured here in 1995 at a town event) and her husband, Larre Smith. Also pictured are sisters Sara (left) and Rachel Nelson of Modena. (Courtesy of the Office of the Plattekill Historian.)

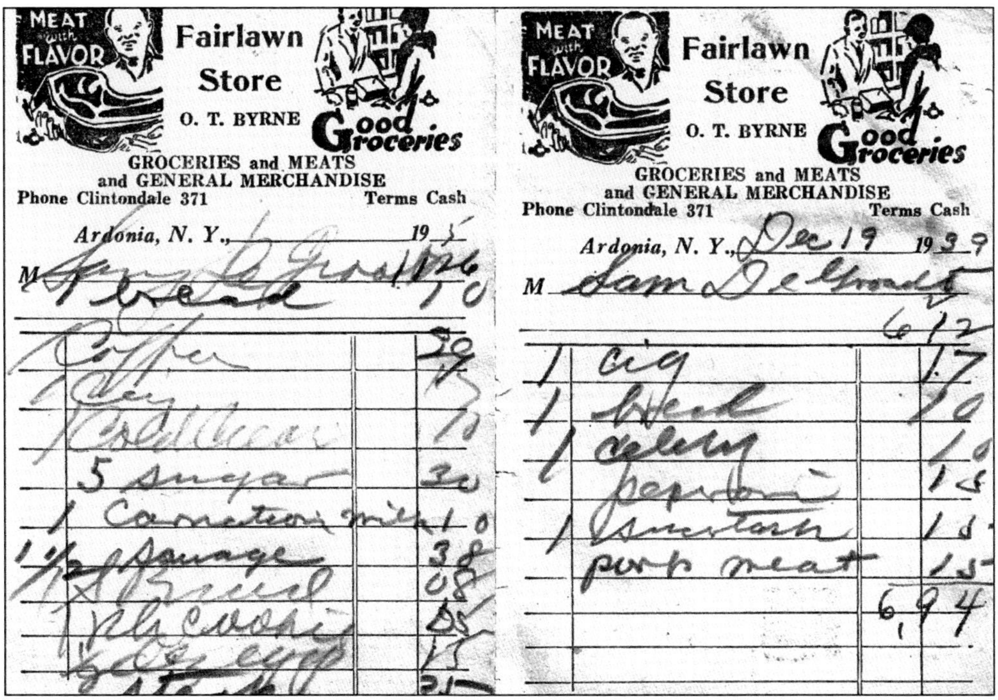

The receipts shown here, from 1938, are from the Oliver Byrne store in Ardonia. In 1938, the Ardonia Post Office moved to the store and remained in the same building until closing on February 28, 1973. The general store was later purchased by Kurt Laser. (Courtesy of the Jesse family.)

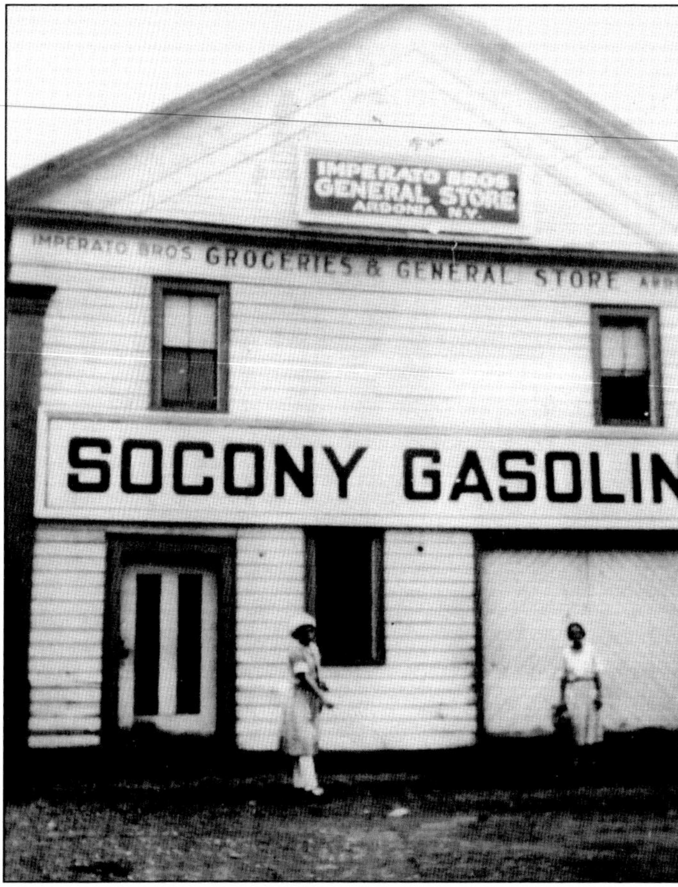

This building, located at the intersection of Milton Turnpike and Route 44/55, was once the Presbyterian church on Chapel Hill Road in the town of Lloyd. It was moved in 1863 to its present location in Ardonia. Members of the Modena Literary Society, organized in 1863, held their meetings in the structure and invited noted speakers such as Horace Greeley to present. By the 1890s, the building served as the Plattekill town clerk's office. Later it was a store, and Socony gas station owned by the Imperato family (left). Since the 1950s, the building has been the Ardonia Market. (Courtesy of Shirley Anson.)

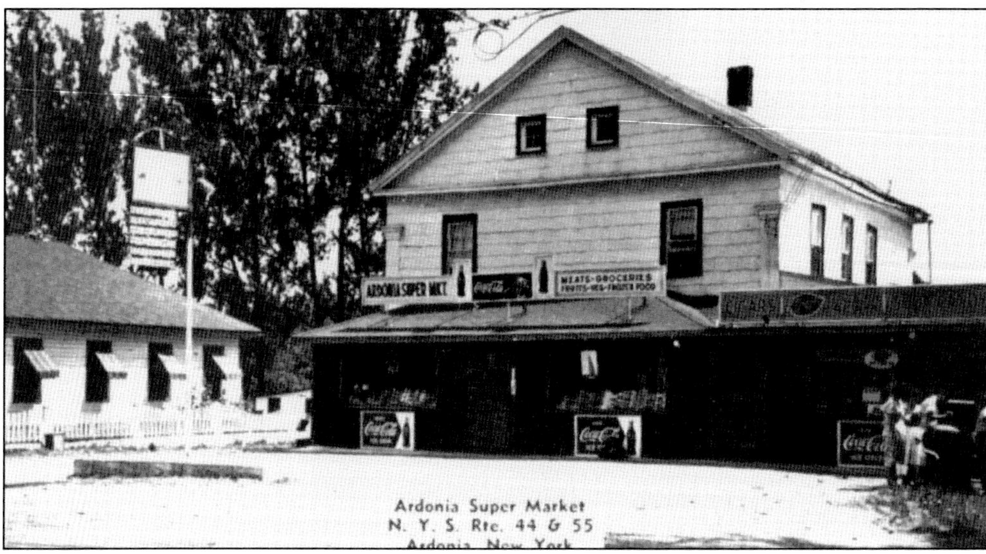

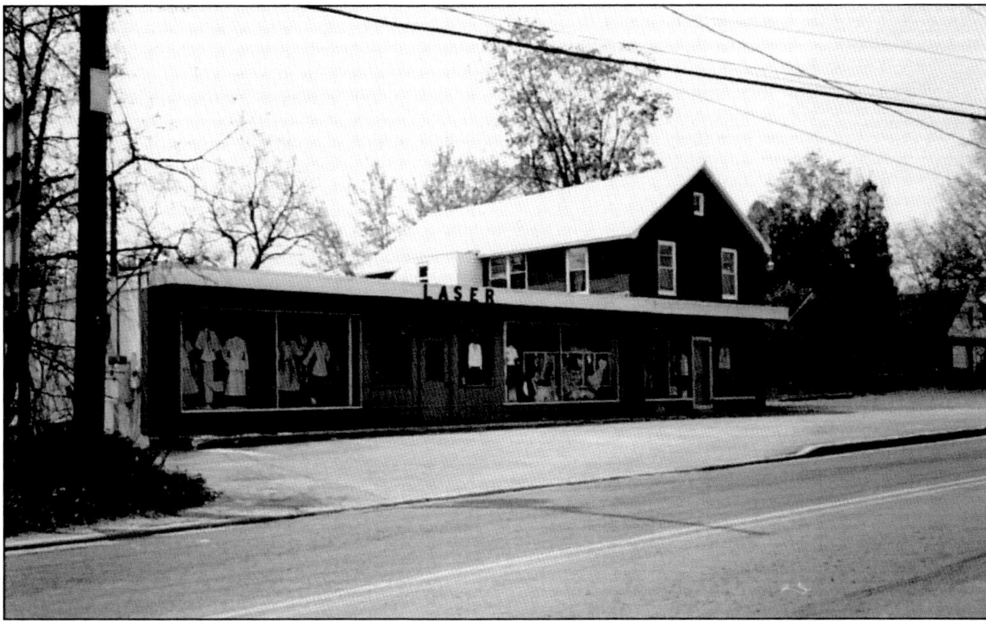

Kurt Laser was the Ardonia Postmaster from 1948 to 1973, when the hamlet's post office was discontinued. He owned a general store that carried everything from hardware to children's shoes. The business later evolved into a women's clothing shop, specializing in blouses, dresses, and pantsuits up to size 60. (Courtesy of *Friends and Neighbors: A Pictorial History of the Town of Plattekill and Southwest Lloyd.*)

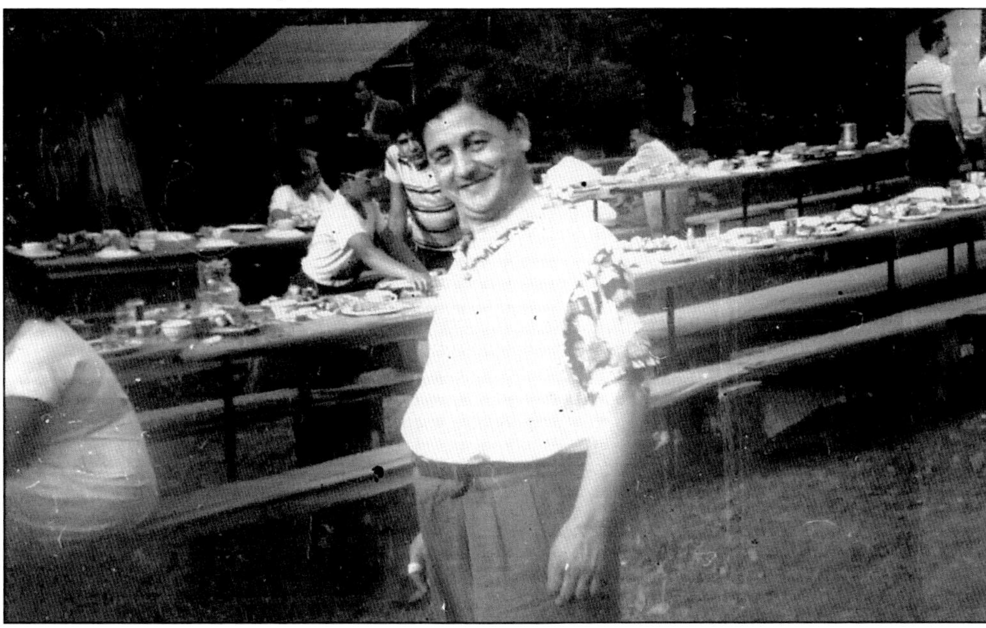

A general store owned by the McDowell family once stood where Primo's Bar and Grill now stands. The Atwood family purchased it and ran it as a general store and post office, with Eugene Atwood acting as postmaster. The store burned to the ground and was later rebuilt as Atwood's Inn. Primo Fiscella (shown here) purchased the building in 1945 and started Primo's Bar and Grill. (Courtesy of author's collection.)

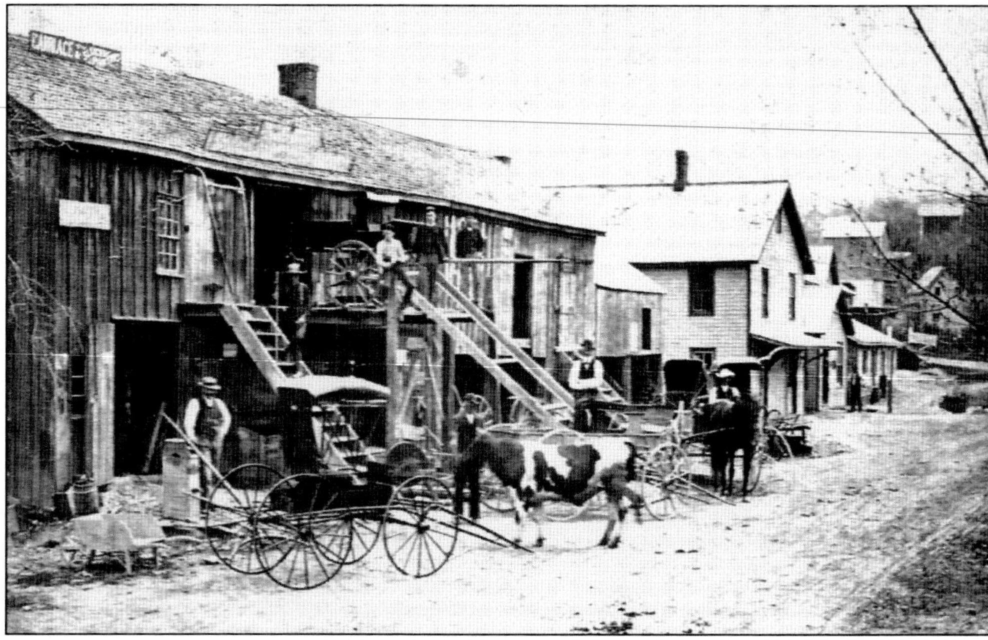

This wagon shop located along the Highland-Modena Turnpike (today Route 44/55) was owned by Hallock W. Sutton. In 1870, Sutton incorporated an undertaking business at the shop as well. By 1985, the shop advertised undertaking and embalming at a reasonable rate. Customers were encouraged to contact the business day or night by telephone or telegraph. This image is from a stereoview photograph taken in 1885. (Courtesy of *Friends and Neighbors: A Pictorial History of the Town of Plattekill and Southwest Lloyd.*)

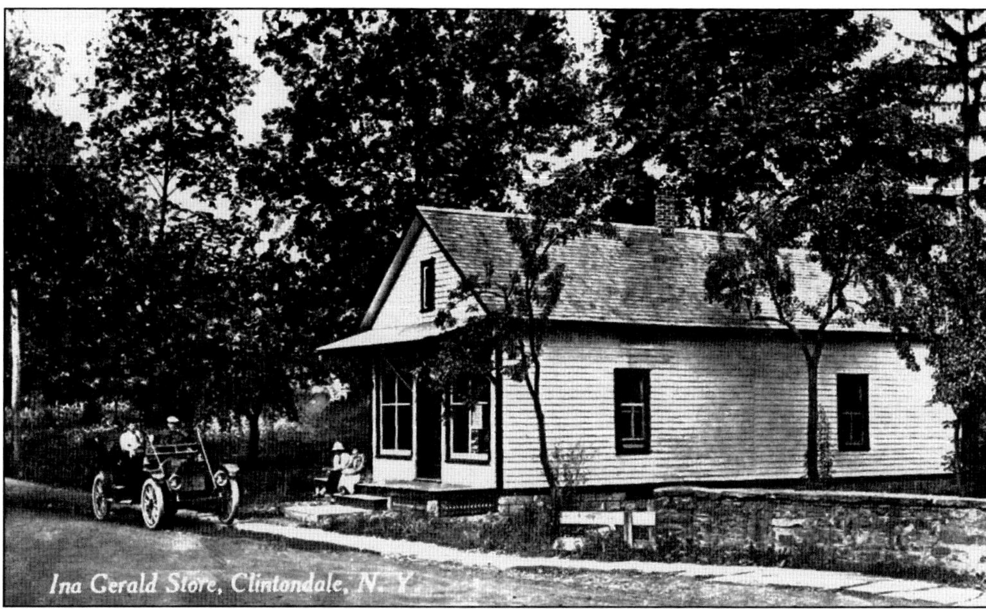

This early postcard shows the Ina Gerald store. Gerald ran a millinery and sold dry goods from this building, located on Maple Avenue in Clintondale. Gerald began her business in 1906 in a rented store; this store was built on a lot purchased in 1910. Gerald ran the store until her death in 1942. (Courtesy of author's collection.)

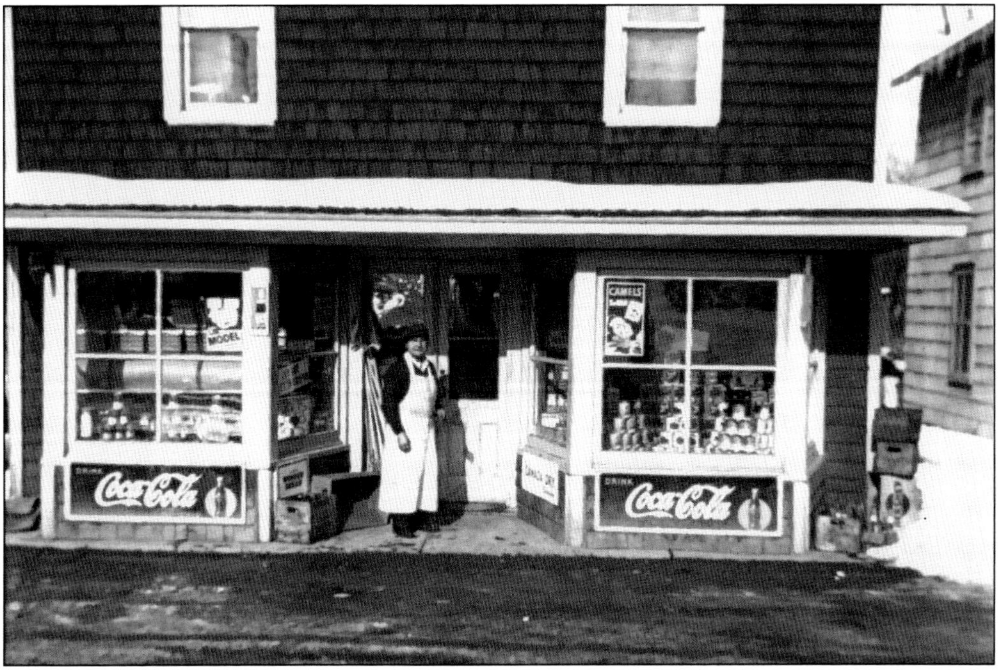

Tobia Capozzi was a well-known businessman in Clintondale. His Capozzi's Clintondale Market still stands on Route 44/55 and is now run by his daughters. Over the years, the building pictured here has housed, among other things, an ice cream parlor, a meat market, a general store, and a barbershop. (Courtesy of Shirley Anson.)

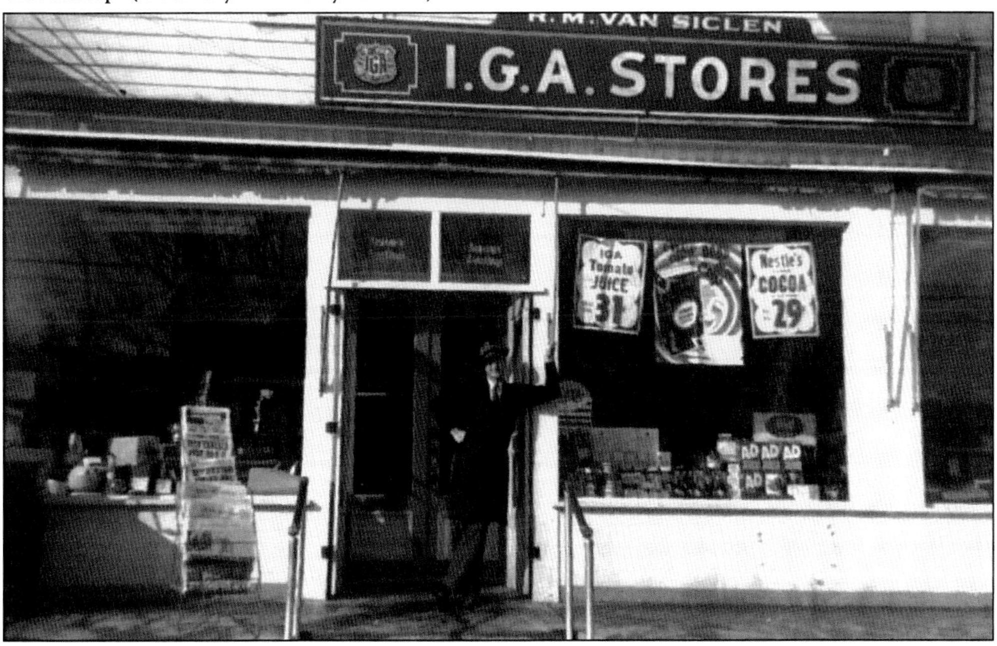

Ralph Van Siclen, pictured here in the early 1950s, operated an I.G.A. store on Maple Avenue. He bought the store in December 1937 from the Capozzi family. The Clintondale Post Office was located in the store for a time, with Van Siclen serving as postmaster. (Courtesy of *Friends and Neighbors: A Pictorial History of the Town of Plattekill and Southwest Lloyd.*)

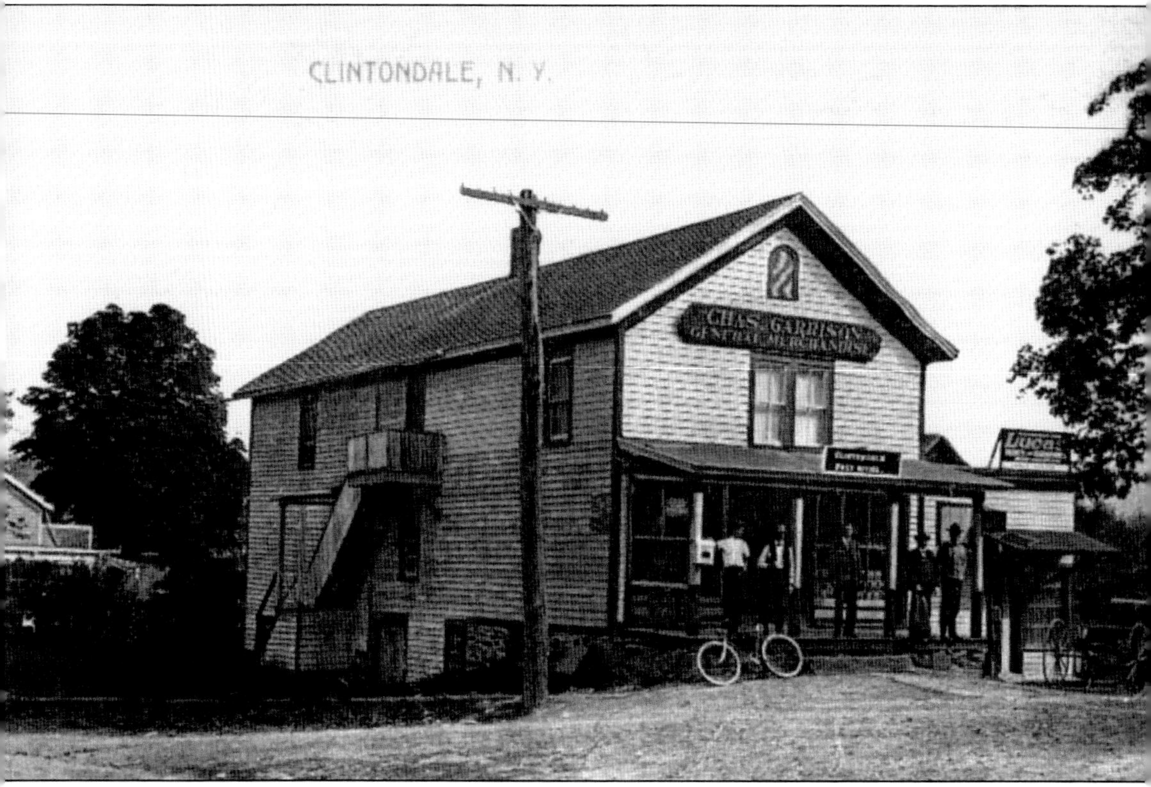

Charles Garrison operated Garrison's Store, located at the corner of Route 44/55 and Maple Avenue, or the "Upper Corner" in Clintondale. The store was built in 1868 by James Hull and was operated by various merchants. At different times, the building housed a bakery, fish market, and general store. An upper part of the building was used as a public meeting hall. A fire at the store in January 1915 destroyed the building. An article in the *New Paltz Independent* stated that the Garrisons were awakened by the barking of the dog they left in the store each night. The post office was housed in the store at the time of the fire. (Courtesy of *Friends and Neighbors: A Pictorial History of the Town of Plattekill and Southwest Lloyd.*)

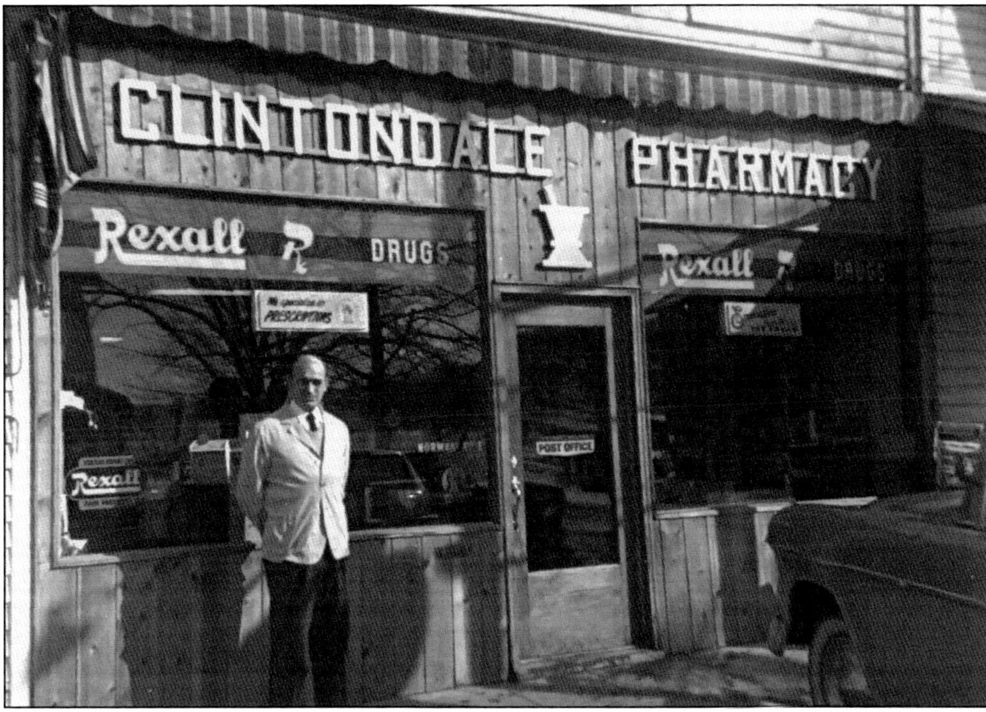

These two c. 1950 pictures show Norman Rice's Clintondale Pharmacy, which also served as the hamlet's post office. Rice, pictured above, was Clintondale's postmaster from August 15, 1945, until August 1973, taking over the position held by Ralph Van Siclen for more than 20 years. In 1945, the post office was moved from Van Siclen's store to Rice's store. The building is still home to the Clintondale Post Office, although no store has been in the building since 1972, when Rice closed his drug store. (Courtesy of Shirley Anson.)

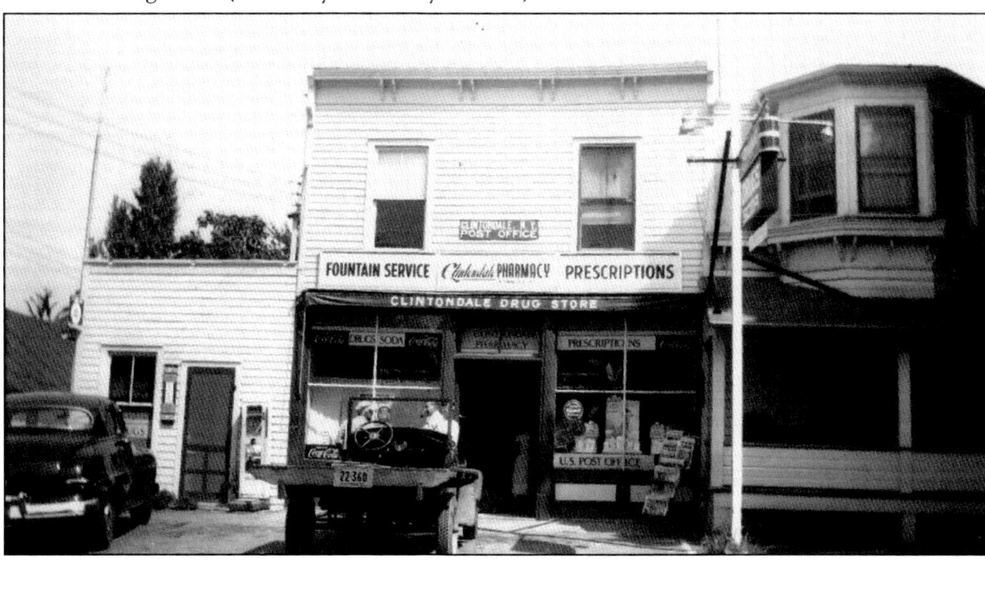

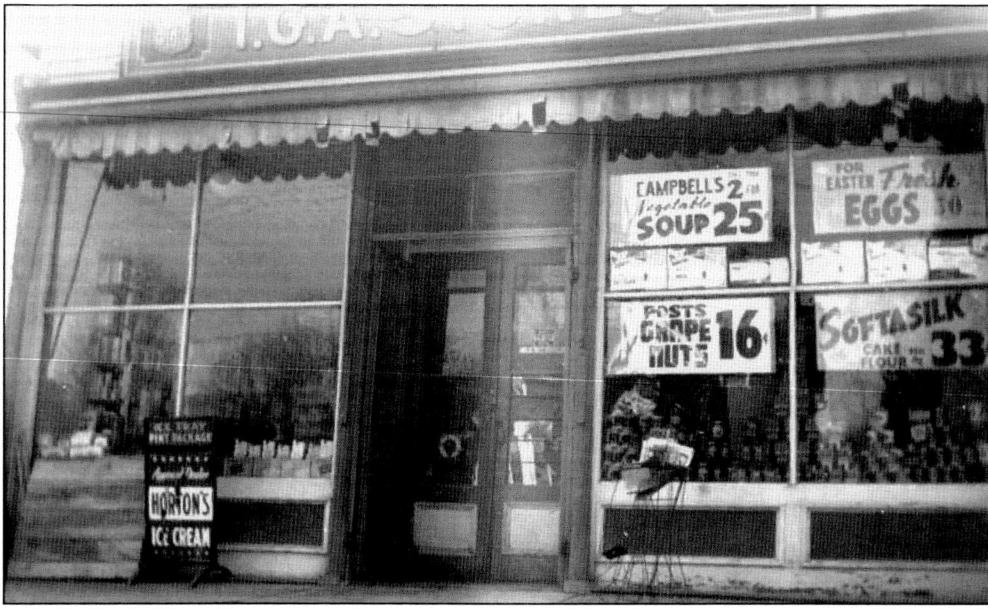

By the late 1950s, Clintondale was down to three stores: the Ralph Van Siclen I.G.A. (pictured here), the Capozzi store on Route 44/55, and the Clintondale Drug store on Route 44/55, owned by Norman Rice. Today the Capozzi store is the last general store in the hamlet. (Courtesy of Shirley Anson.)

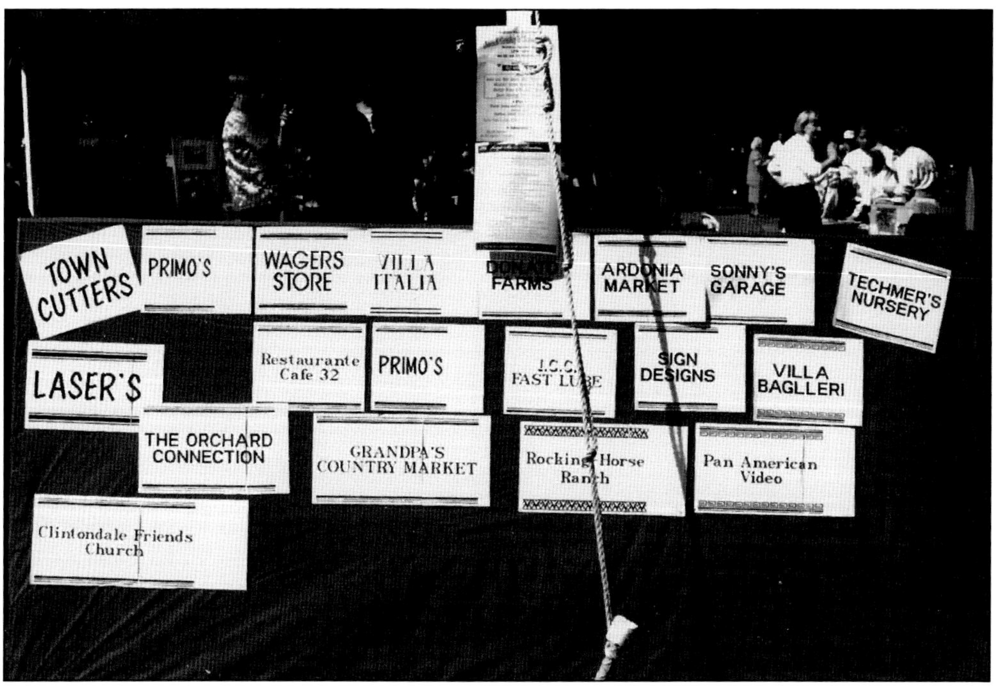

A booth at a Plattekill Day celebration during the 1990s shows off some off the Plattekill businesses still operating at that time within the various hamlets. Most of the businesses depicted here are still in existence, while many new businesses have opened in town since that time. (Courtesy of the Office of the Plattekill Town Historian.)

Five

The Boardinghouses, Villas, and Resorts

Its attractive natural features make Plattekill an ideal vacation spot, as an untold number of tourists have discovered in the last century. During the late 1800s and early 1900s, boarding houses flourished throughout the town as guests would take the train or drive from New York City to spend a summer in the country. Guests were invited to enjoy the farms, gardens, and, in the case of the Elixir Spring House in Clintondale, the mineral waters of the town. Many of those same boarding houses gave way to villas by the 1920s and 1930s.

When New York City newspapers began touting the Plattekill area as the "Spanish Alps at the base of the Catskills," tourists began arriving by the thousands to spend a day, a weekend or a summer. In his 1995 memoir, Ed Wager, a former town constable, recalls busses arriving in town "thirty, forty at a time." Wager recalled many of the busses parking for the day at the Plattekill firehouse and the town purchasing another patrol car to deal with the influx of visitors. As many as many as 5,000 guests each weekend would head to the numerous Italian, Spanish, and Puerto Rican villas in Plattekill and Clintondale, as well to the boarding houses still scattered throughout the town.

Problems arose when the influx of visitors caused traffic jams and packed villas by the hundreds. Illegal villas that sprung up throughout Plattekill provided a home for cockfights, gambling, and drugs, and many clashes occurred between residents and tourists.

The villa era ended by the early 1980s, with only a few still operating. Most of the former villas are now used as apartment buildings and have given way to family oriented resorts. Despite the tumultuous times, the villa era left a lasting legacy on the town. Many tourists chose to make Plattekill their home and still reside there today. Responsible villa owners worked closely with the Plattekill constables to ensure that everything remained orderly, which led to long term relationships. Said Lester Wager, Plattekill's head constable during the villa era, "we made a lot of good friends during that time."

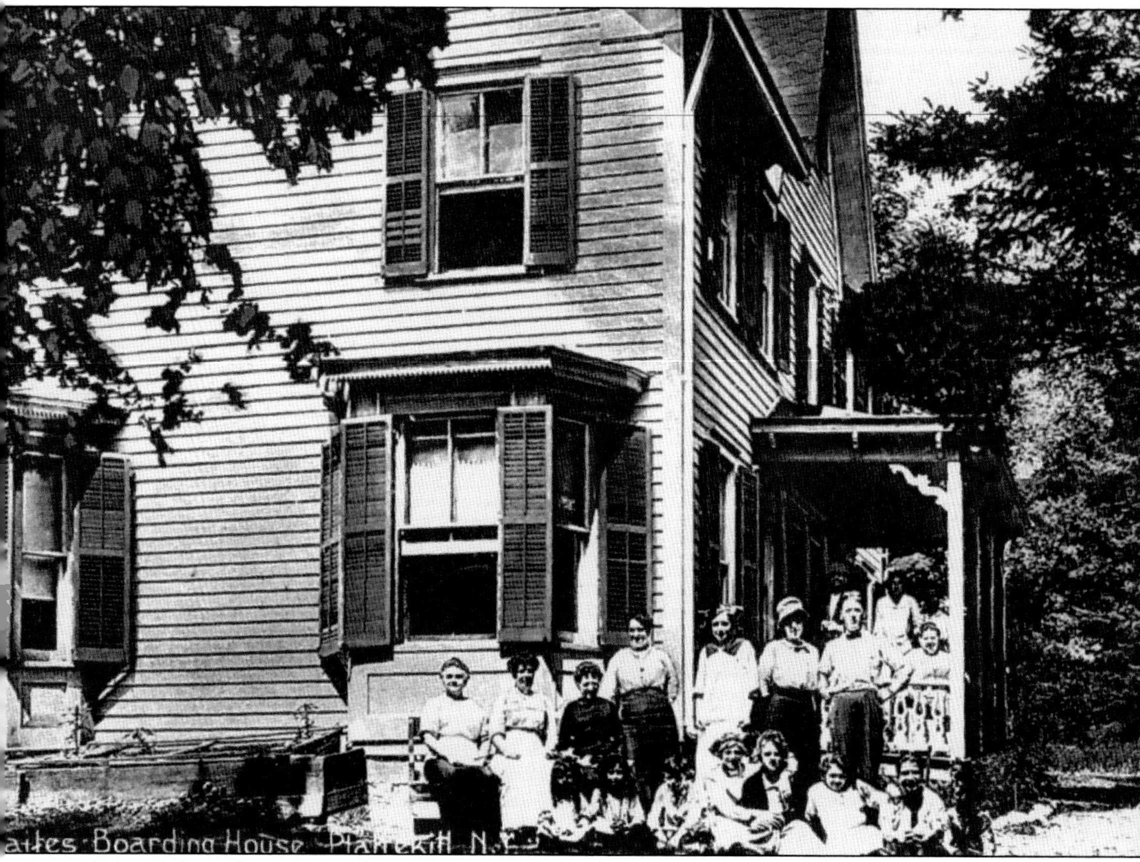

Waite's Boarding House, located on Plattekill-Ardonia Road, was run by Matilda Waite until the 1940s. It is shown here on a postcard around 1920. Later it became the Villa Galicia, one of many popular villas along Plattekill-Ardonia Road and still later a tennis club. Today the structure is used as apartments. (Courtesy of *Friends and Neighbors: A Pictorial History of the Town of Plattekill and Southwest Lloyd.*)

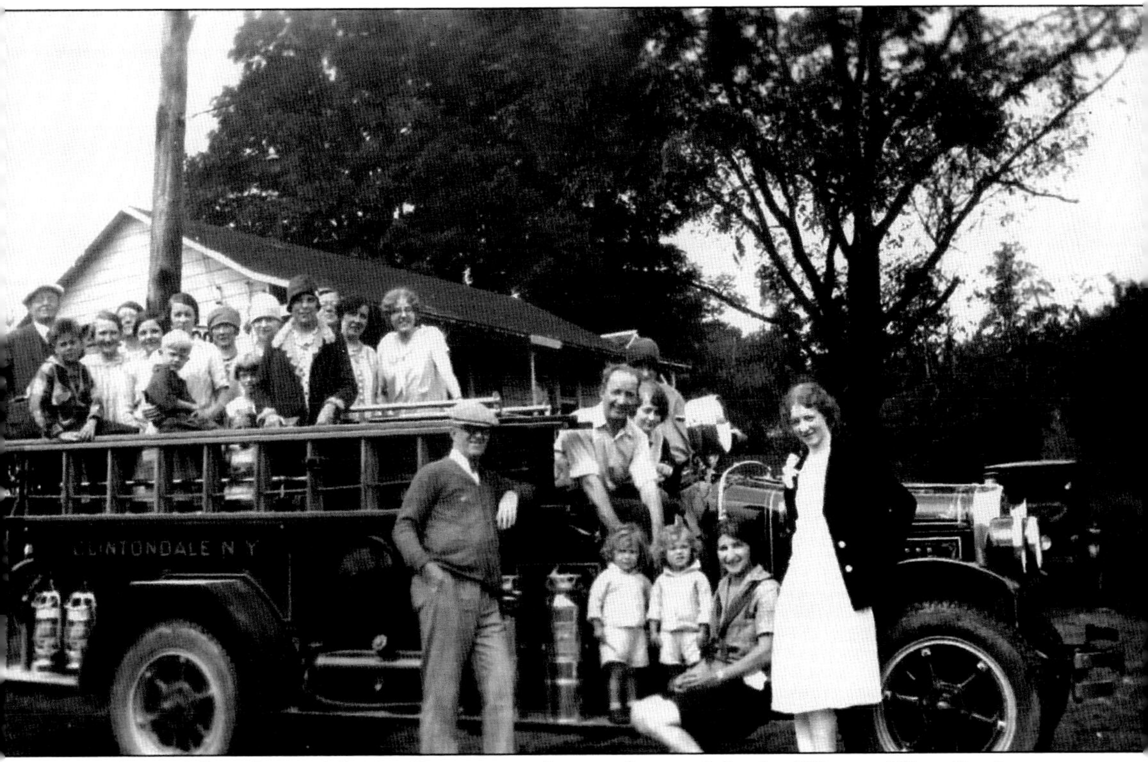

Members of the Clintondale Fire Department bring a fire truck by the Elliswood Boardinghouse on Crescent Avenue in Clintondale in September 1936. At one time, the hamlet of Clintondale was home to several popular boardinghouses, including the Elixer Spring House and the Bonnie Brae Inn. Elliswood Boardinghouse, owned by Clemmie Ellis White during the 1920s and 1930s, was a popular resort featuring cottages and bungalows. Tourists from New York City could reach Clintondale by the Hudson River Day Boat Line or by a train to Poughkeepsie, Newburgh, or Beacon. An early advertisement for the resort touted "Garage for Automobiles. Good road all the way, either side of River." The rate was advertised as $3 a day or $15 to $18 a week, with special rates for families. Today the structure is used as apartments. (Courtesy of *Friends and Neighbors: A Pictorial History of the Town of Plattekill and Southwest Lloyd.*)

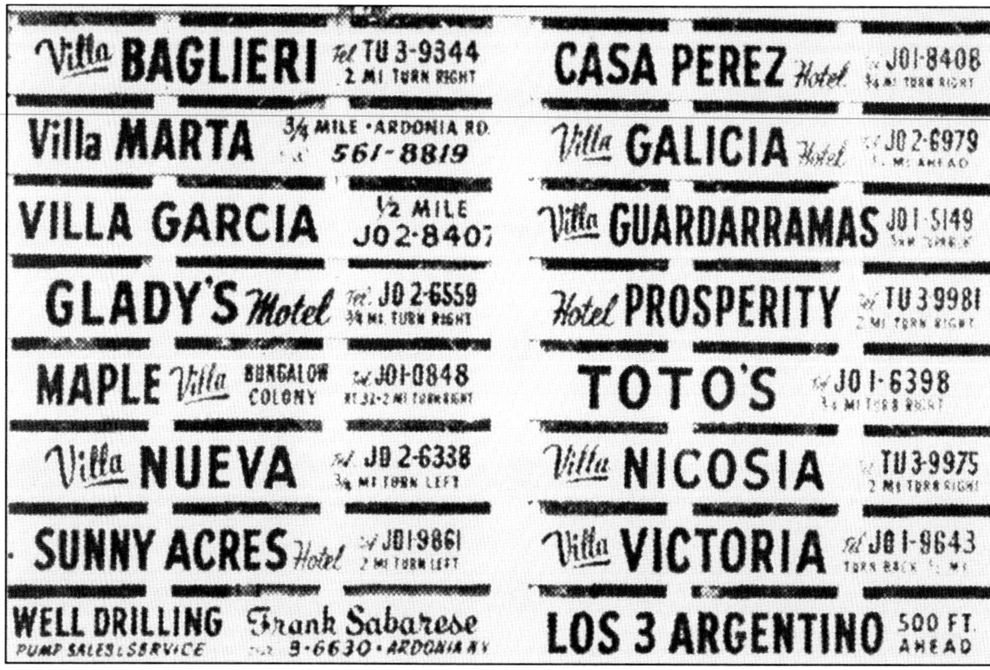

A large sign advertising the many Italian, Spanish, and Puerto Rican villas and associated businesses once stood at the intersection of Route 32 and Plattekill-Ardonia Road in Plattekill. The sign seen above provides a picture of the area during the height of the tourism era in the mid-1960s, while the picture below, taken in 1989, shows the last of the villas. At present, the sign still stands and advertises only a single resort—the Garden Cathay resort and golf course, on the grounds of the former Villa Nueva. (Above, courtesy of Sonny Wager; below, courtesy of *Friends and Neighbors: A Pictorial History of the Town of Plattekill and Southwest Lloyd.*)

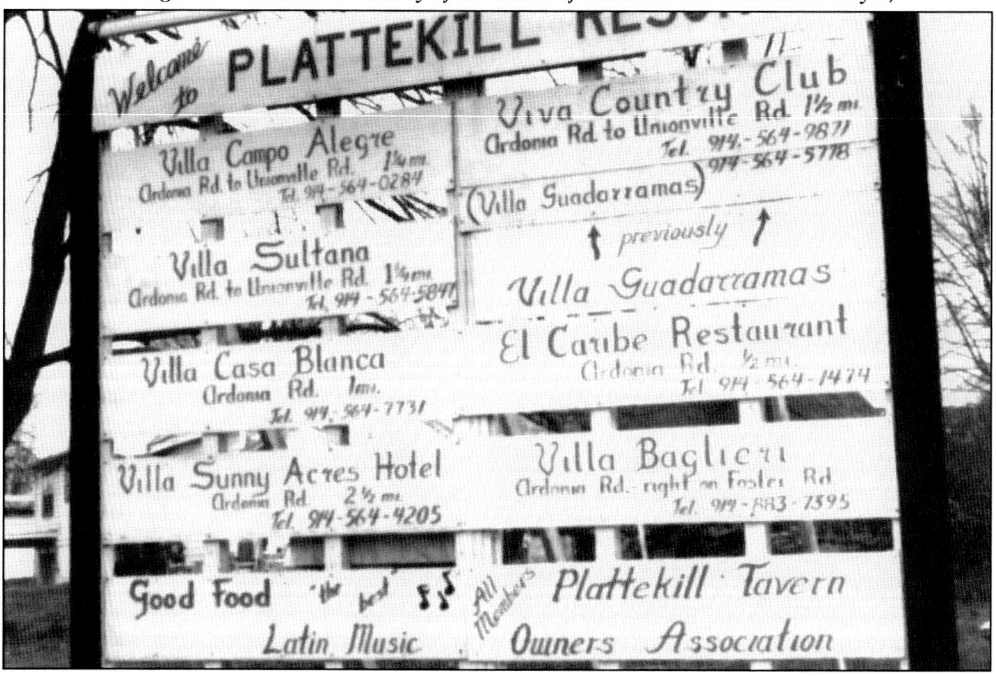

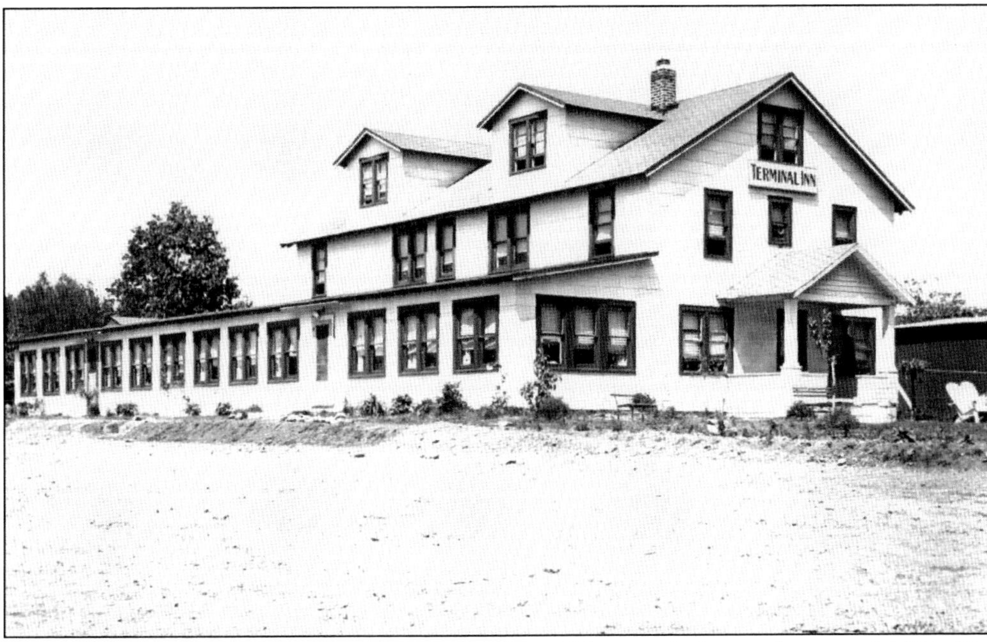

Guests of the Terminal Inn pose in front of the well-known Italian villa around 1950. The resort's heyday was in the 1950s, when tourists from New York City and surrounding areas would come for a day, a week, or the entire summer. Residents can recall villa guests purchasing eggs, flowers, and vegetables from them at their roadside farm stands and taking walks along South Street. The Terminal Inn was owned and operated by the Monforte family. Today the building, located on South Street in Plattekill, is an apartment house. (Courtesy of the Office of the Plattekill Historian.)

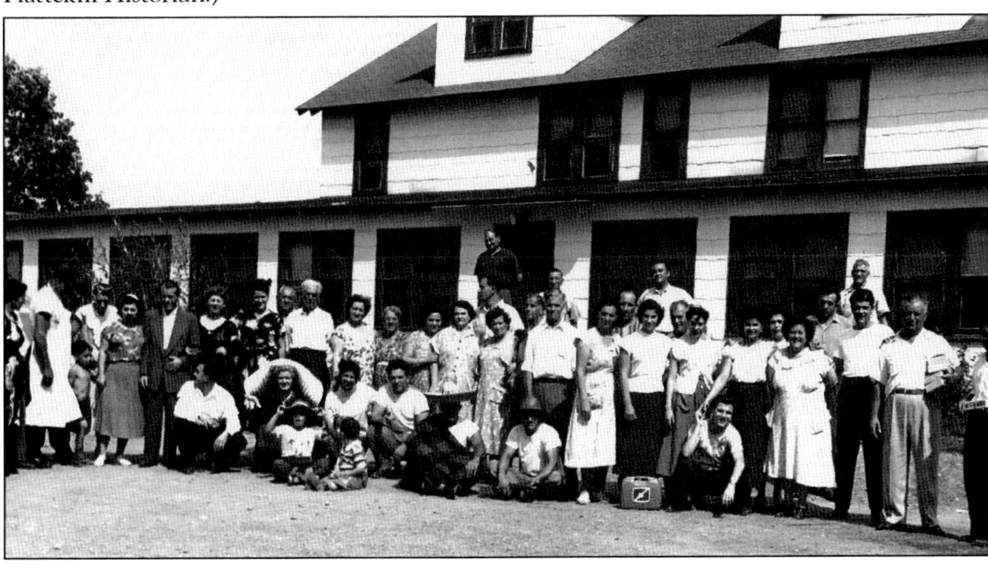

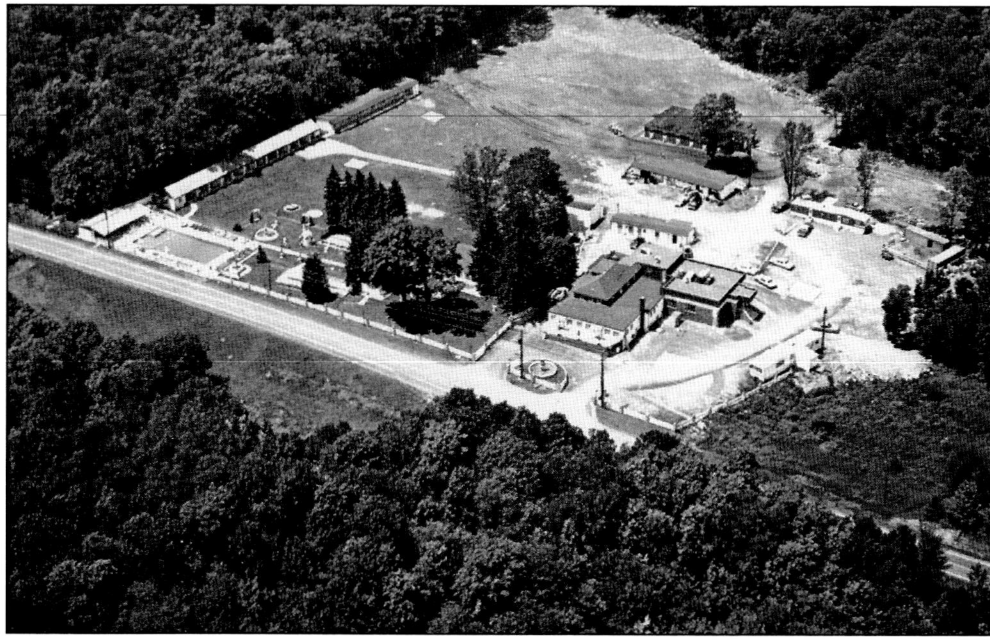

The Villa Baglieri, located on Fosler Road, was billed as "a modern resort, family owned since 1946." The Italian villa, which sat on more than 100 acres, featured an Olympic-sized heated pool, horseback riding, a free midnight buffet every Friday, and social directors leading a variety of activities. The resort touted itself as being family friendly, with planned adult activities and counselors to lead games for children. The resort was popular into the mid-1990s, when it was used as a catering and banquet facility and hosted many weddings. Today the buildings are used primarily as efficiency apartments. (Courtesy of the Office of the Plattekill Historian.)

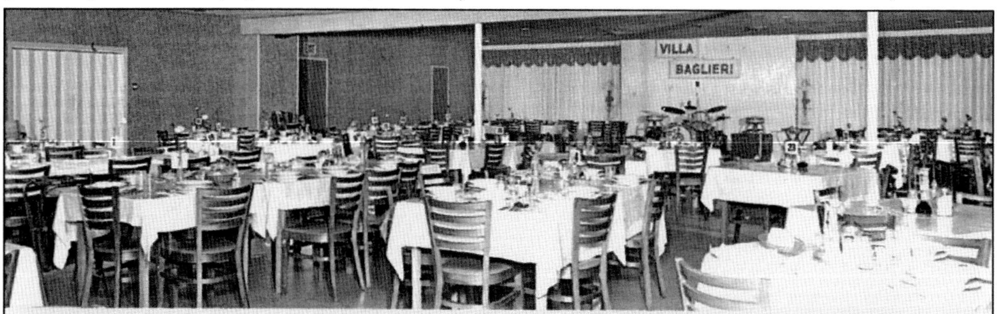

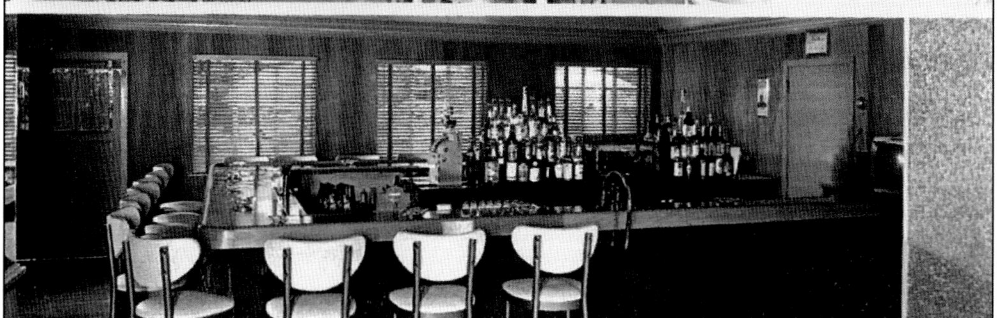

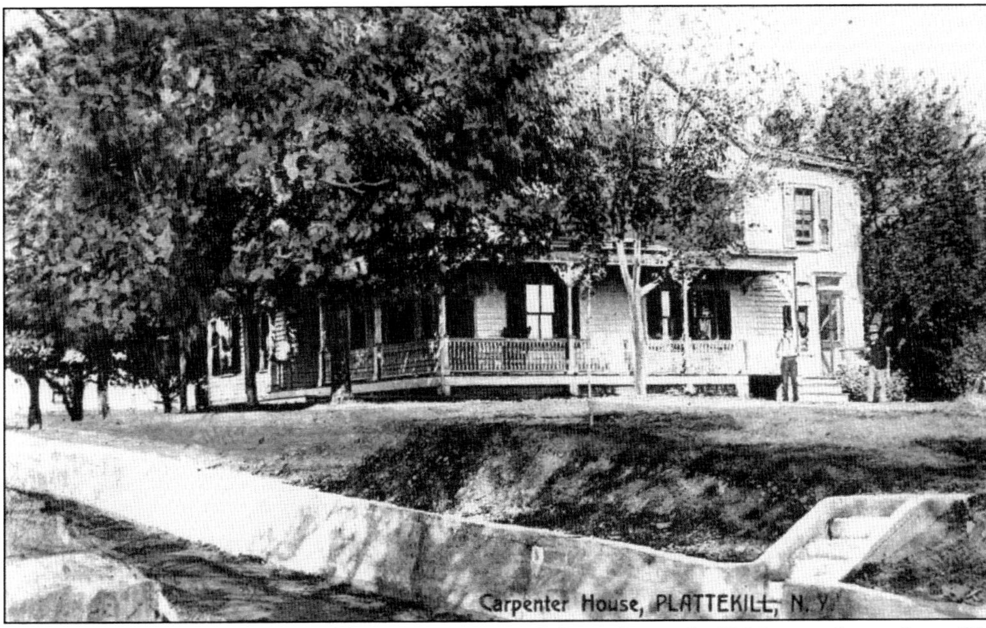

The Carpenter House, pictured here on a postcard from the early 1900s, was located on Old Route 32 and Church Street in Plattekill. The house later became the Casa Los Andes, a popular Puerto Rican villa. (Courtesy of author's collection.)

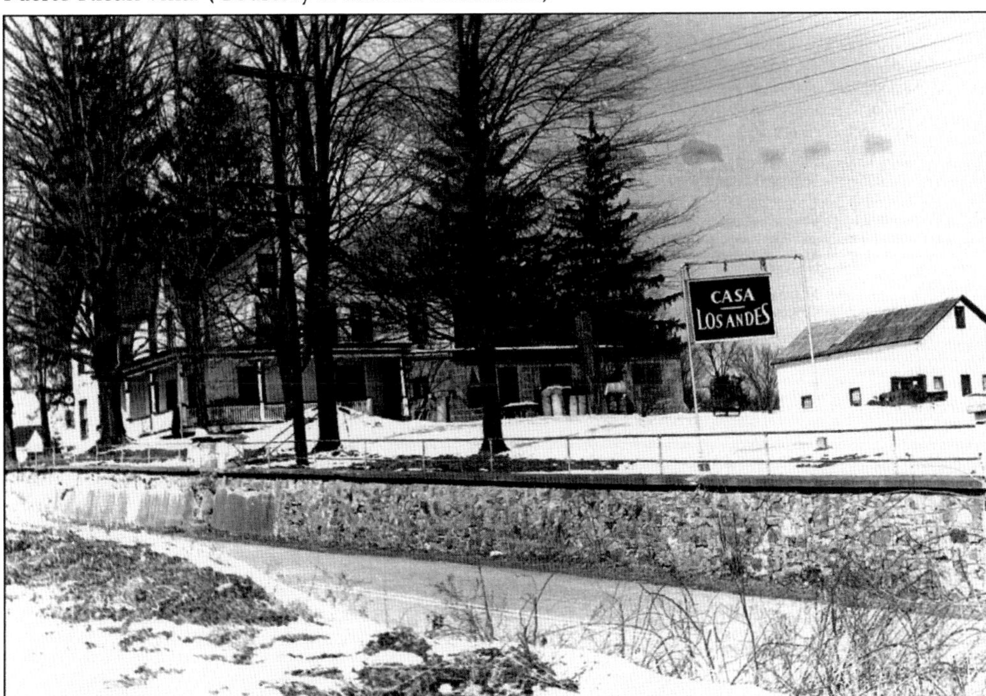

The Casa Los Andes, around 1950, was owned by Isidore Romero. Some of the land was taken over in the 1950s by the New York State Thruway Authority and today the New York State Thruway runs through part of the original property. Today a smaller section of the house still stands on Plattekill's Church Street. (Courtesy of the Office of the Plattekill Historian.)

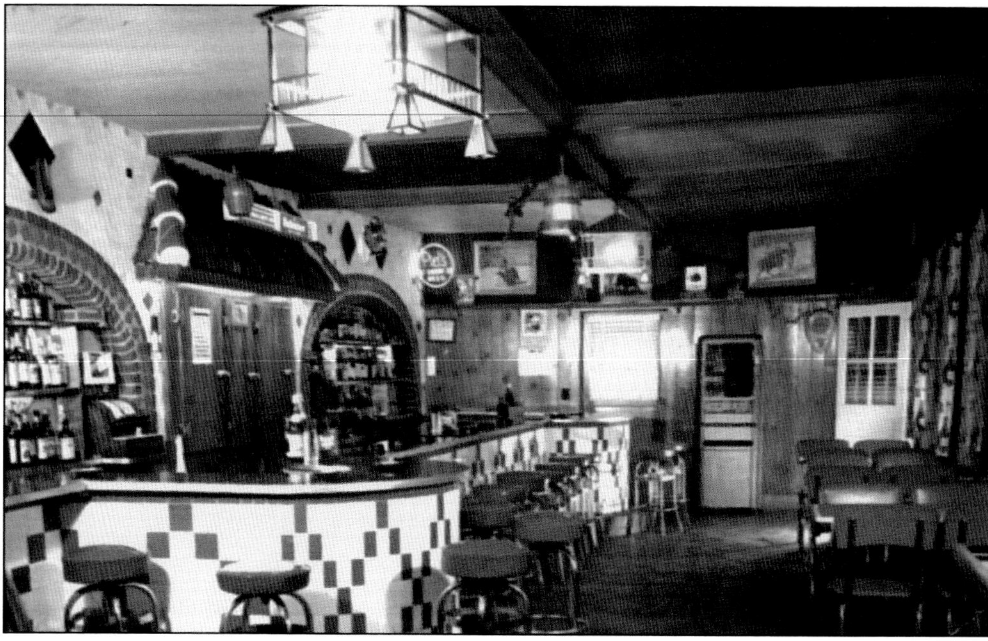

The Villa Nueva, pictured here on a 1940s postcard, was a Spanish villa located on Plattekill-Ardonia Road. The well-known villa was often written about in newspaper articles describing Plattekill's "Spanish Alps" feel. A 1965 article in the *New York Times* noted that while other villas were "rustic," coats and ties were "de rigueur" in the Villa Nueva's "plush, modern dining room." Recipes from the villa's kitchen were reprinted in the *New York Times*. The resort was not only popular with tourists, many area service organizations held their annual banquets and meetings at the villa. Today the buildings and grounds are part of the Garden Cathay resort. (Above, courtesy of the Office of the Plattekill Historian; below, courtesy of Shirley Anson.)

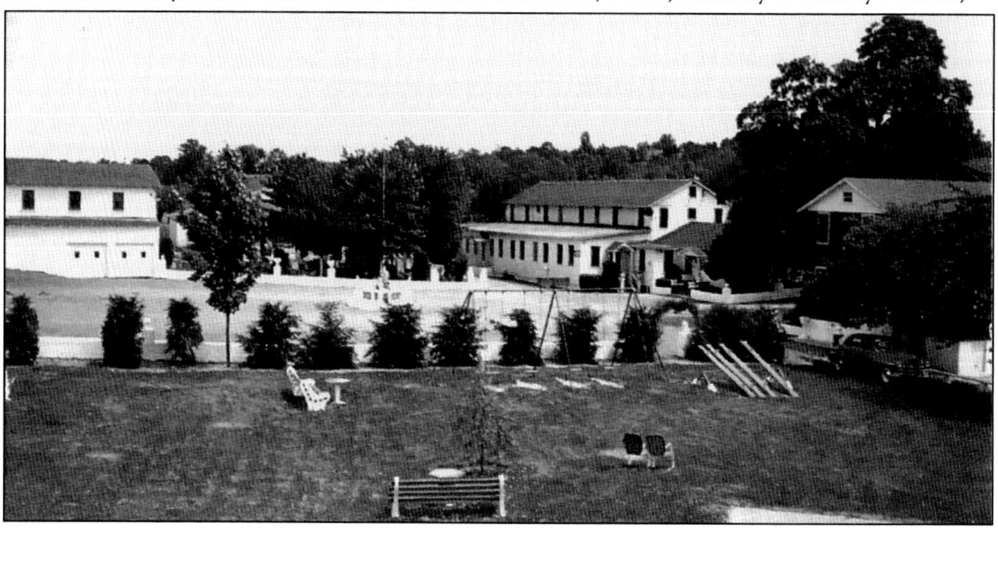

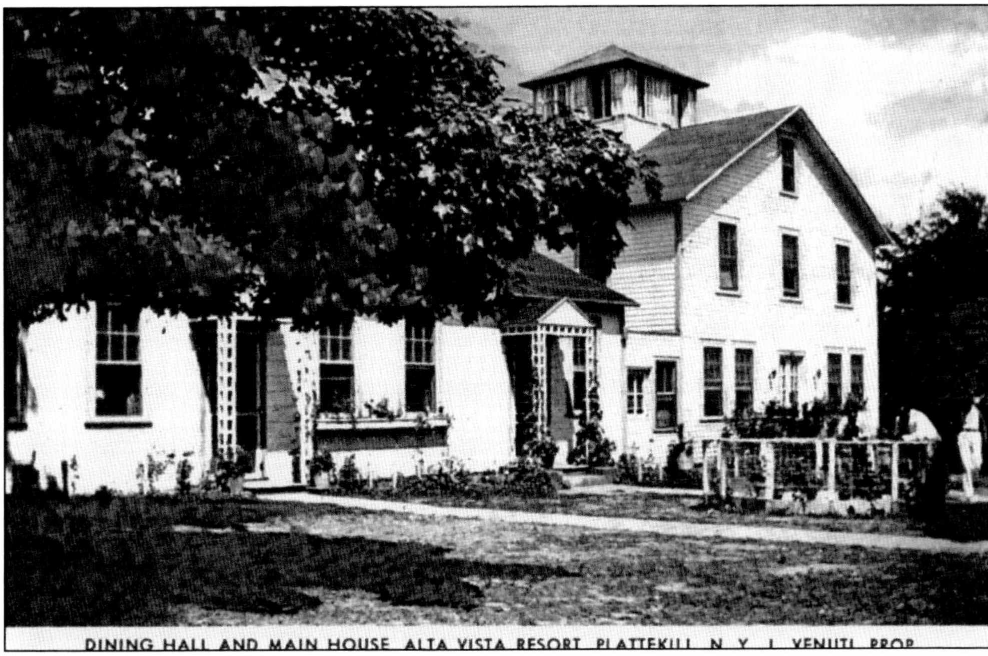

The Alta Vista Resort was an Italian villa located on what is today called Venuto Road. The dining hall and main house are pictured here in an early postcard. The villa was owned and operated by the Venuti family. Much of the property near the villa was taken over by the New York State Thruway Authority in the 1950s, while Venuto Road became a dead end. (Courtesy of Shirley Anson.)

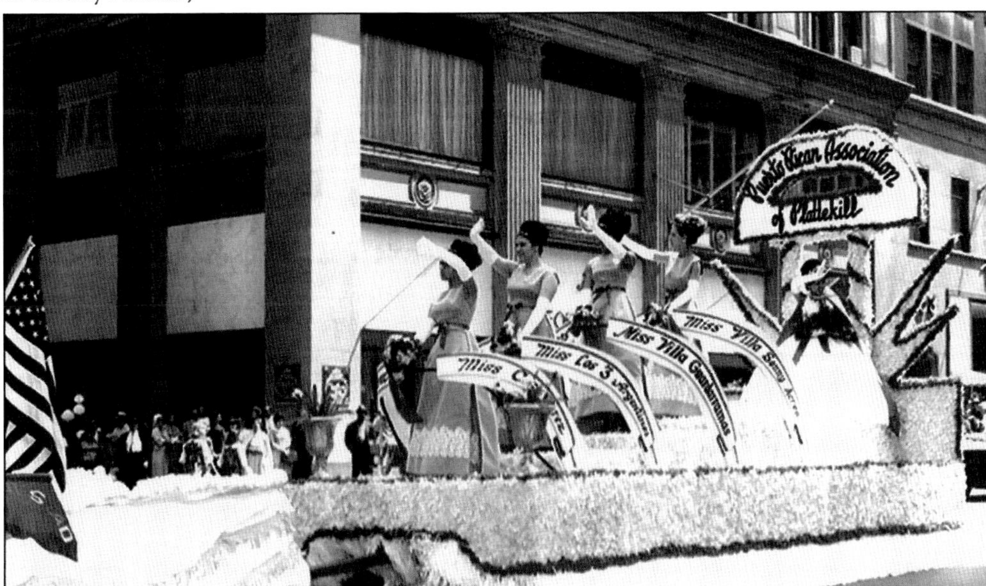

A 1965 photograph shows representatives of Plattekill's Puerto Rican villas on a float in a New York City parade. Representing the Casa Perez is Gloria Velasquez, the Los 3 Argentino is Minnie Ortiz, the Villa Guadarramas is Linda Comulalada, and the Villa Sunny Acres is Linda Comulalada. Linda Sifre (right) was named Miss Puerto Rican Association of Plattekill. (Courtesy of the Office of the Plattekill Historian.)

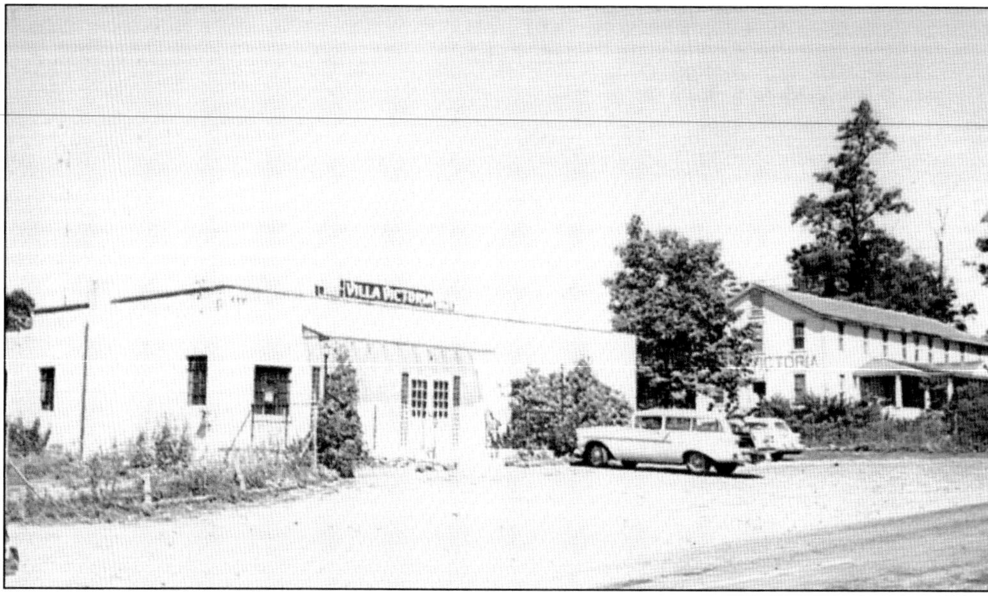

One of the most notorious villas in Plattekill was the Villa Victoria, located on Route 32 near the Orange County border. Hundreds of guests would visit each weekend, often spilling out onto the street and disrupting the flow of traffic along Route 32. Today the building in the foreground is the Café 32 restaurant, while the building in the back is apartments. (Courtesy of the Office of the Plattekill Historian.)

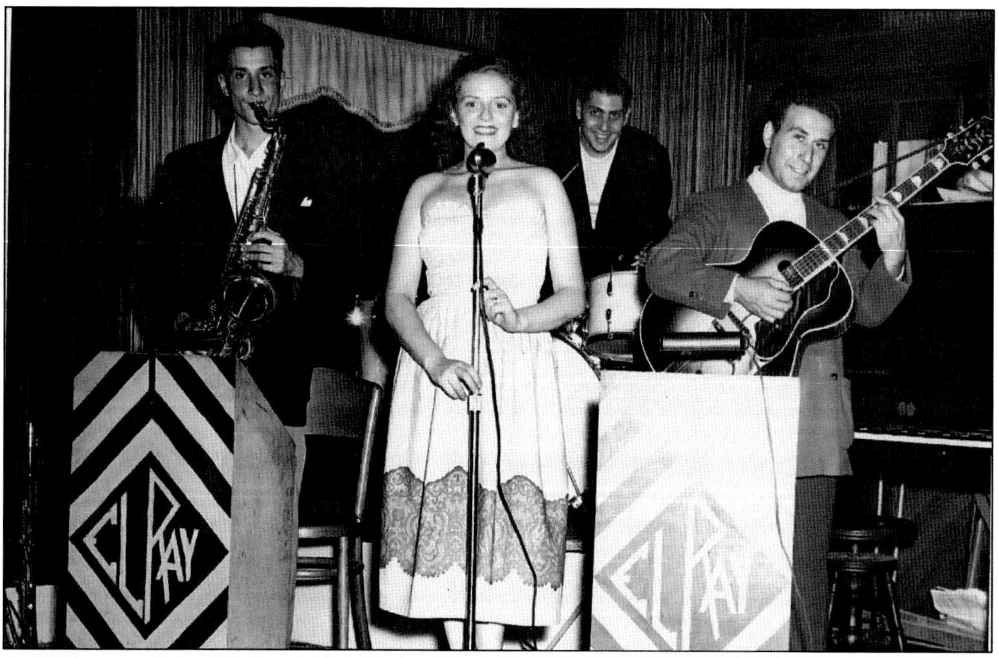

A 1965 issue of the *Highland Mid-Hudson Post* explained the villa nightlife: "Usually at 2 p.m. on Saturdays and Sundays the Latin bands start filling the dance halls and the surrounding hills with merinques, cha-chas and rumbas. They take a break for dinner and then return until the 3 a.m. closing." Shown here are singers at the Club El Rey. (Courtesy of the Office of the Plattekill Historian.)

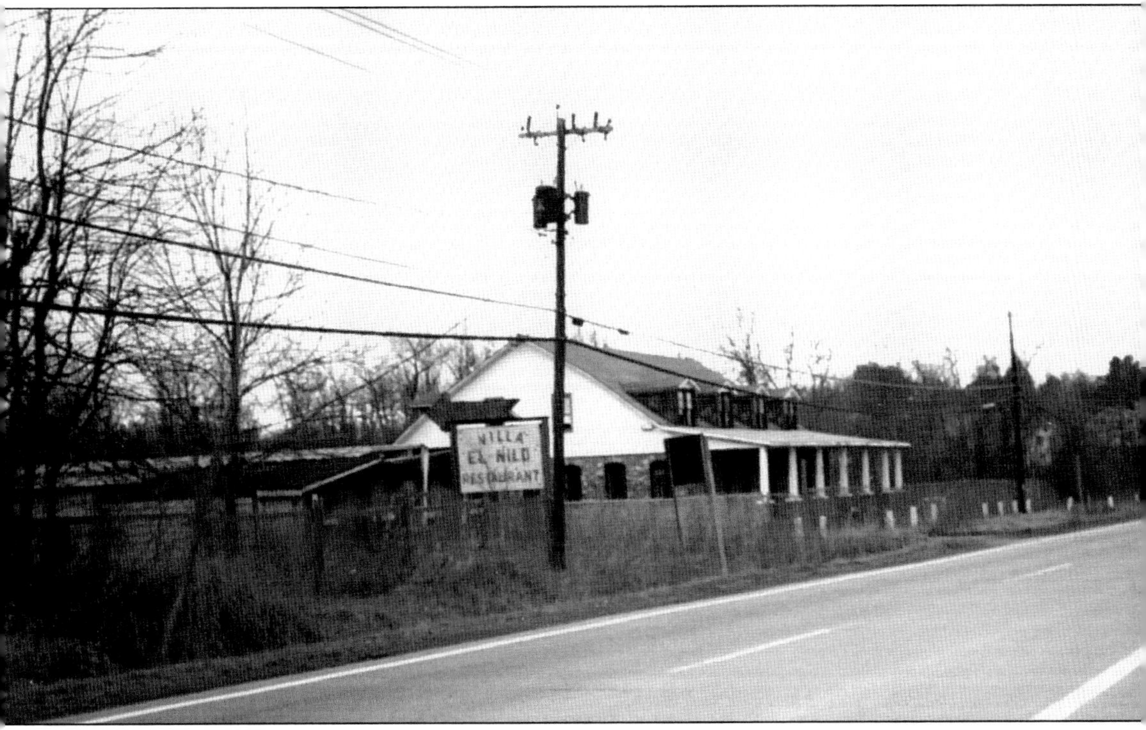

A picture taken of the crumbling remains of the former Club El Rey or Villa El Nilo on Route 32 near the Orange County border is seen here. Before it was the Club El Rey, it was a club known as the Cat's Meow. In his 1995 memoir, former Plattekill constable Ed "Pop" Wager recalls the reaction of the town to this new venture: "This was the first saloon in the village—a real fancy place. You could buy any kind of drink that you could think of. People came from all over, well dressed, in big cars with chauffeurs driving them." Wager also wrote of one particular Sunday morning when the police were called for a traffic backup along Route 32. Showgirls from the club were sunning themselves on the roof sans clothing, much to the chagrin of many residents who were driving to church. (Courtesy of the Office of the Plattekill Historian.)

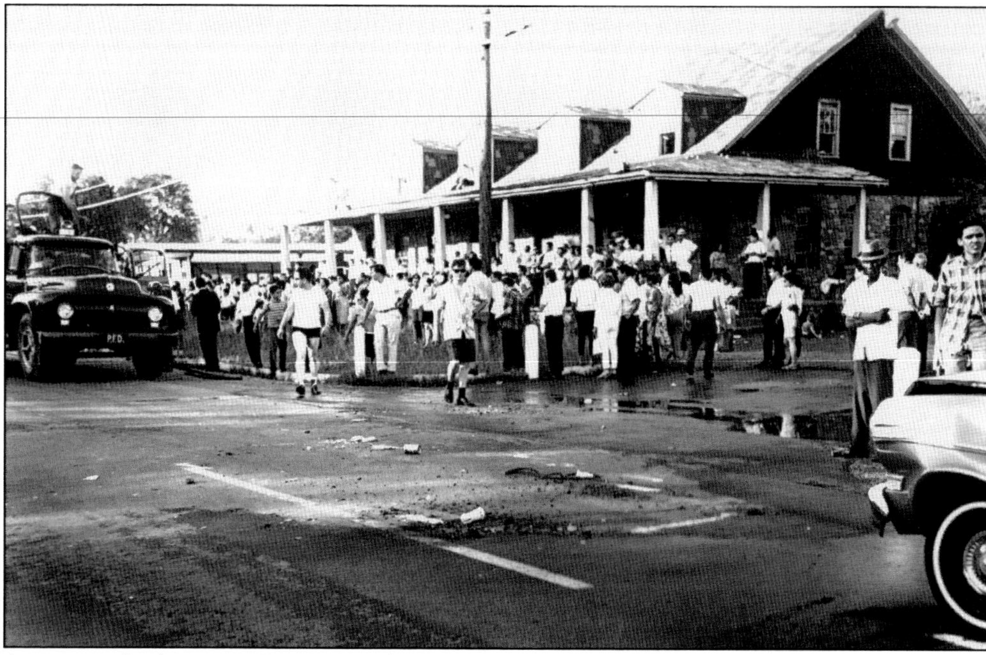

A near-riot broke out on Route 32 in between in the Villa El Nilo and the Villa Victoria in July 1965, after a fatal automobile accident killed a young tourist over the Fourth of July weekend. A car crashed into the back of a vehicle that had stopped in the road, killing a 15-month-old boy who was a passenger in the stopped car. A crowd of more than 500 people who had been visiting the villas refused to disperse and allow firefighters to clear the scene. Fire hoses were used to push back the crowd, who responded by throwing beer bottles and rocks at firefighters and police. No injuries were reported. Pictured at the left of the bottom photograph is Plattekill chief constable Lester "Sonny" Wager. (Courtesy of Sonny Wager.)

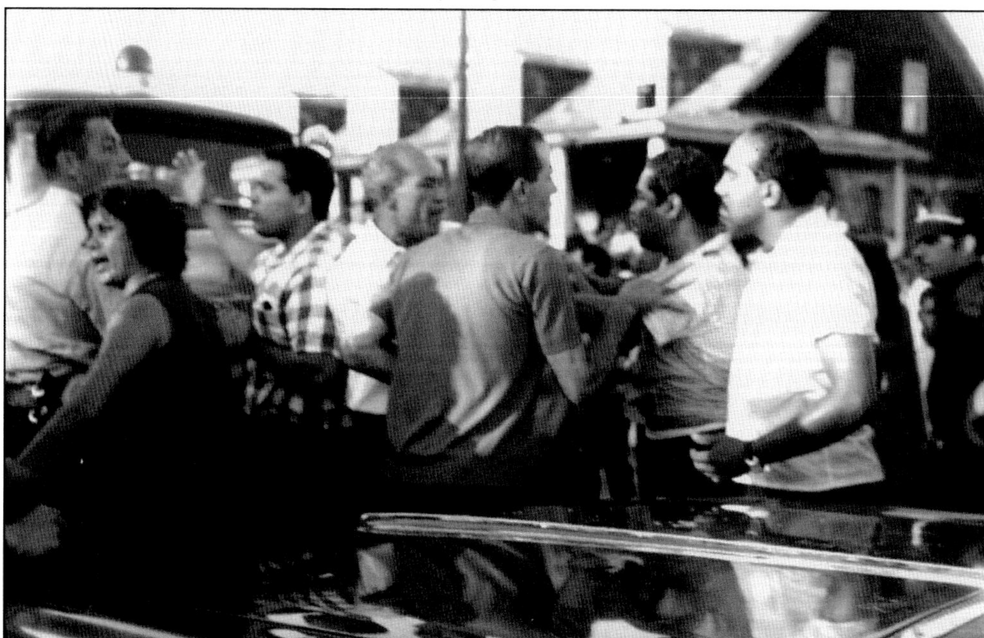

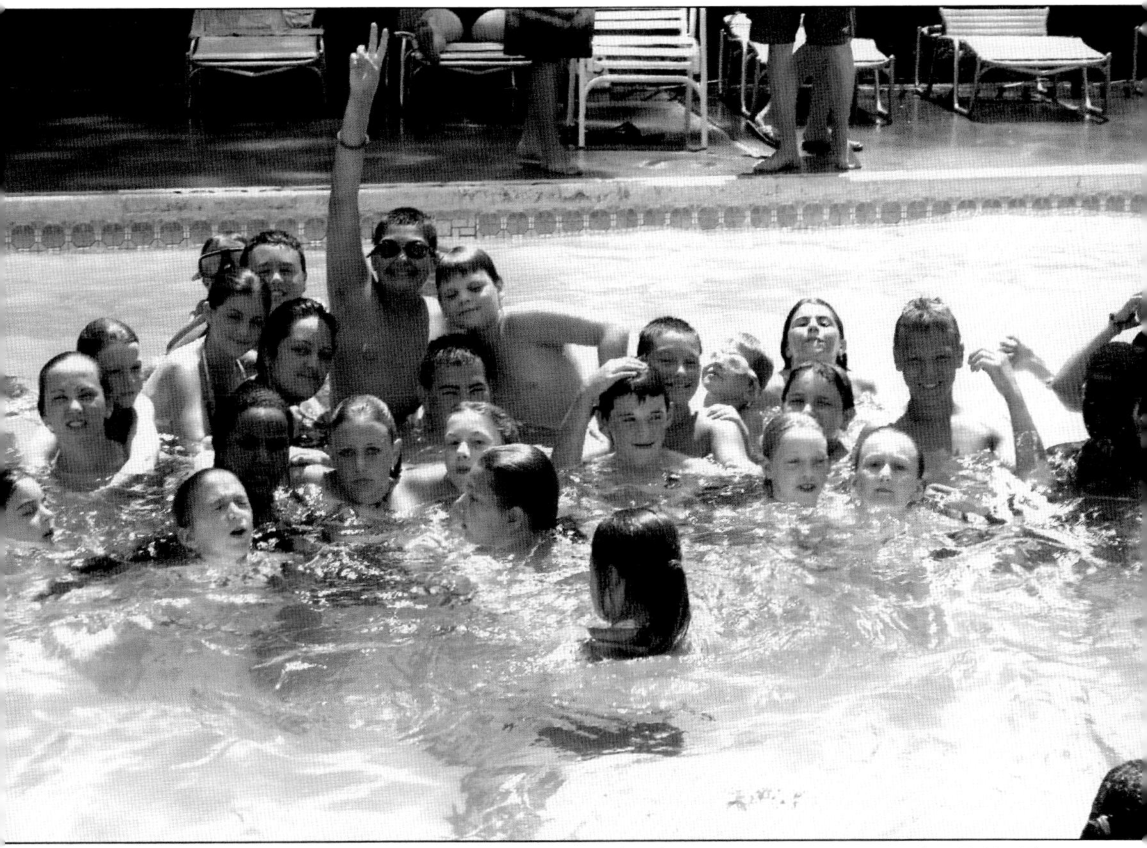

The KOA Kampground resort on Freetown Highway has been in operation since the 1960s. For more than two decades, it was run by Wes and Rita Conklin. Today the Town of Plattekill runs part of their summer camp program at the resort, as seen in this 2006 photograph. Campers are able to swim, take hayrides, and participate in various activities at the campground. (Photograph by Elizabeth Werlau, reprinted from the *Southern Ulster Times*.)

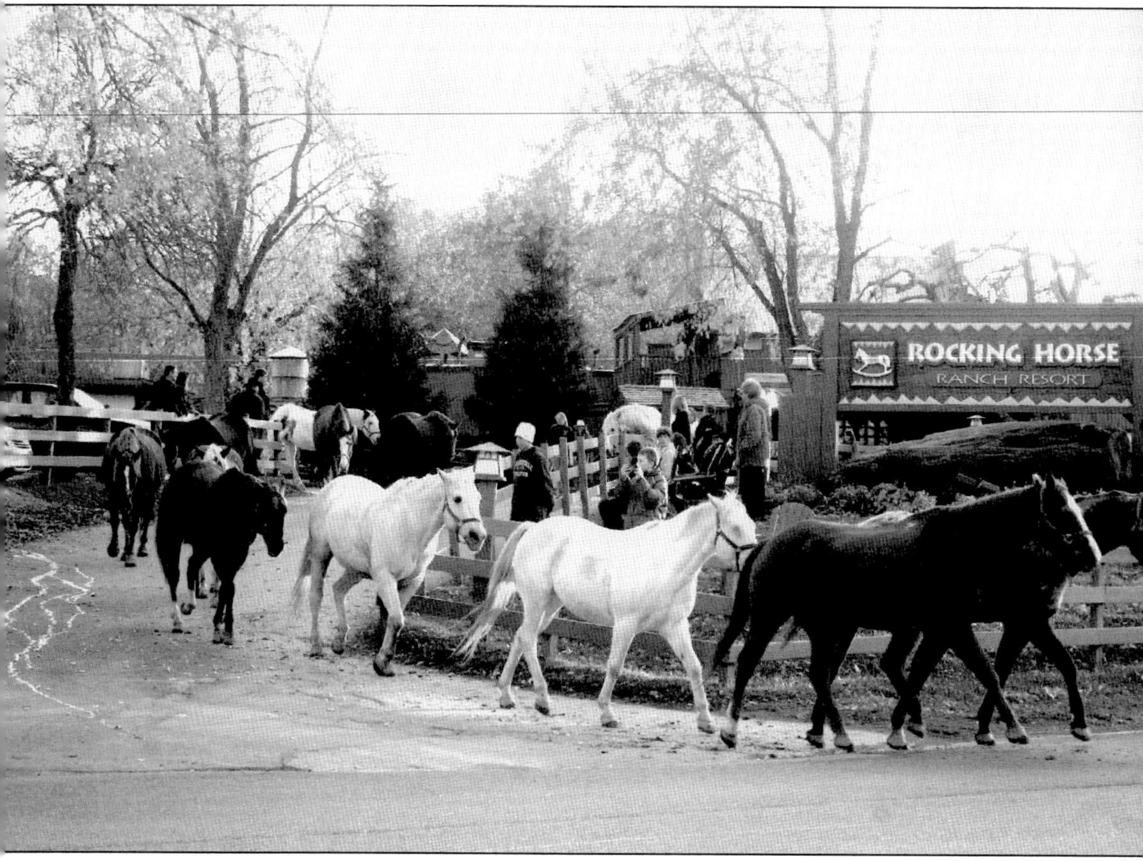

A common sight in Clintondale has been the horses at the Rocking Horse Ranch Resort. Twice a day, the horses are led across Route 44/55 by their handlers to the resort, where they provide trail, wagon, and hayrides through the resort's more than 500 acres and back to their stable area for the night. Traffic is stopped in order for the horses to cross the busy road, and guests can often be seen on the lawn taking pictures of the event. The Rocking Horse Ranch Resort recently celebrated its 50-year anniversary. (Photograph by Elizabeth Werlau, reprinted from the *Southern Ulster Times*.)

Six

Plattekill's Veterans

In 1880, historian Nathanial Bartlett Sylvester wrote, "the military history of the town is necessarily brief." Early records show that several Plattekill men served in the war of 1812, while many more served in the Civil War. World War I saw soldiers from the various hamlets head overseas after town-wide celebrations to see them off. World War II saw a true community effort throughout the town, as residents compiled lists of soldiers who were serving and erected honor rolls throughout the town. At the same time, the town organized a civil defense program so that residents could volunteer at air raid warning towers and learn first aid procedures, while organizations such as the Clintondale Service Cheer Committee organized to ensure soldiers would receive care packages and letters form home.

The community spirit that was alive back then is still present throughout the town. A veteran's committee is in the process of compiling an honor roll of all Plattekill veterans, so that a permanent structure can be installed at the Thomas Felten Park. Several services and breakfasts to honor veterans take place throughout the year, the largest being the town's Tri-Town Memorial Parade. The celebration includes the laying of wreaths at monuments at the Plattekill Elementary School, the Plattekill Firehouse, and at the Plattekill Library.

In 2007, the town purchased signs to stand at the main entrances to the town along Routes 32 and 44/55. Along with a large sign welcoming people to the community stands a smaller sign reading "The Town of Plattekill Honors Our Veterans."

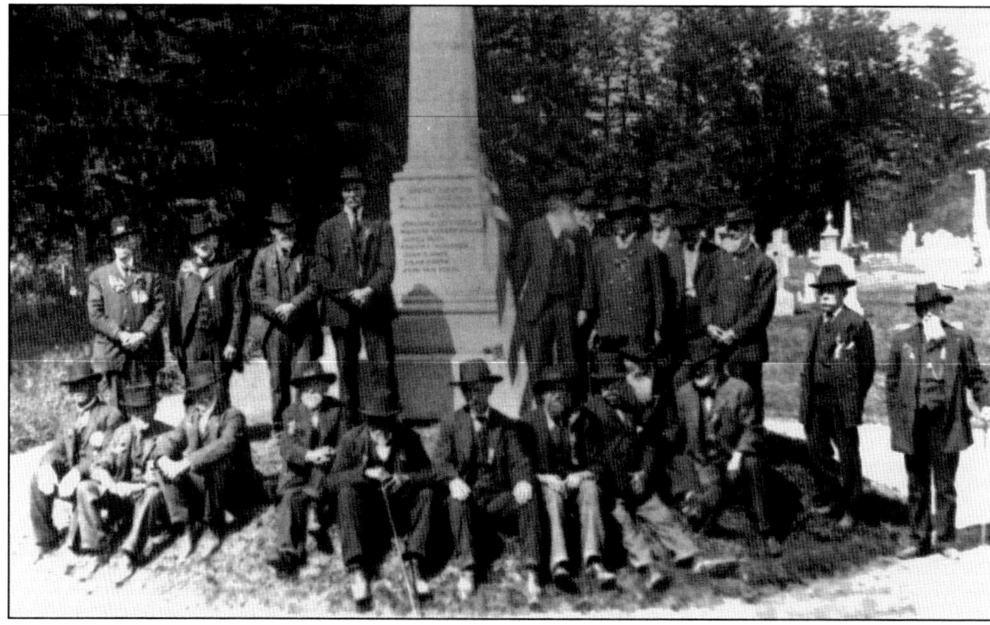

For many years, area veterans of the Civil War, including some from Plattekill, gathered for reunions in the town of New Paltz. This particular picture was taken at the New Paltz Cemetery on Plains Road. More than likely early settlers in the area that was to become Plattekill fought in the Revolutionary War, although some of the earliest records come from the Civil War. (Courtesy of *Friends and Neighbors: A Pictorial History of the Town of Plattekill and Southwest Lloyd.*)

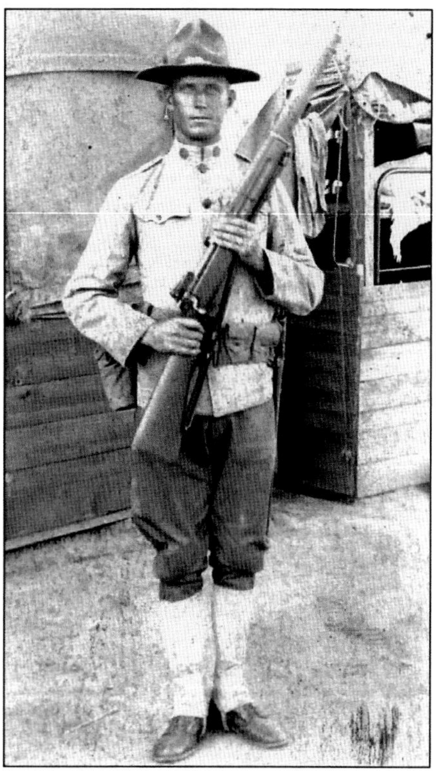

An early postcard shows an unidentified Modena World War I soldier and was sent to R. Ward of Modena in 1918. The soldier, stationed in Spartanburg, South Carolina, spoke of his plans for visiting Modena before being sent overseas: "130 degrees down here . . . will be home before I go over . . . am coming north in a few days." (Courtesy of Shirley Anson.)

John Leonard Coy of Modena, shown here around 1917, was an army cook during World War I. He would have been in his early 20s when this picture was taken, at an army camp in Alabama. Coy passed away in 1951. (Courtesy of Russ Coy.)

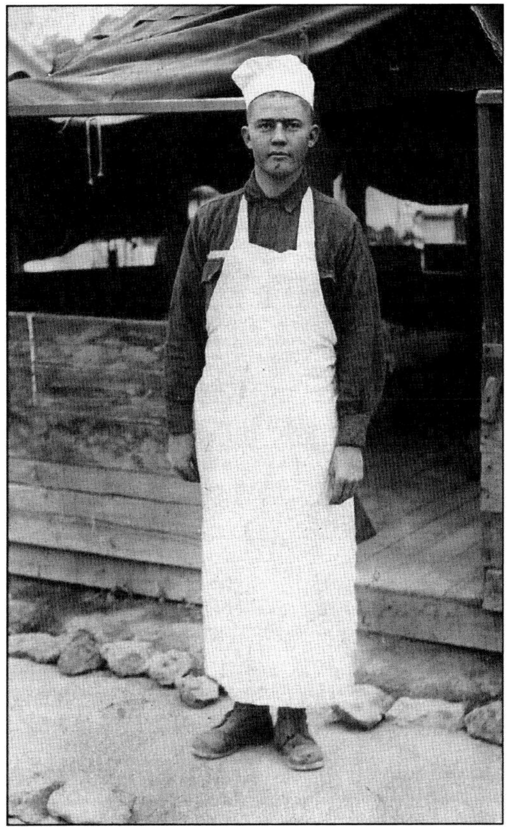

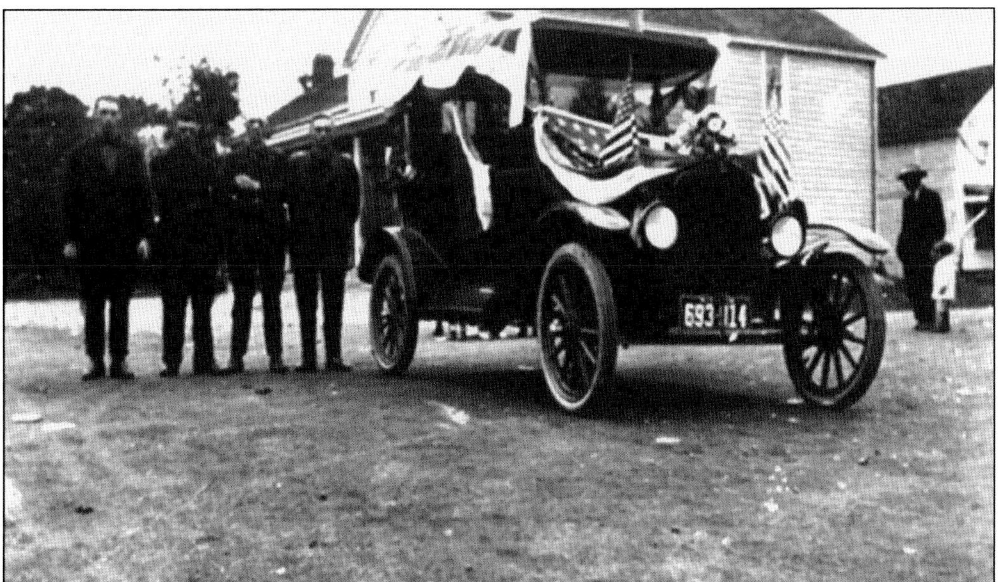

World War I soldiers pose for a picture in Modena before reporting for enlistment in September 1918. Among those who reported at the same time were Byron Paltridge, Lewis Hickey, Ambrose Ronk, Guy Rappleyea, and George Alsdorf. The picture was taken at the four corners in Modena, looking south. (Courtesy of Shirley Anson.)

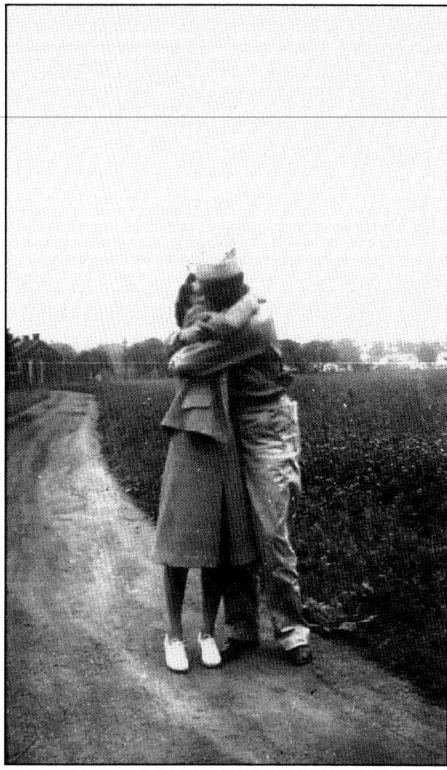

Brothers Oscar and Martin Feldt both joined the army during World War II. Oscar returned home from service in 1944 and is pictured at left with his wife, Jennie. Martin, pictured below, was a staff sergeant in the army from 1942 to 1945. Martin's family recalls Oscar relating a story about a care package Martin's wife, Ruth, sent while her husband served overseas. The package was mistakenly delivered to his brother Oscar, who made sure to devour its contents and report to his brother how good everything had been. Another care package from home did make it to Martin Feldt, containing hard-boiled eggs that had gone bad after the package was delayed. (Courtesy Daniel and Carol Feldt.)

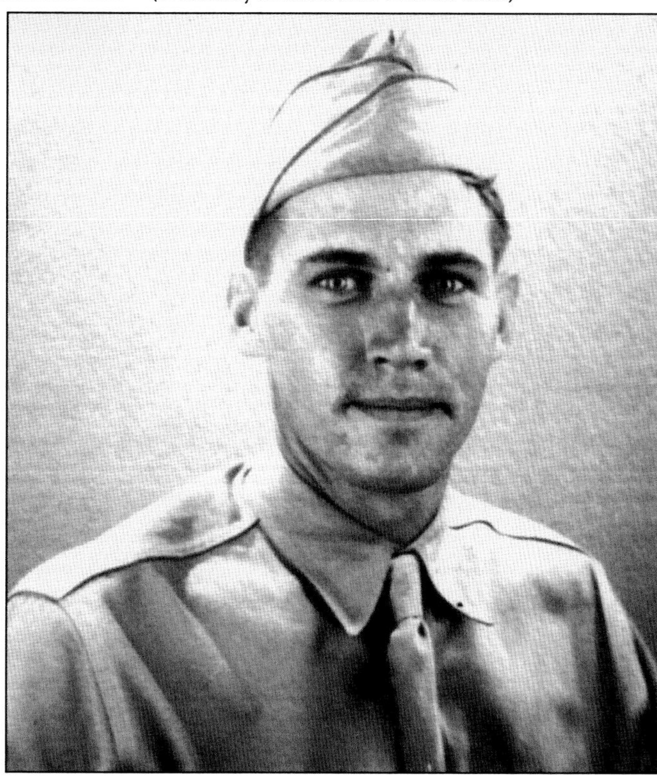

Russ Coy of Modena tried to join the Merchant Marines as a 16-year-old in 1945. He remembers wanting, along with his friends, to serve the country during World War II. He was turned away because of his age, but was able to join the U.S. Navy the following year. He is shown here in front of his Modena home in 1946 during leave. (Courtesy of Russ Coy.)

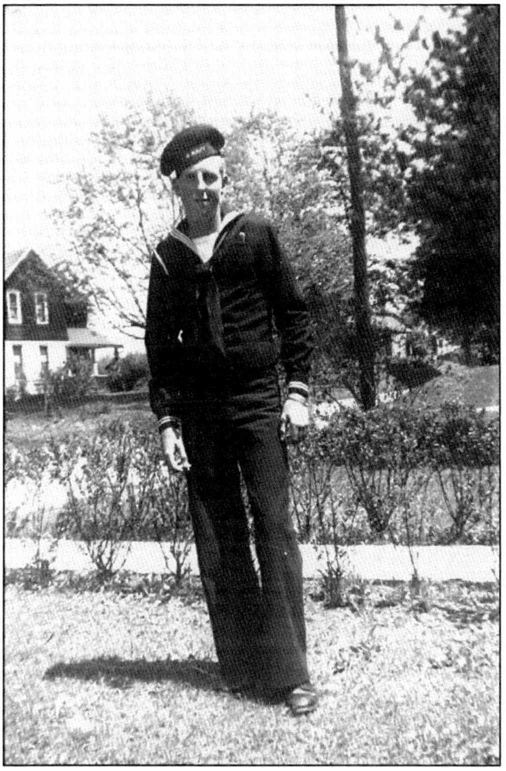

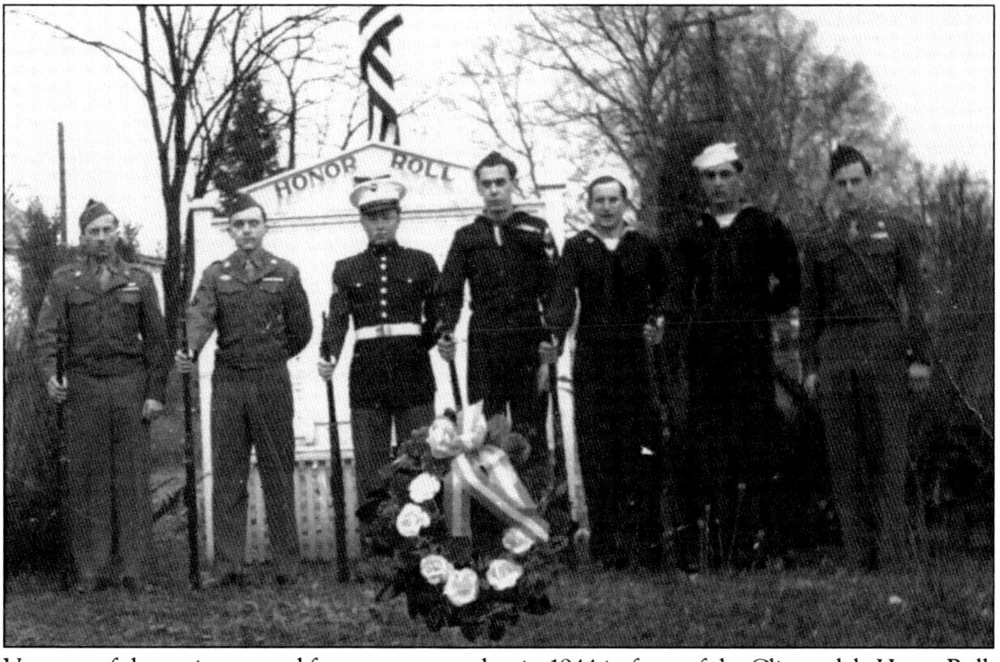

Veterans of the various armed forces came together in 1944 in front of the Clintondale Honor Roll. The honor roll was set up by the Clintondale Service Cheer Committee, which also sent letters and care packages to those serving overseas. At the time, the honor roll was still set up along Route 44/55. It was later moved to Maple Avenue near the I.G.A. (Courtesy of author's collection.)

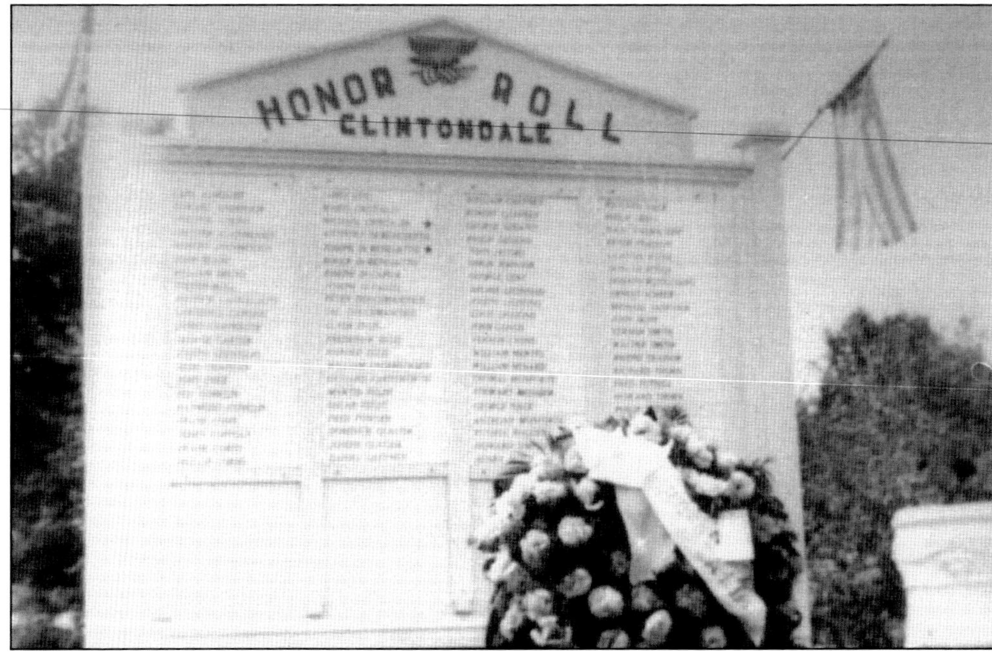

Clintondale's honor roll, built by Lawrence Morse, first stood at the intersection of Hull and Maple Avenues and Route 44/55. The monument was set up by the 4-H Club. The Clintondale Service Cheer Committee compiled the names of the 87 veterans listed. According to the 1959 *History of Clintondale*, about 54 Clintondale men were drafted or volunteered for service during World War II. (Courtesy of *Friends and Neighbors: A Pictorial History of the Town of Plattekill and Southwest Lloyd.*)

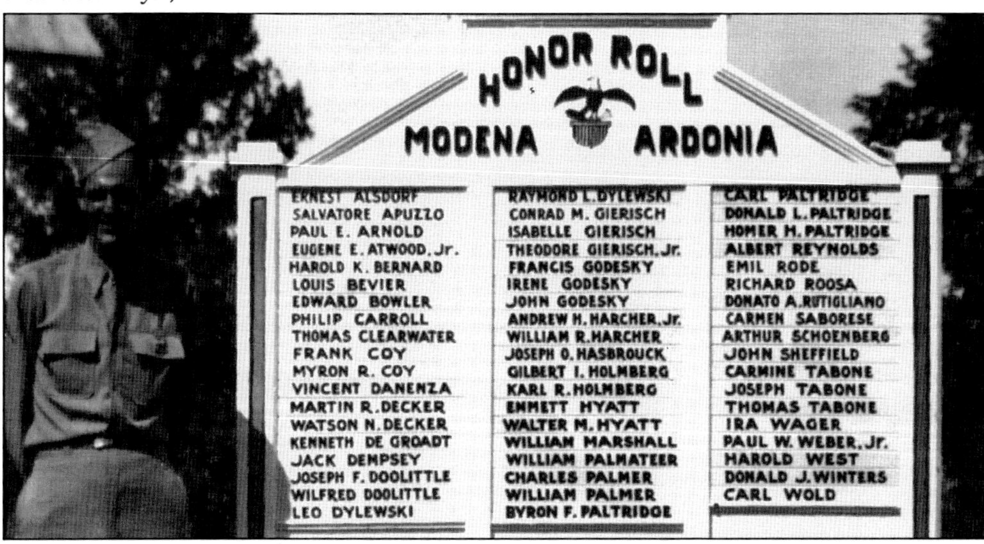

The Modena Honor Roll was set up at the four corners in 1944, on property owned by the Hasbrouck family. Veteran Charles Palmer, who was on leave at the time, stands beside the new monument, which featured the names of both Modena and Ardonia veterans. Ardonia's honor roll contained the names of 19 veterans and was set up on property owned by Frank Sabarese in Ardonia. (Courtesy of *Friends and Neighbors: A Pictorial History of the Town of Plattekill and Southwest Lloyd.*)

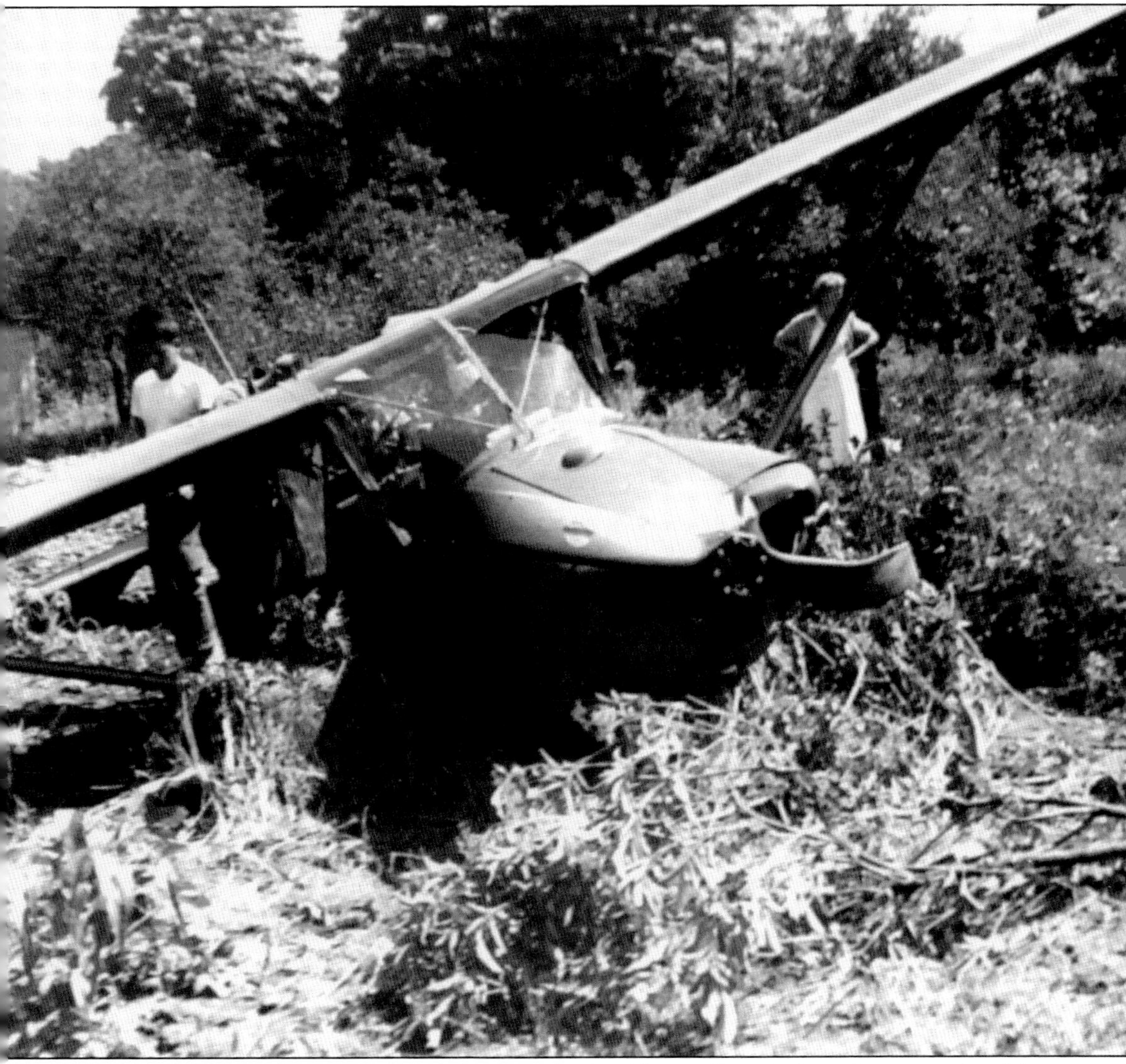

Since the 1940s, at least four planes have crashed in Plattekill, including this one, piloted by Lt. Richard D. Nace. Nace's L-19A Field Artillery Observation plane crash-landed in Clintondale in June 1953. The plane landed near South Street. In 1943, a plane from the U.S. Military Academy at West Point crashed near Tucker's Corners, killing one cadet and seriously wounding another. Another crash occurred in November 1969, when a T33 jet trainer from Stewart Air Force Base crashed on the Pennsylvania Central Railroad tracks in Modena. In that crash, the pilot and copilot were able to safely parachute to the Stanley Orchard property. (Courtesy of *Friends and Neighbors: A Pictorial History of the Town of Plattekill and Southwest Lloyd.*)

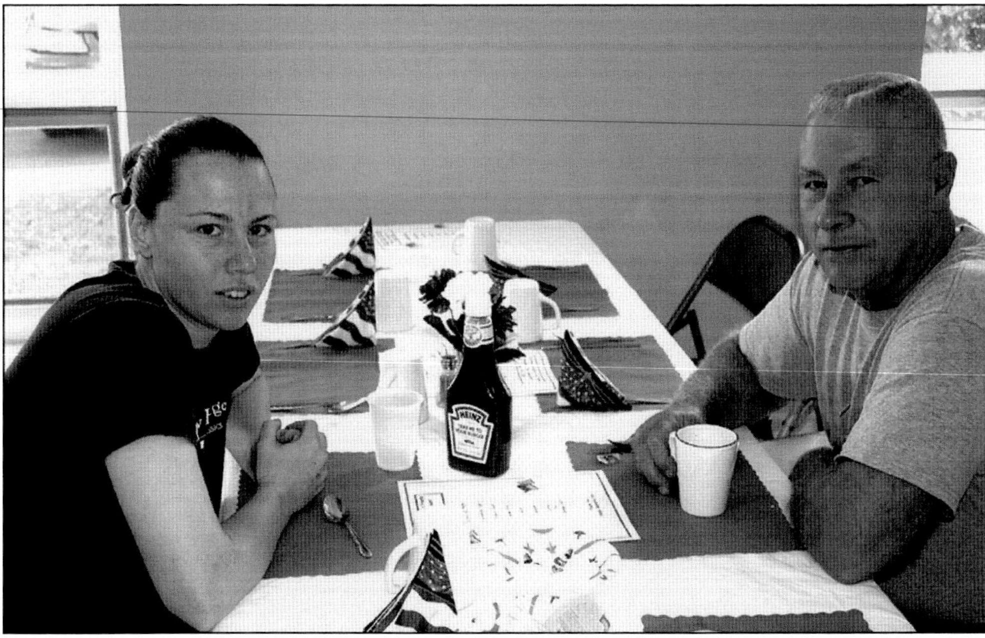

Veterans Bob Roberts and his daughter Amanda Roberts, both of Modena, enjoy a 2006 Memorial Day breakfast hosted by the members of the Modena Fire Department in honor of all local veterans. Bob served during the Vietnam War, while Amanda was deployed to Iraq as a member of the Air National Guard. (Photograph by Elizabeth Werlau, originally appeared in the *Southern Ulster Times.*)

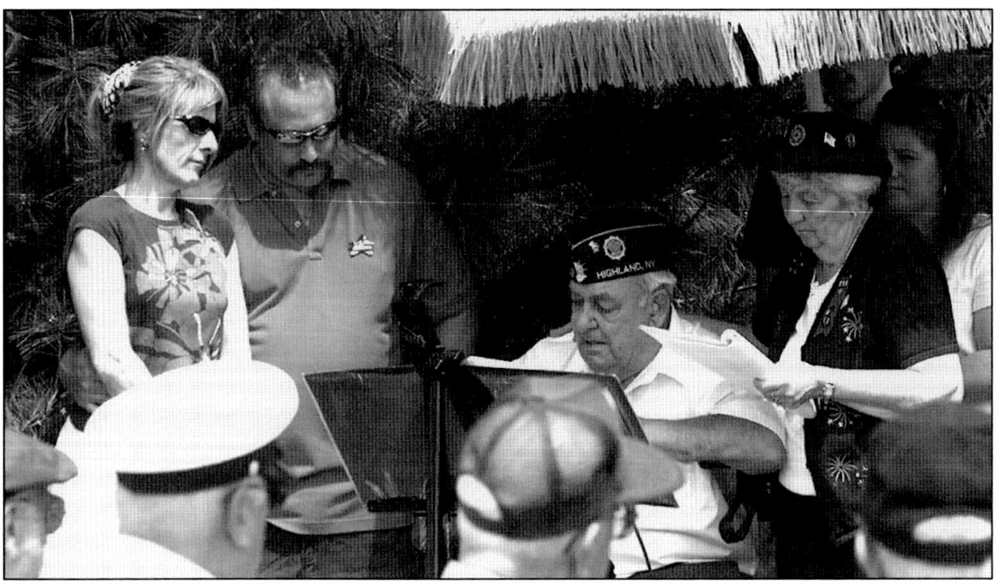

For many years, Ed Longbard of the Aloha Home Acres Senior Community has conducted a service honoring veterans every Memorial Day and Veterans Day. Longbard, a veteran of World War II, designed the service to include prayers, a salute by the members of the Cadet Squadron of the Civil Air Patrol, and a roll call of all local veterans, living and deceased. He is pictured here with Laura and Michael Baum (left), owners of the Aloha Park, and his wife, Dot Longbard. (Photograph by Elizabeth Werlau, originally appeared in the *Southern Ulster Times.*)

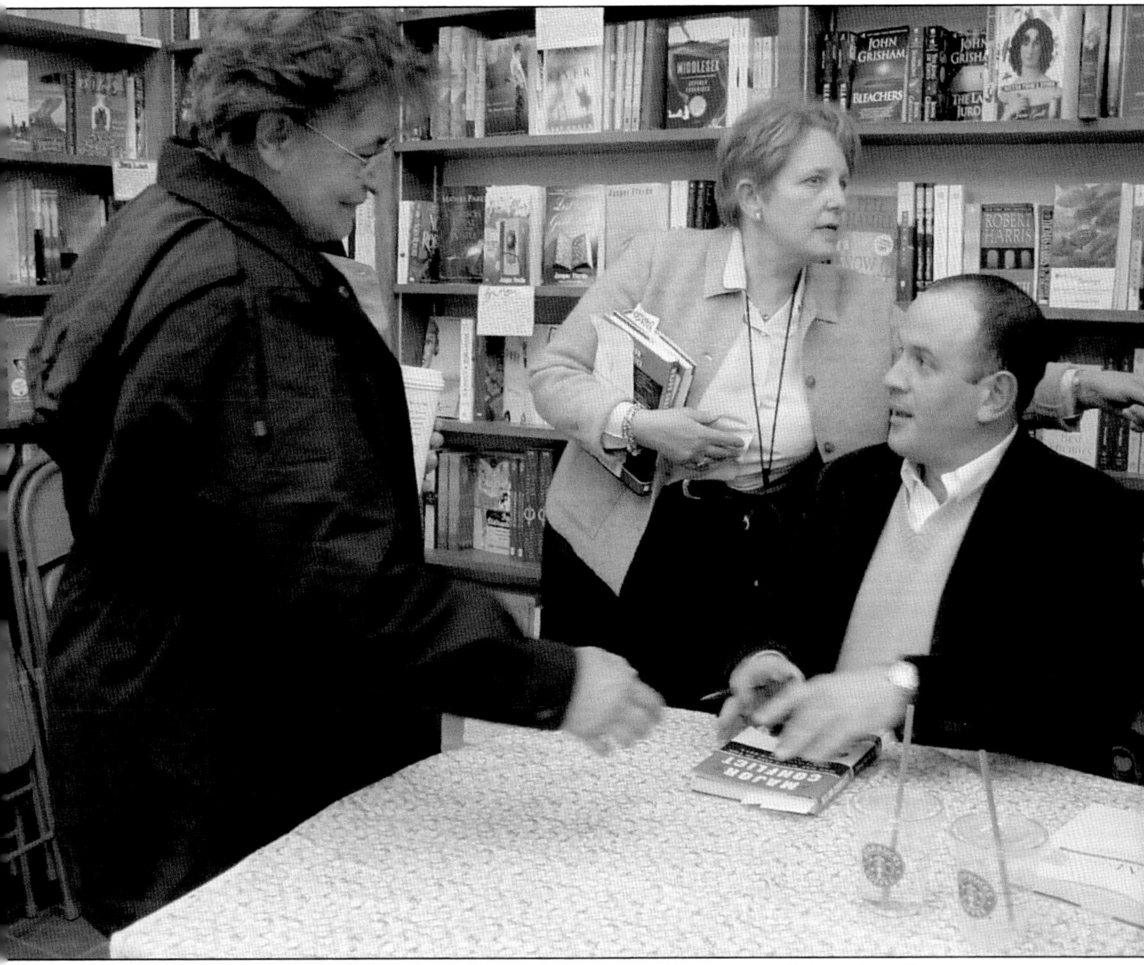

In 2005, Maj. Jeff McGowan (Ret.) of Clintondale released his memoir *Major Conflict*, an account of his experiences being a gay officer in the military. McGowan made national headlines in 2004 when he and his partner Billiam Von Roestenburg were married in a ceremony presided over by then-mayor of New Paltz, Jason West. Their same-sex marriage was followed by many similar ceremonies in that town. New York State refused to recognize the ceremonies and West was charged with breaking the state's marriage law, but the ceremonies continued. Pictured here is McGowan and Clintondale resident Shirley Anson at McGowan's 2005 book signing event at Ariel Booksellers in New Paltz. (Photograph by Elizabeth Werlau, originally appeared in the *Southern Ulster Times*.)

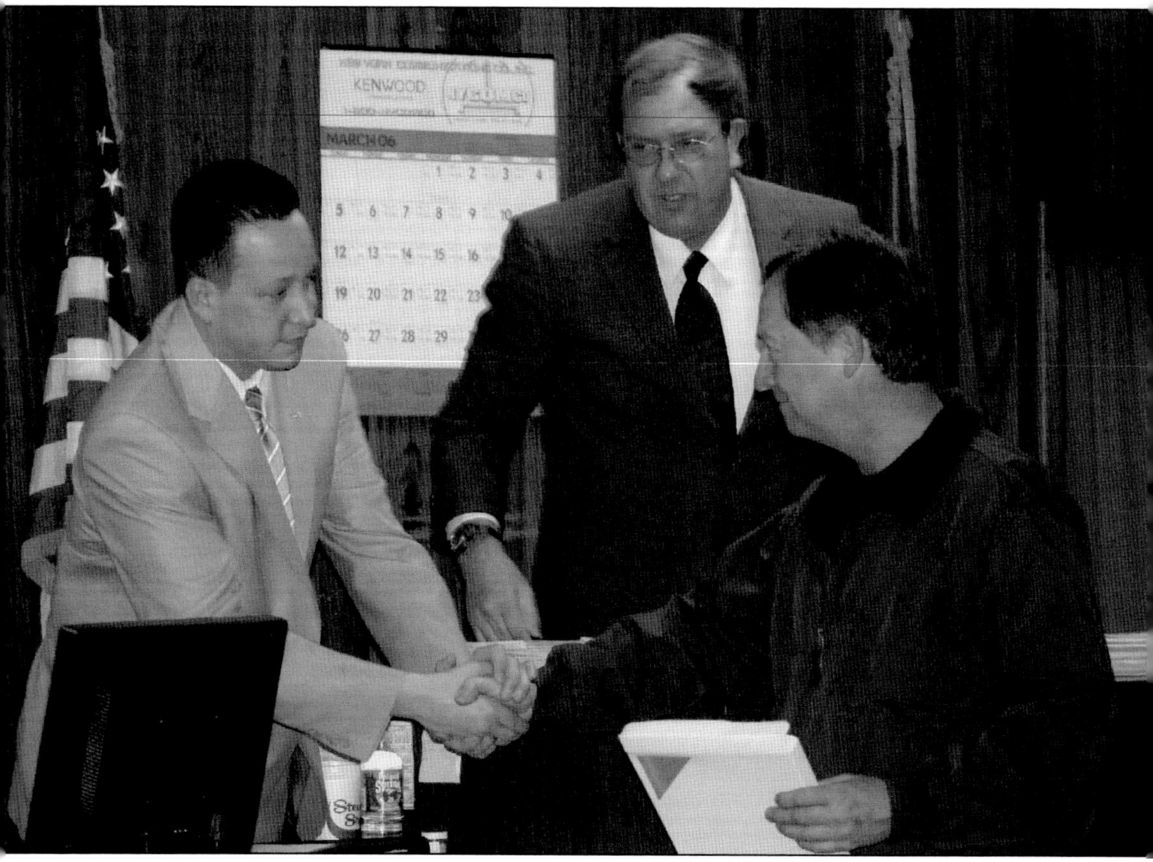

Lt. Mark Dooley, who grew up in Plattekill and was a 1997 graduate of Wallkill High School, died in action in Iraq on September 19, 2005, while serving with the Vermont National Guard. In March 2006, the Town of Plattekill declared that March 26 would be declared Lt. Mark Dooley Day. Pictured here, from left to right, are town councilman Steve Martinez and Plattekill supervisor Bruce Loertscher with Dooley's father, Peter, after the proclamation was read. Before he left for service in Iraq, Dooley had written a letter to his parents and brother in the event he did not return. After his death, the Dooleys shared the letter with family and friends. The letter circulated, eventually making its way to the White House. In 2006, the Dooleys were invited to Arlington National Cemetery on Memorial Day to hear Pres. George W. Bush use Dooley's words in his Memorial Day address to the nation: "Remember that my leaving was in the service of something that we loved, and be proud. The best way to pay respect is to value why a sacrifice was made."

Seven

THE FIRE DEPARTMENTS

The town of Plattekill is served by three all-volunteer fire departments, the Plattekill Fire Department, the Modena Fire Rescue Department, and the Clintondale Fire Department. Both Plattekill and Modena have rescue squads that work with the departments and all three departments have auxiliary groups that help out with a variety of events and fund-raising.

The Plattekill Fire Department was organized in 1926 as a bucket brigade. The first firehouse was a one-bay garage standing near the site of the current station No. 1. The current firehouse was built in the 1950s and has been added onto over time. In 2006, station No. 2 was built on Forest Road. The department's first truck was purchased in 1928. In 1964, the Plattekill First Aid Unit became part of the department.

The Modena Fire Rescue Department originated in May 1928 as the Hasbrouck Chemical Company. The company was formed by volunteers in response to several fires during the 1920s that caused considerable damage to structures in the hamlet. The first firehouse was erected in 1932, on land donated by the Hasbrouck family. Over the years, the additions brought the building to what it is today. The department's first truck was a used 1924 Dodge. The Modena Rescue Squad was established in 1965.

The Allied Communities (Clintondale) Fire Department was formed in 1927 by residents Howard Atkins, Adam Roland, John Thorn, William Carr, George A. Conklin, John Glecker, and Savior Albano. The department purchased its first truck in 1928, and the first firehouse was purchased in 1938.

Although each fire district handles several hundred fire and rescue calls each year, all three departments have remained 100 percent staffed by volunteers who leave their homes and families at all hours of the day and night to help out the community.

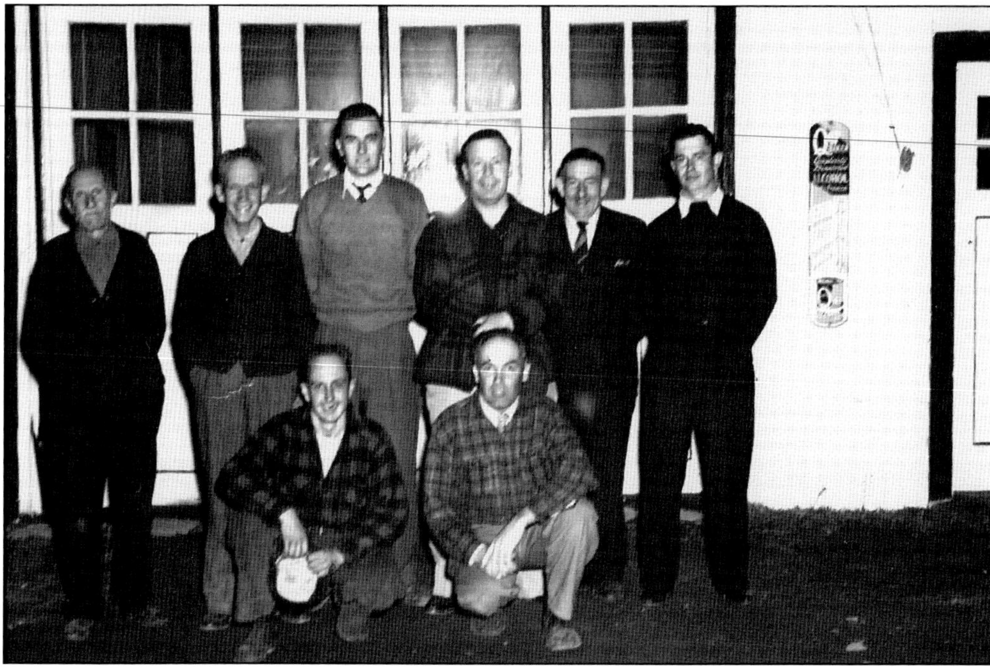

This picture, taken in front of the Plattekill firehouse about 1950, features some of the charter members of the Plattekill Fire Department. Seen here, from left to right, are (first row) John O'Dell and Tom Dawes; (second row) unidentified, Vernon Wager, George Sisti, Ed Wager, and two unidentified. The men shown here received 25-year service pins from the department. (Courtesy of the Office of the Plattekill Historian.)

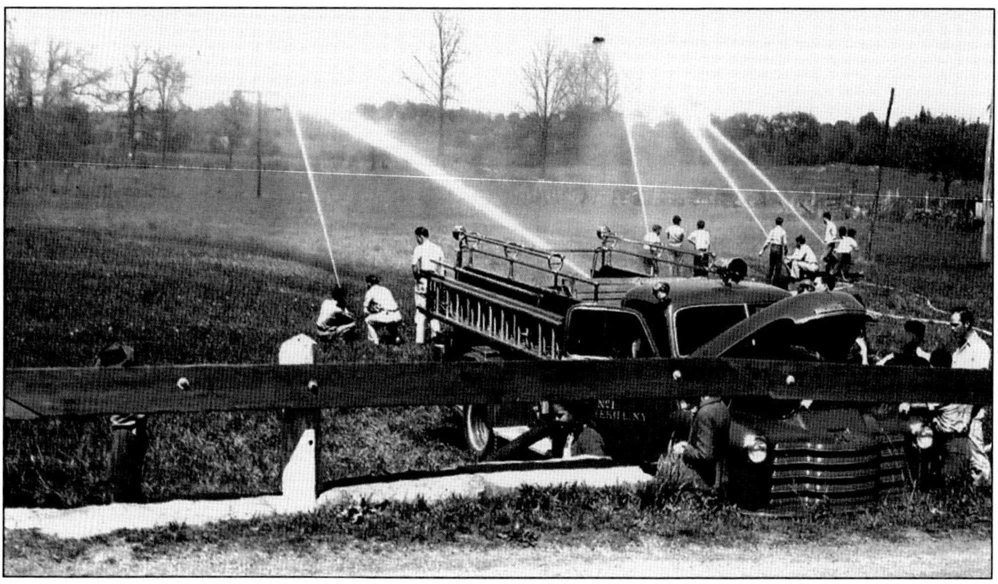

The Plattekill Fire Department drills on the field behind the firehouse around 1950. The landscape around the firehouse changed dramatically with the coming of the New York State Thruway in the mid-1950s. State Road 32 no longer ran in front of the firehouse; instead the road was rerouted to a bridge at the rear of the department's property. (Courtesy of the Office of the Plattekill Historian.)

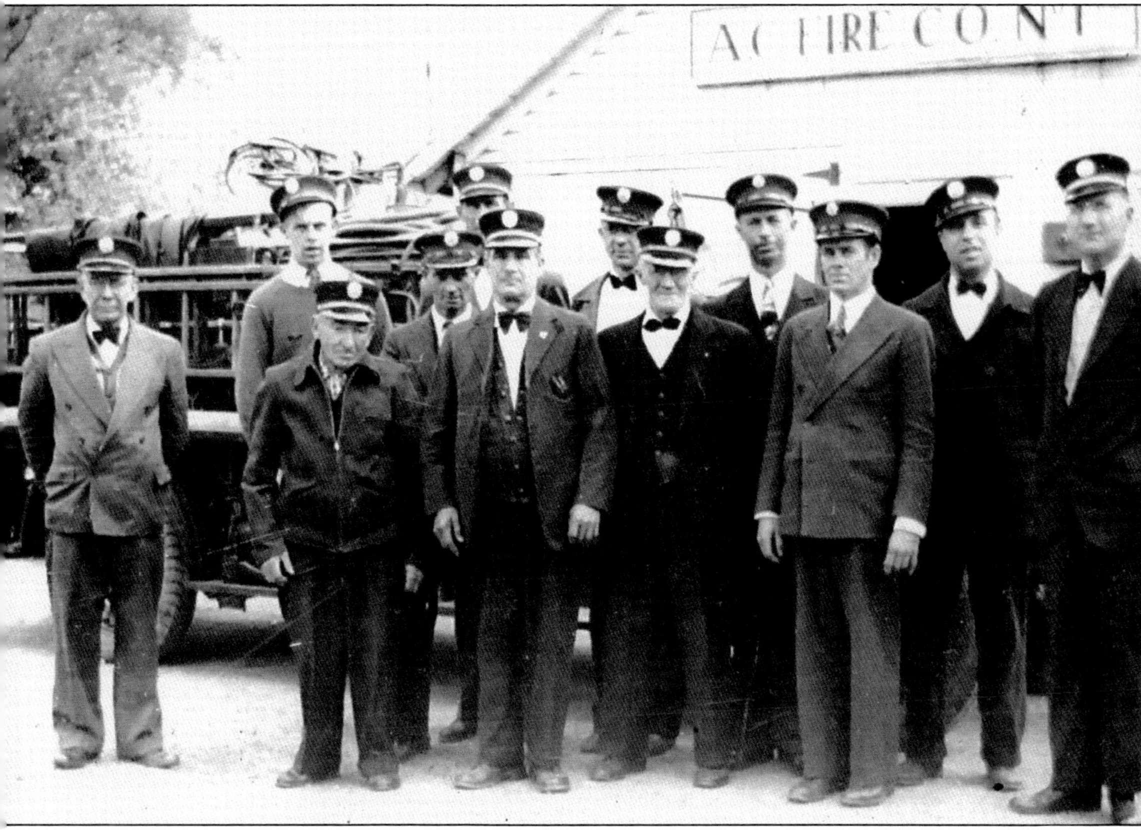

Members of the Allied Communities Fire Company No. 1 in Clintondale stand in front of the original one bay firehouse in May 1945. This structure sat close to the site of the present building. The original building was rented for $35 a year by the department from William Carr, who owned the adjacent general store. The building and property were purchased from Carr in 1939 for a total of $2,500. In 1968, plans were made for a new firehouse on the same property, and by May 1970, the department was able to hold the dedication of that building. Pictured here in 1945 are, from left to right, (first row) Leslie Ackert, Pete Coutant, Angelo Albano, Adam Roland, and Myron Ronk; (second row) Harry Ronk, George Ronk, Gus Conklin, Herbert Lyons, Pete Rosenkranse, Joe Pampinella, and George Conklin. Chief Leslie Ackert was the fire chief from 1943 to 1947. (Courtesy of Shirley Anson.)

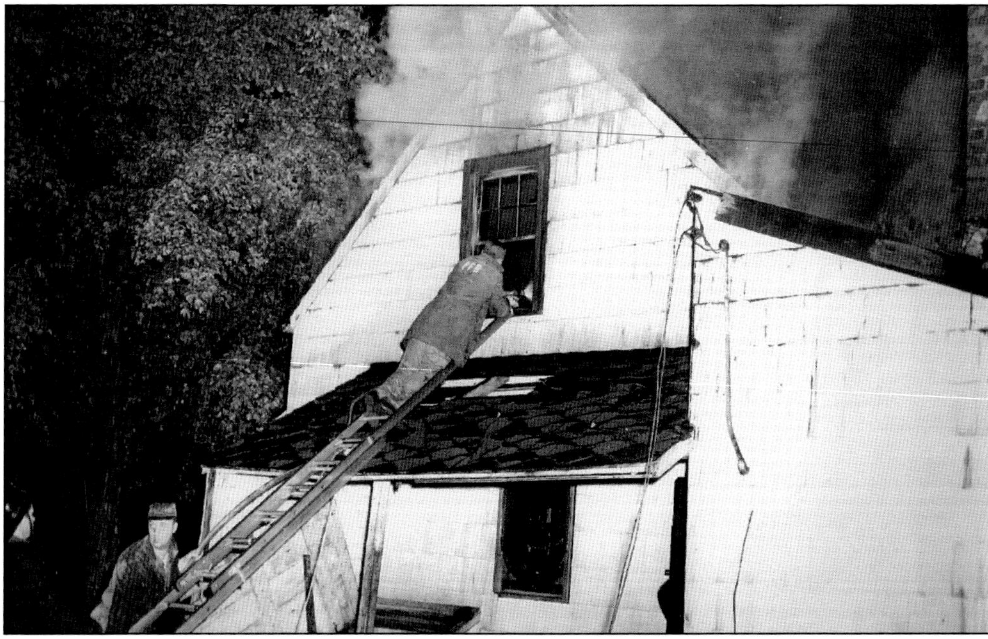

Several destructive fires have damaged structures and taken lives within the town of Plattekill. Before radios and pagers were common, firefighters would carry buckets of lime on the fire trucks. The siren would sound, and, if no one stayed to staff the fire station, small piles of lime would be dropped along the road so that firefighters could find the fire scene. Firefighters from Plattekill and Modena are shown here in the 1960s, fighting a fire on Orchard Road in the Modena Fire District. The fire in a rental home claimed the lives of several children. The firefighter seen facing the camera in the photograph above is George Dougherty Sr. of Modena. (Courtesy of Russ Coy.)

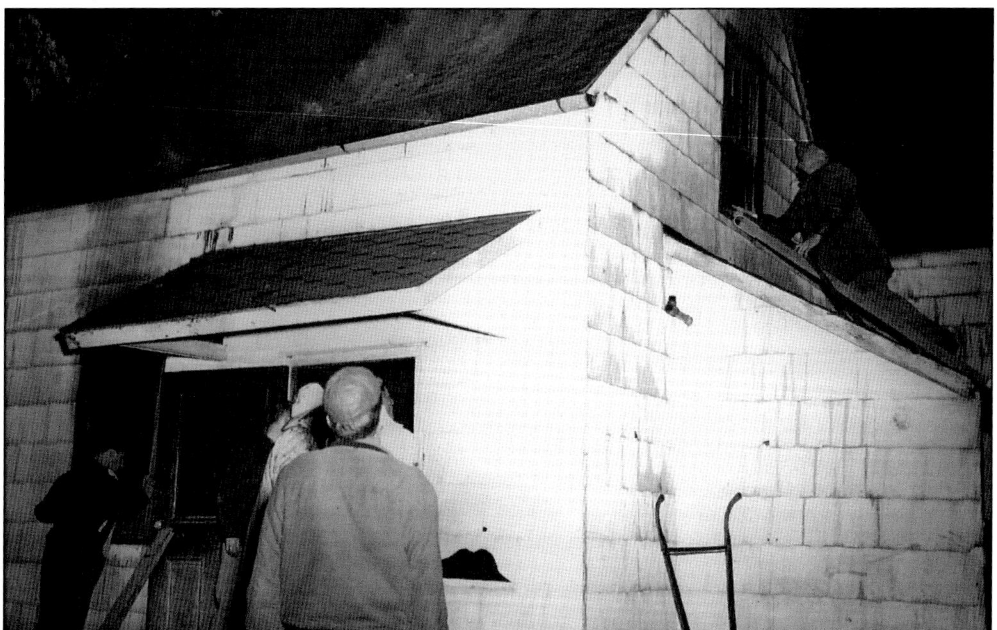

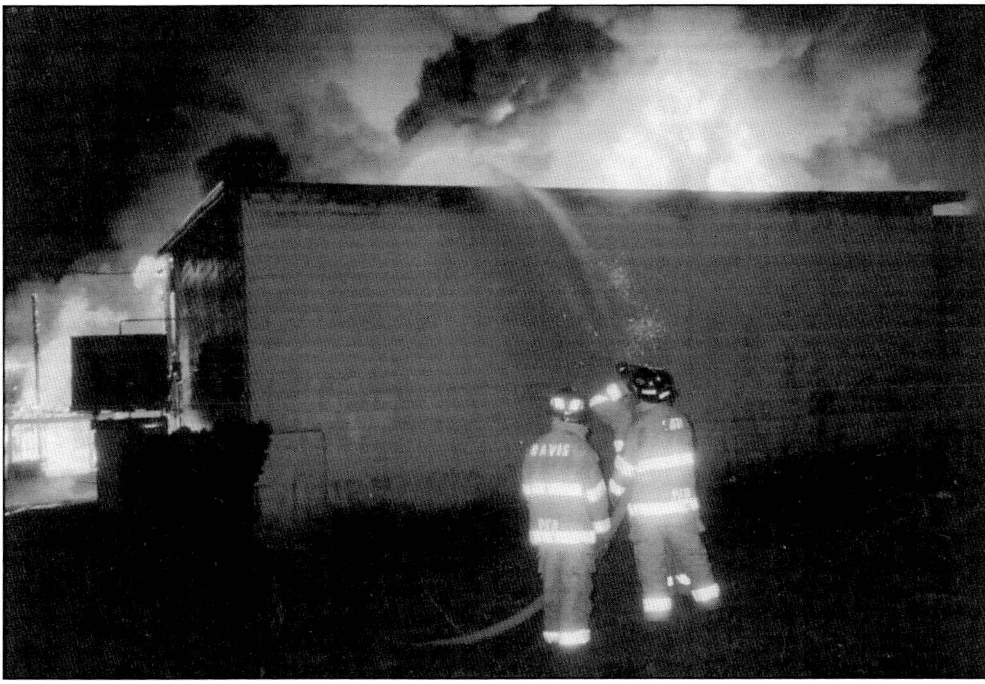

Arguably the largest structure fire in the town of Plattekill occurred in the early morning hours of Monday, June 24, 2000, in Modena as the Stanley Orchard warehouse burned. Ten fire departments, including three ladder companies, responded to the scene on Route 32 and Orchard Drive. Damages to the 70-year-old business were estimated at over $1 million. The fire was extinguished that day, although firefighters remained on the scene for several days afterward to control hot spots in the cork used to insulate the building. The picture below shows some of the apples and pears that had been stored in the warehouse. (Courtesy of Jeffery Zupan.)

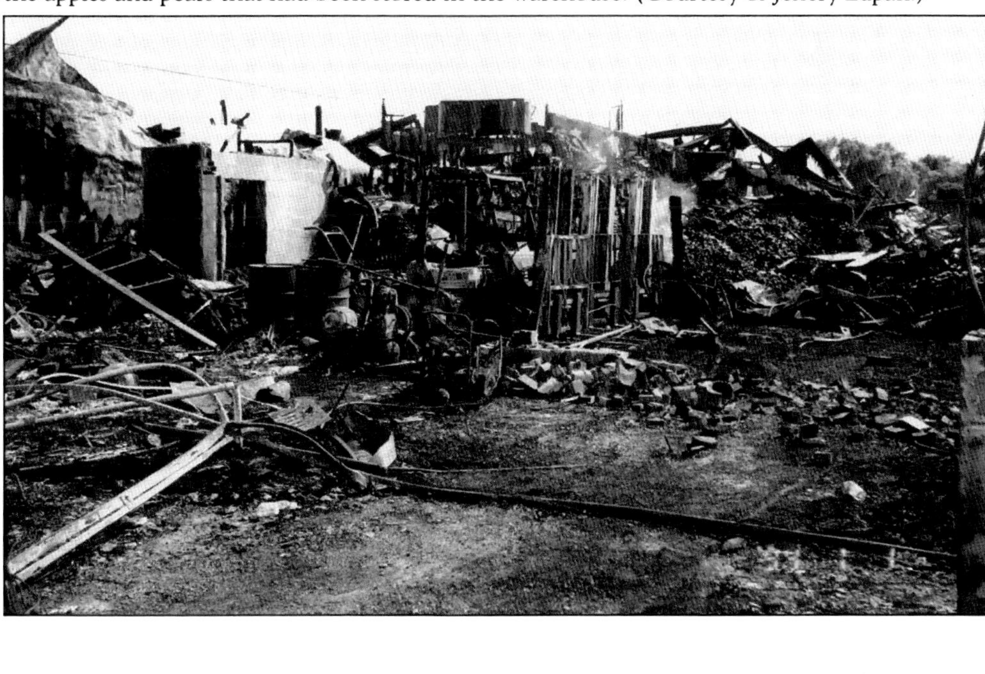

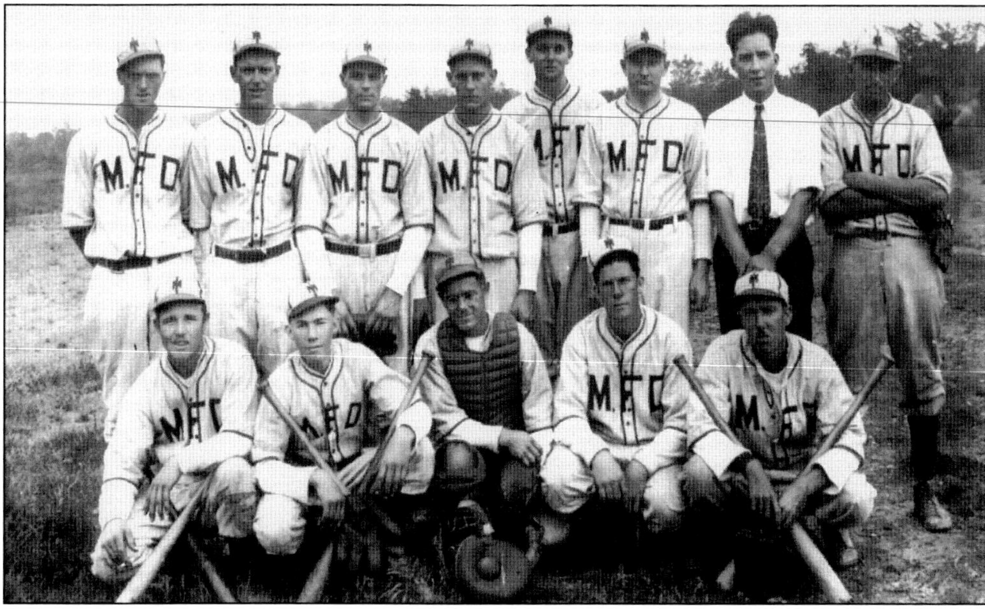

Dating back to their inception, the three fire departments in the town of Plattekill have a long-standing tradition of friendly competition. Over the years, members have formed baseball and softball teams, played in a pinochle league, helped celebrate new apparatus with daylong "wet-downs" and attended each other's social functions, as well as those of neighboring departments such as New Paltz and Gardiner. Shown above is the Modena Fire Department baseball team in a 1935 photograph. Members include, from left to right, (first row) Conrad Geiresh, Orville Coy, Eddie Rhynhart, Richard Coy, and Claude "Strawberry" Wager; (second row) Ike Wager, Burton Ward, George Ackert, Alex Rooney, Myron Miller, Frank Miller, Les Wager, and Russ Smith. Below are members of the Clintondale Fire Department after participating in a competition held at the New Paltz Elks Club. (Above, courtesy of Russ Coy; below, courtesy of Shirley Anson.)

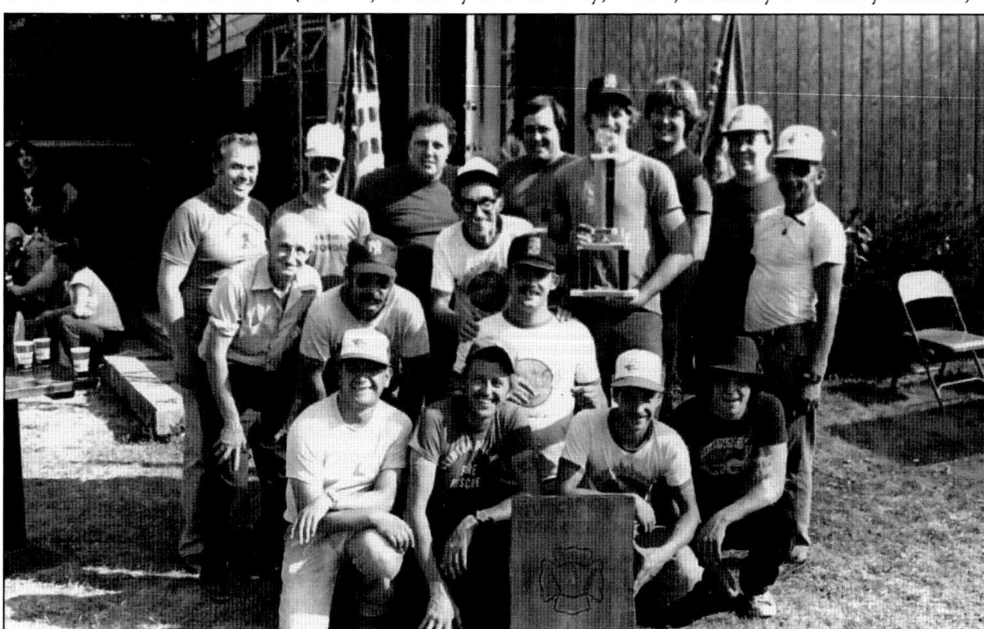

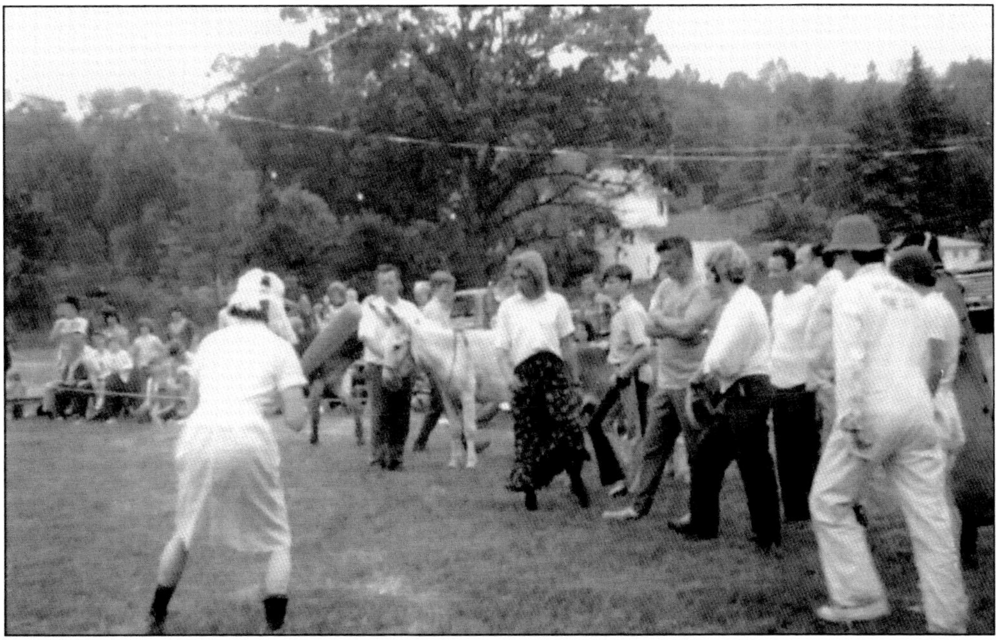

Members of the Clintondale Fire Department (above) and the Modena Fire Department (below) are pictured during donkey baseball games. For many years, donkeys were brought onto the playing field via tractor trailer and participants would ride them in a comical game. Clintondale played on the field behind the firehouse, while in Modena, the Grimm property across from the Modena firehouse or the field at the Plattekill Library were used for such competition. Modena Fire Department life member Russ Coy recalls one game in the town of Gardiner, when the department arrived to find donkeys that had gotten free and stubbornly refused to be rounded up. Pictured below are (first row) Lou Sekunda and Fran McDowell; (second row) Charlie Henry, Sonny Wager, Ronnie Wager, Wayne Smith, Bill Depew, George Dougherty, Dick Marquard, unidentified, and Russ Coy. (Above, courtesy of Shirley Anson; below, courtesy of Russ Coy.)

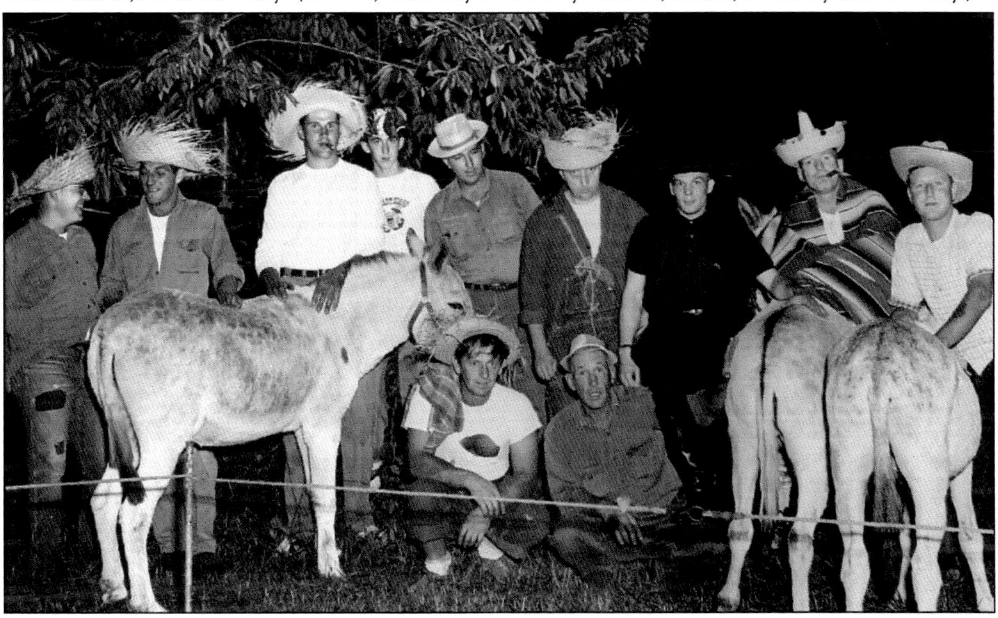

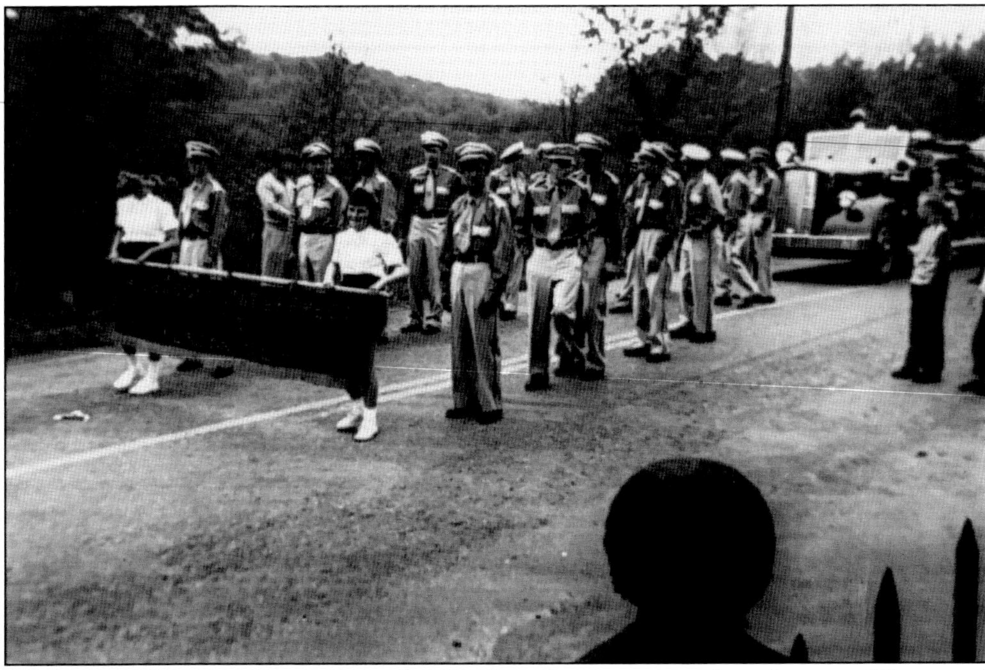

Parades are a long-standing tradition for the three departments within the town. The annual Tri-Town Memorial Parade rotates yearly between the hamlets of Plattekill, Modena, and Clintondale. In addition, the departments attend various other town, county, and state parades. Pictured above are members of the Allied Communities Fire Company No. 1 (Clintondale) marching in a parade while below, the late Harry Marschall, a life member of the Modena Fire Department, drives a truck in the hamlet of Wallkill's annual St. Patrick's Day Parade, around 1995. (Above, courtesy of Shirley Anson; below, courtesy of author's collection.)

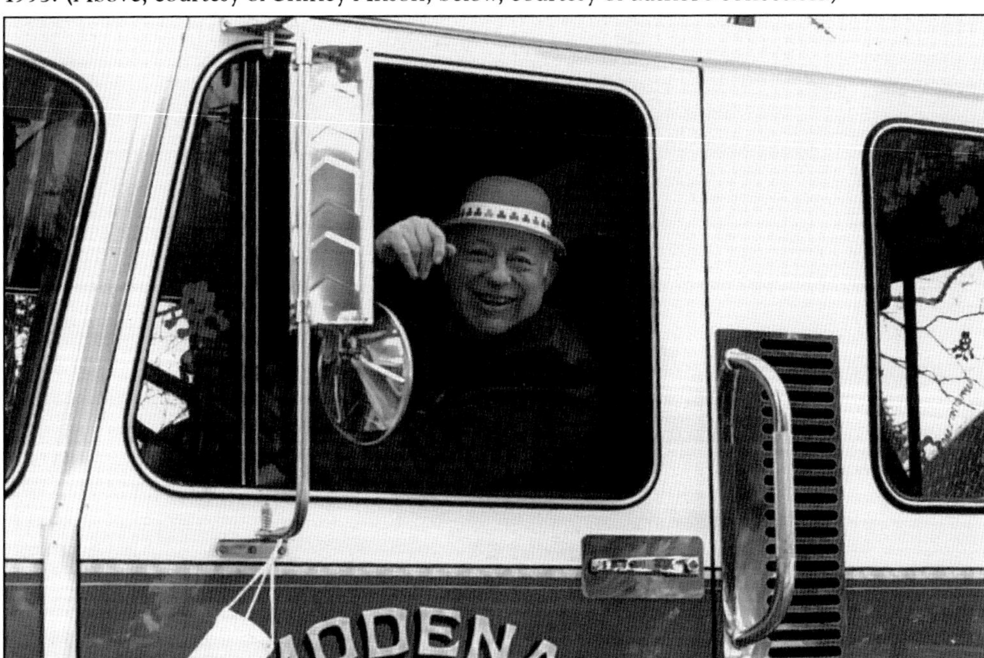

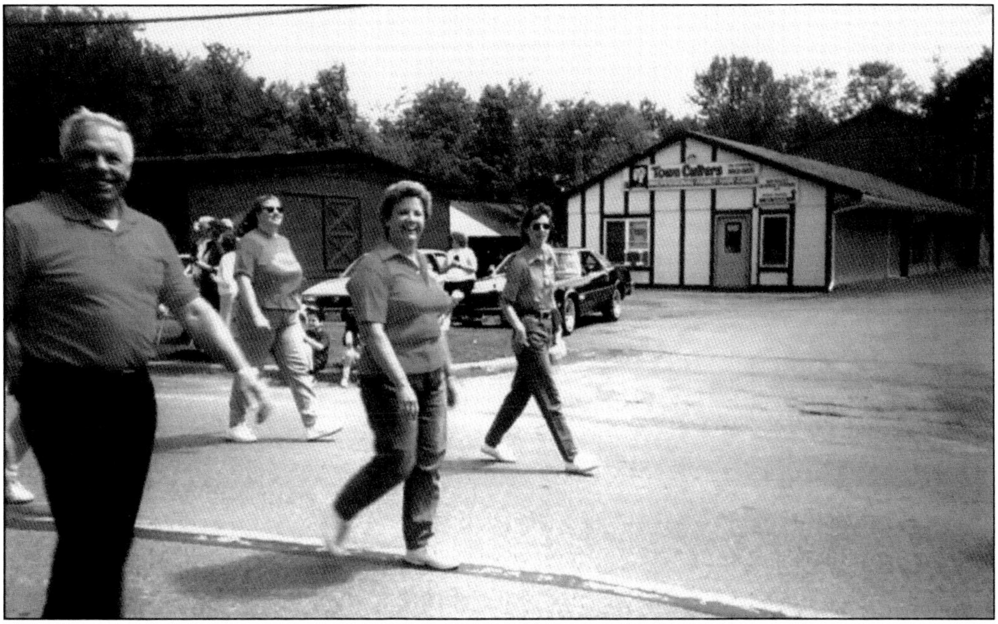

Members of the Modena Rescue Squad march west on Route 44/55 in the 1996 Memorial Day Parade. In 2002, the Modena Fire Department and the Modena Rescue Squad consolidated into the Modena Fire Rescue Department. Pictured here are Robert Werlau, Kimberly Meyer, Sharon Ostrander, and Kelly Nelson marching west toward the four corners in Modena. (Courtesy of author's collection.)

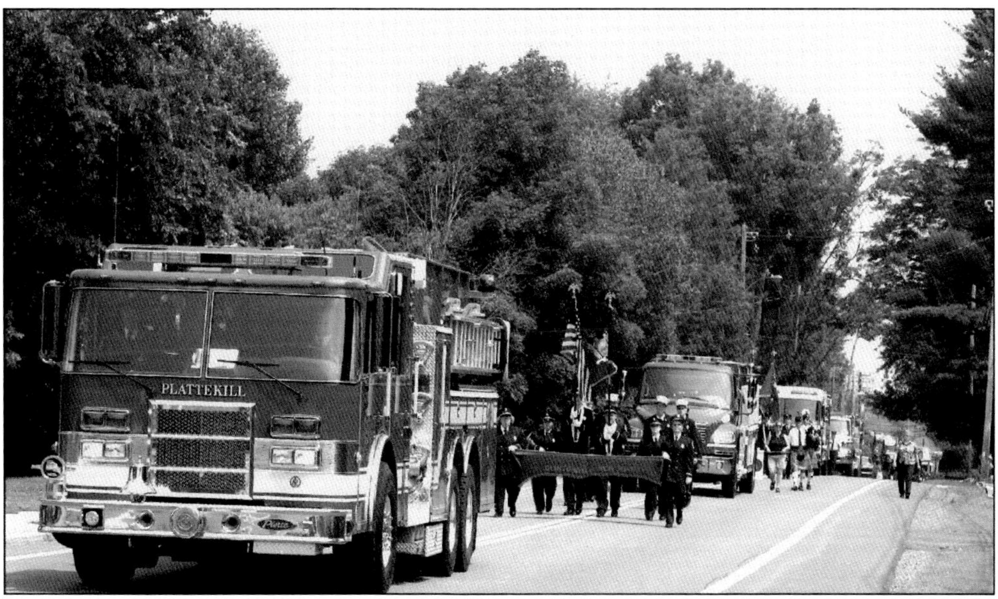

Each year, departments in Ulster County take turns hosting the Ulster County Volunteer Firemen's Association (UCVFA) parade. The parade is traditionally held in the UCVFA president's home fire district. In 2007, George Eason of the Modena Fire Rescue Department served as the association's president, and so in August 2007, the Modena Fire Rescue Department hosted the prestigious parade. (Photograph by Elizabeth Werlau, originally appeared in the *Southern Ulster Times.*)

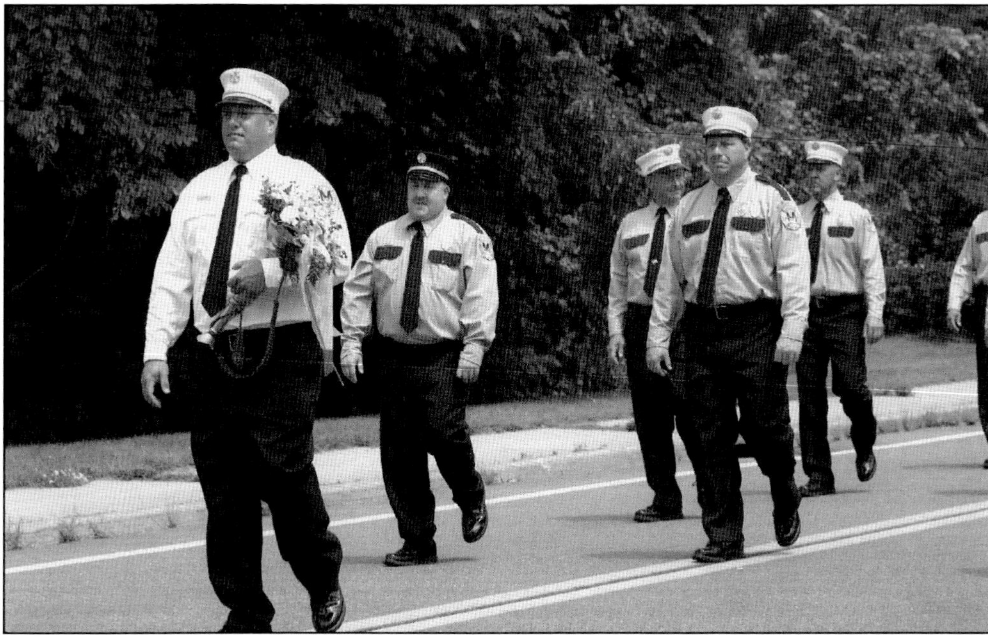

The parade featured representatives from 35 fire districts, as well as local rescue squads, police organizations, and community organizations. Modena Fire Rescue volunteers shown here are, from left to right, Fire Chief Jeffery Zupan, Second Assistant Chief James Nelson, former Chief David Winters, First Assistant Chief Dwight Dougherty, and former Chief Tom Nelson. (Photograph by Elizabeth Werlau, originally appeared in the *Southern Ulster Times.*)

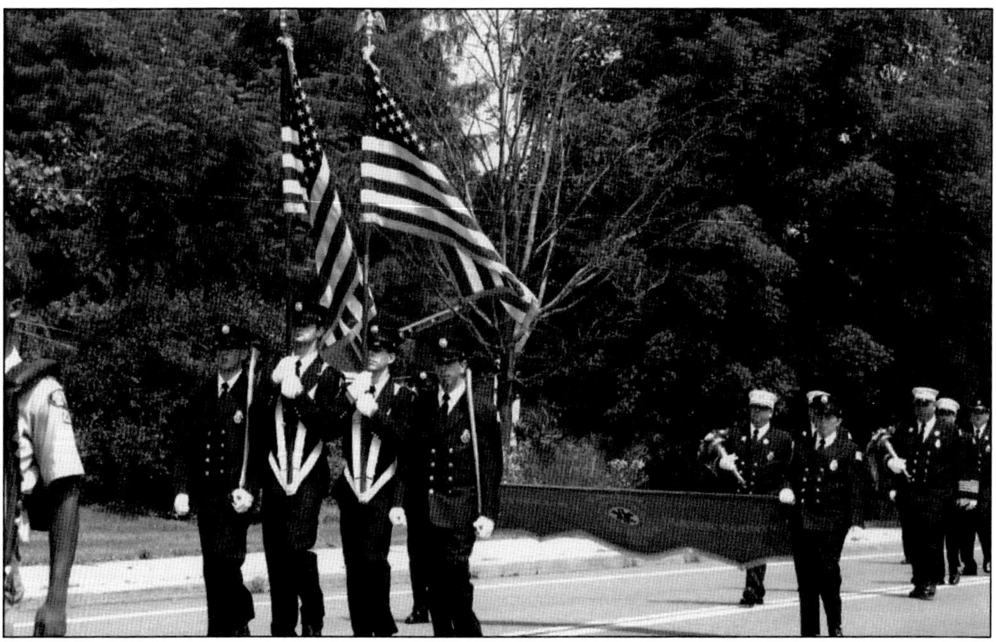

Members of the Plattekill Fire Department participate in the UCVFA parade. The parade started at the Thomas Felten Park and moved along Patura Road, Freetown Highway, Route 44/55, and ended back at the park. Firefighters shown here are marching west on Route 44/55 in Modena. (Photograph by Elizabeth Werlau, originally appeared in the *Southern Ulster Times.*)

Eight

Community

With several distinct hamlets, the town of Plattekill could very easily be considered a group of small communities. In some cases, that is true. The three main hamlets of Modena, Clintondale, and Plattekill each have their own fire department, businesses, post offices, and history. Many service organizations have sprung up over the years with allegiances to particular hamlets. What continues to run through the town, however, is a strong sense of community despite the separation of school districts, churches, and various organizations.

Service organizations such the Boy and Girl Scouts, the Grange, the Rotary, and the Knights of Columbus have remained very active over the years, while organizations such as the Plattekill Library provide common ground for the community. The creation of the Thomas Felten Community Park in 1996 further served to unite the hamlets as town-sponsored activities throughout the year provide an opportunity to get together. Every year, the town celebrates Plattekill Day, a daylong event highlighting the businesses and service organizations throughout the town. Community breakfasts and dinners, church events, penny socials, book clubs, and sports leagues provide additional opportunities for residents to meet, socialize, and work together.

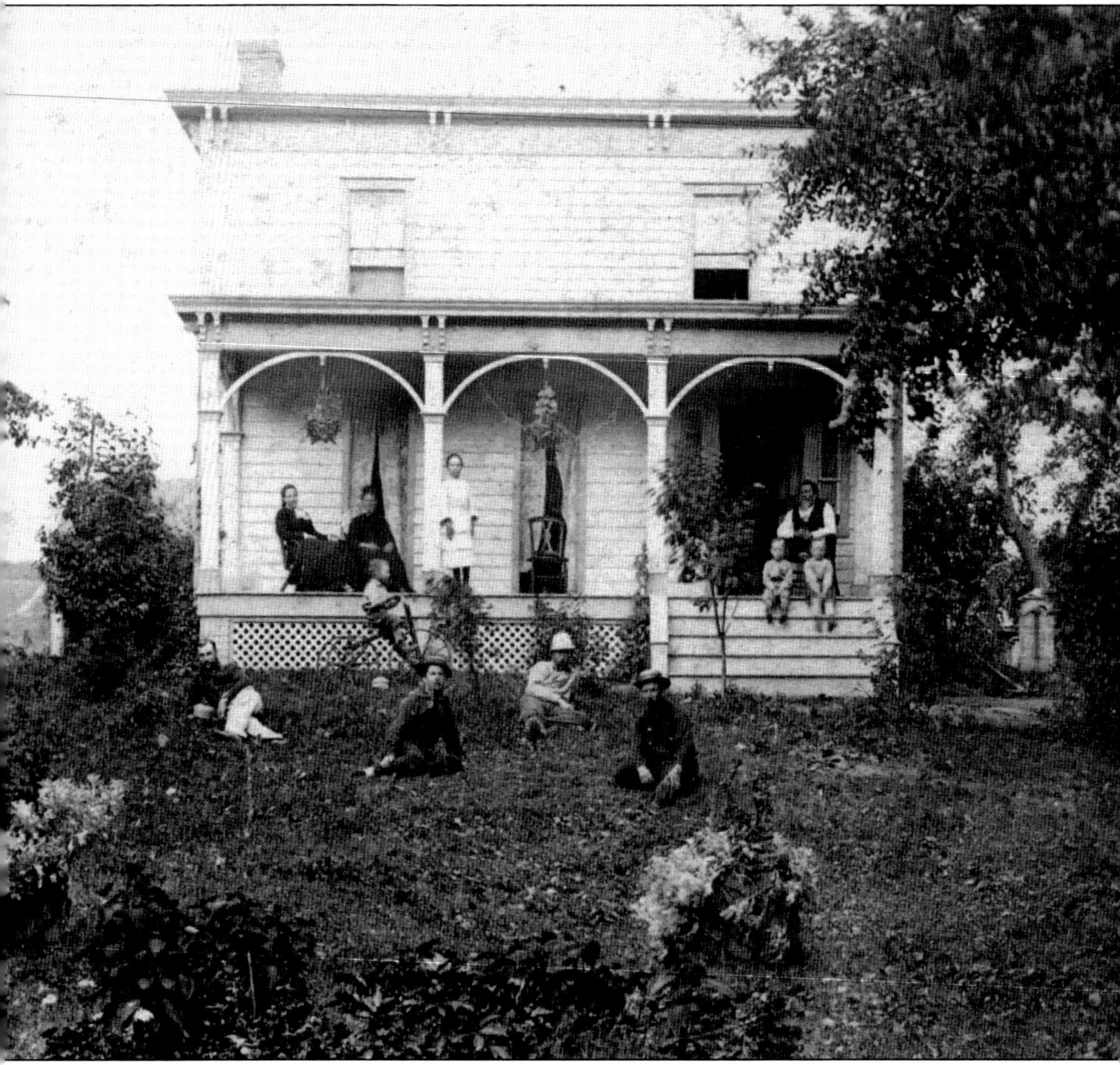

A line in the November 18, 1880, edition of the *New Paltz Independent* newspaper noted that a "Mr. D. J. Auchmoody has been taking stereoscopic views of a number of residences in this village." A week later, the paper noted, "a literary society was organized last Friday evening at the house of M. L. Moore." The Moore house, shown here in a stereoscopic photograph from the 1880s, was more than likely captured as a result of Auchmoody's work in the hamlet. Literary societies remain active to the present, as several book clubs continue to meet regularly within the town. (Courtesy Jeffrey Kraus and antiquephotographics.com.)

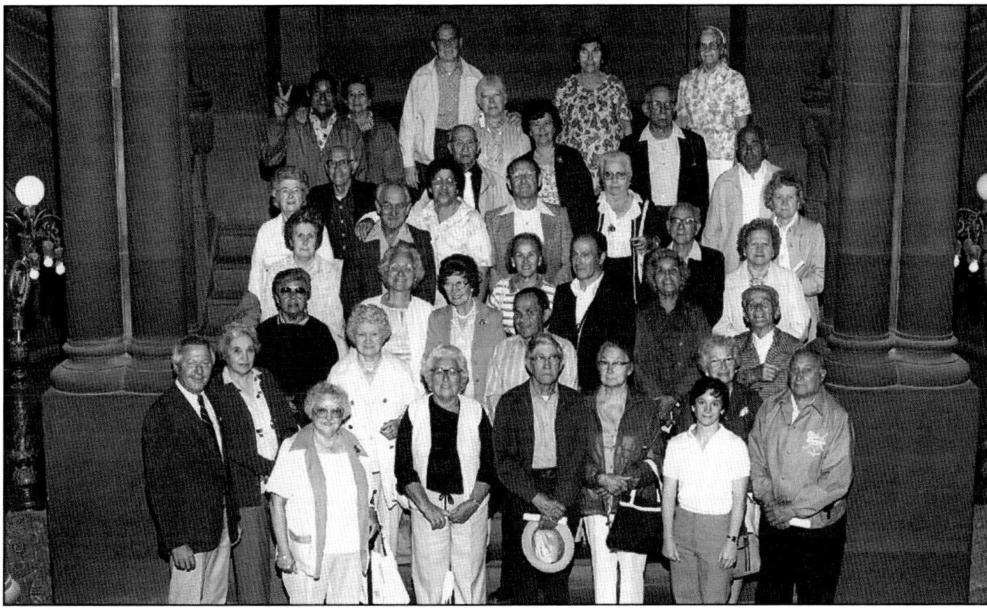

Plattekill has three active senior citizen groups—the Golden Years Club, the Plattekill Senior Citizens Club, and the Aloha Home Acres Social Club. The groups hold weekly meetings and take a variety of trips. Shown here are Plattekill seniors in 1983, who took a trip to the state capitol in Albany and met with New York State senator Richard Shermerhorn. (Courtesy of Shirley Anson.)

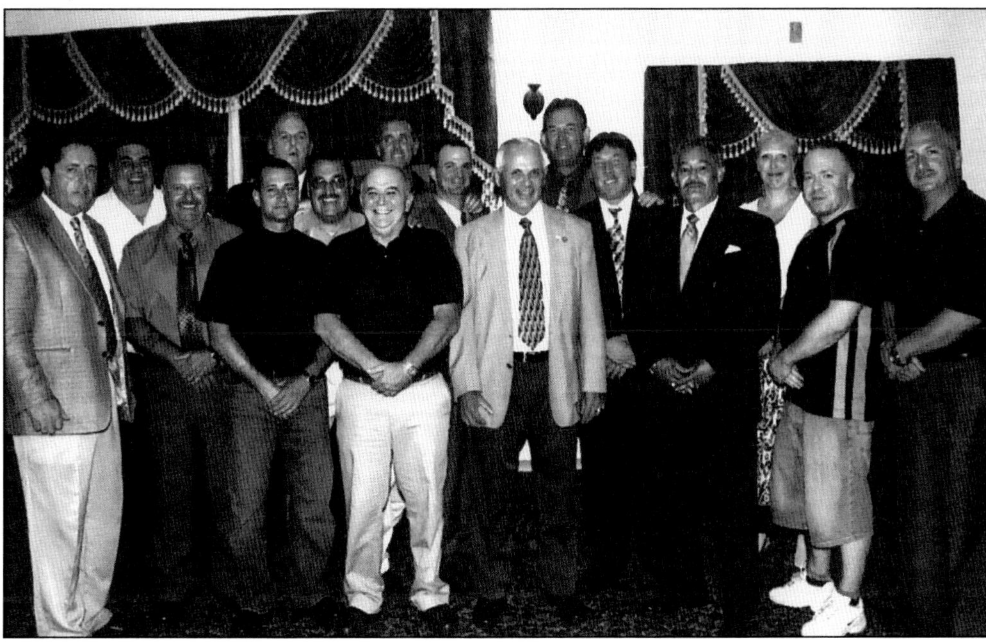

A retirement party for Plattekill Police Department's Chief Gunter Henrich was held in July 2007. Henrich, pictured here in the center, retired after 25 years of service. The Plattekill Police Department was formed in the 1970s, replacing a constable force. Henrich was also an award-winning varsity soccer coach for the Wallkill Central School District. (Photograph by J. Daniels, courtesy of Shirley Anson.)

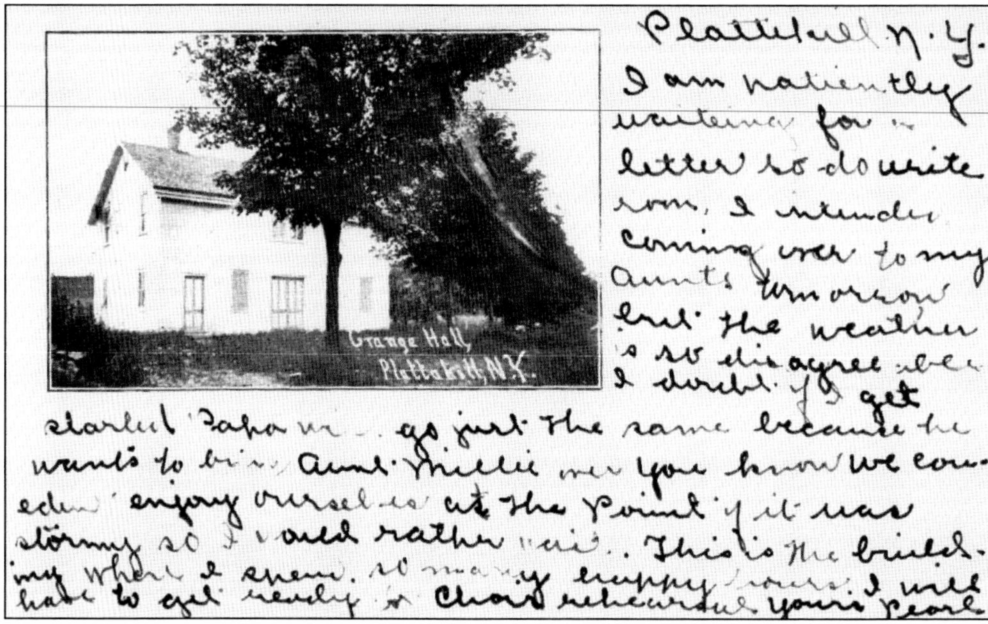

The Plattekill Grange building, pictured here in an early postcard, was built in 1903. Plattekill's first Grange was formed in 1876. The existing Grange organization, Plattekill No. 923, was formed in 1902. Meetings of the Plattekill Grange are still held in the hall, located on Church Street. (Courtesy of Shirley Anson.)

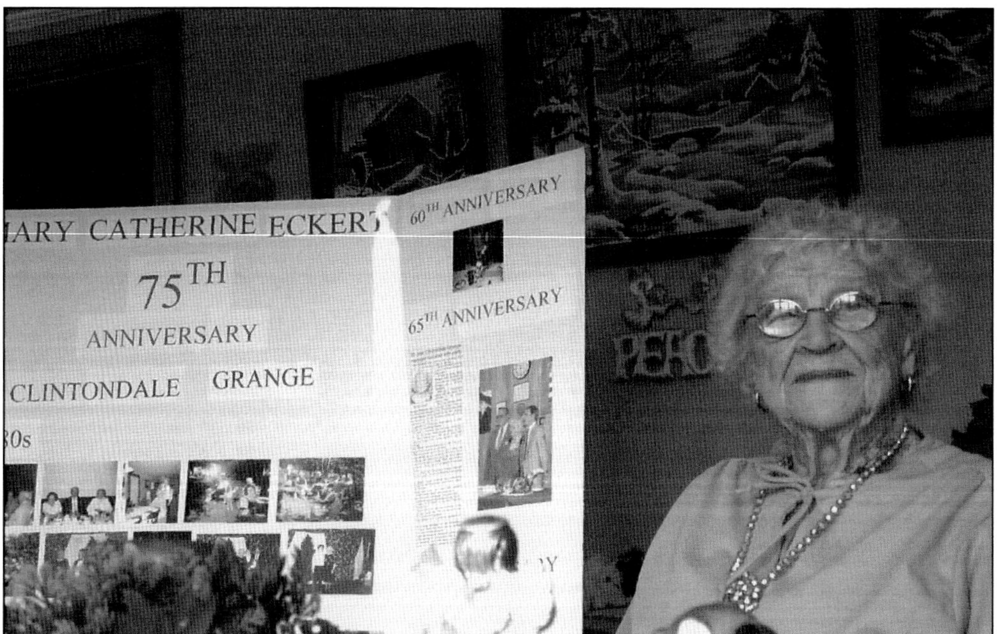

Mary Eckert of Clintondale, shown here in 2005 at age 90, was a member of the Clintondale Grange for more than 75 years and secretary of the group for more than 40. In a 2005 interview, Eckert recalled that when she joined in 1929, most of her friends, including her future husband, Fred, belonged to the active group, which formed in 1903. (Photograph by Elizabeth Werlau, originally appeared in the *Southern Ulster Times*.)

PROGRAMME

"Oh, Kay!"

Mystery Comedy in Three Acts,
written by Adam Applebud

At Plattekill Grange

Wednesday, March 11th, 1931

- 8 P. M. -

SYNOPSIS:

The entire action of the play takes place in the Living Room of the Whitman home in the course of one evening.

A few minutes elapse between Acts I. and II.

Acts II. and III. are continuous.

CHARACTERS:

Edith Whitman .... Hazel Lippincott
Evelyn Whitman—her mother .... Mrs. Seth Lippincott
Arthur Whitman—her brother .... Wilson Edmunds
George Whitman—her father .... C. E. Thorne
"Gram Pembroke" .... Bessie Harris
Alice Borden .... Lolita Harris
Captain Whitman .... Eugene Stevens
"Gramp Pembroke" .... Charles Everett
Jim Hayes .... Arthur Fosler
Kay Millis of the Millis Detective Agency .. Mrs. Harold Mills
Fred Alden .... Sheldon Edmunds

Specialties: Myron Fosler, Baritone Soloist.
Rev. J. W. Taylor, Reader.
Orchestra.

The Goodnough Press, 140 Water Street

Through the 1960s, families would meet at the Plattekill and Clintondale Granges for a wide range of activities including plays, such as the one in Plattekill depicted on the program at right and in the c. 1940 photograph of the Plattekill Grange below. Grange-sponsored dinners were so popular that customers would purchase tickets in advance and wait in line for an opportunity to eat in the packed hall. "If you didn't have a ticket, you didn't eat," recalled Muriel Fosler Obermeyer, whose family members were active in the organization for decades. (Courtesy of Micki Obermeyer.)

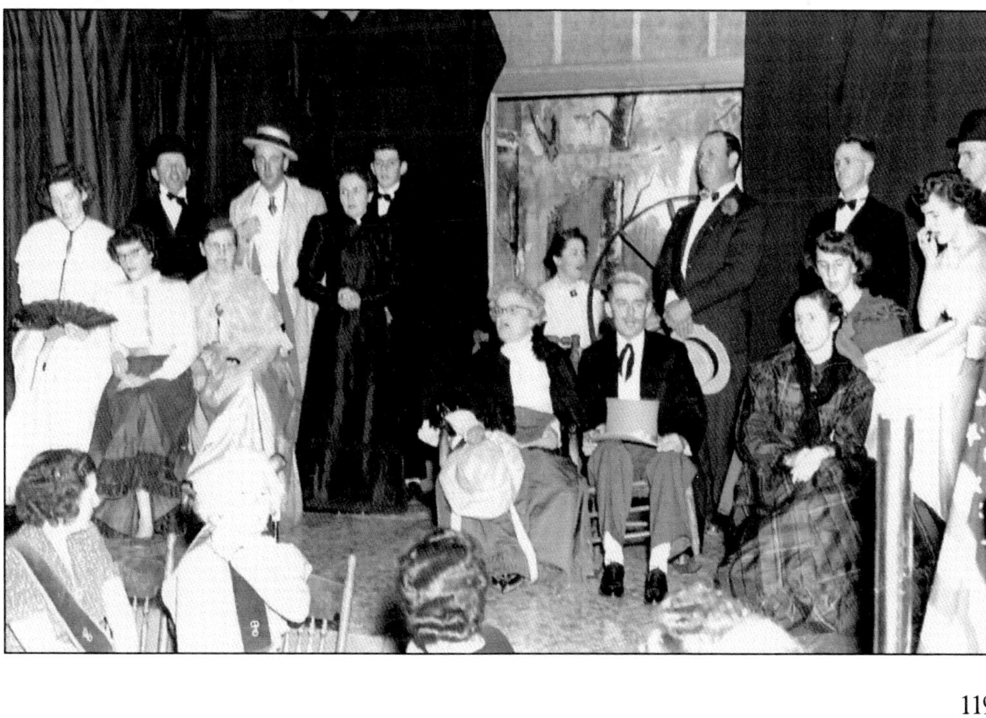

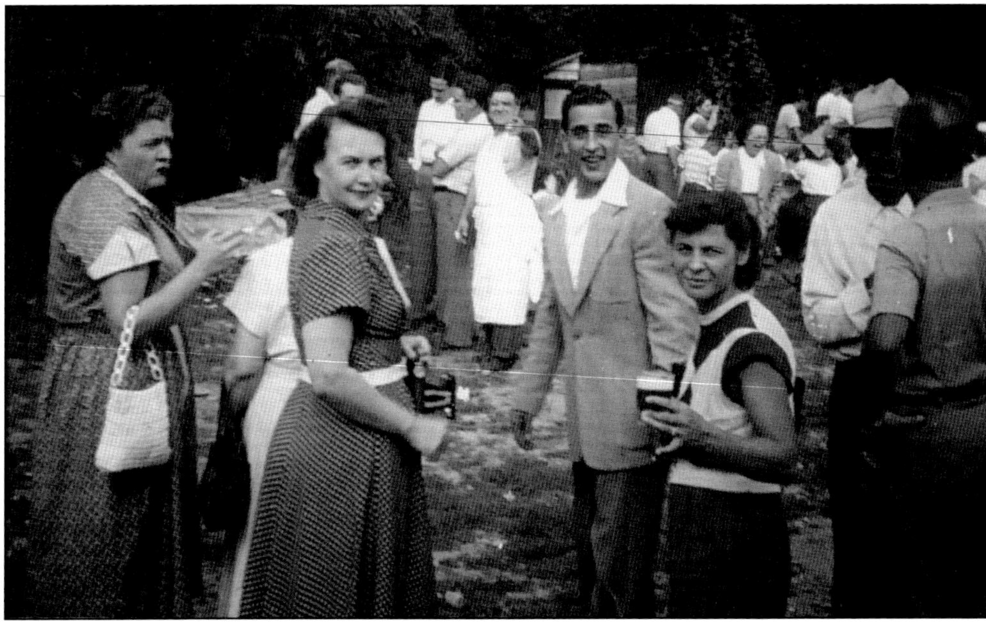

In his 1880 *History of Ulster County, New York,* Nathanial Bartlett Sylvester points out that taverns long served as local meeting places in the town: "nearly every prominent farmer's house was in one sense a 'tavern' around whose fireside the people of the locality congregated, exchanging the gossip and news of the day." This tradition took on new life in the 1940s and 1950s, as the local bars hosted daylong outdoor dinners and clambakes such as the ones at Primo's Bar and Grill in Ardonia (above) and McCabe's Bar in Clintondale (below). Extended families and friends used the dinners as a chance to get together and catch up with each other. (Courtesy of author's collection.)

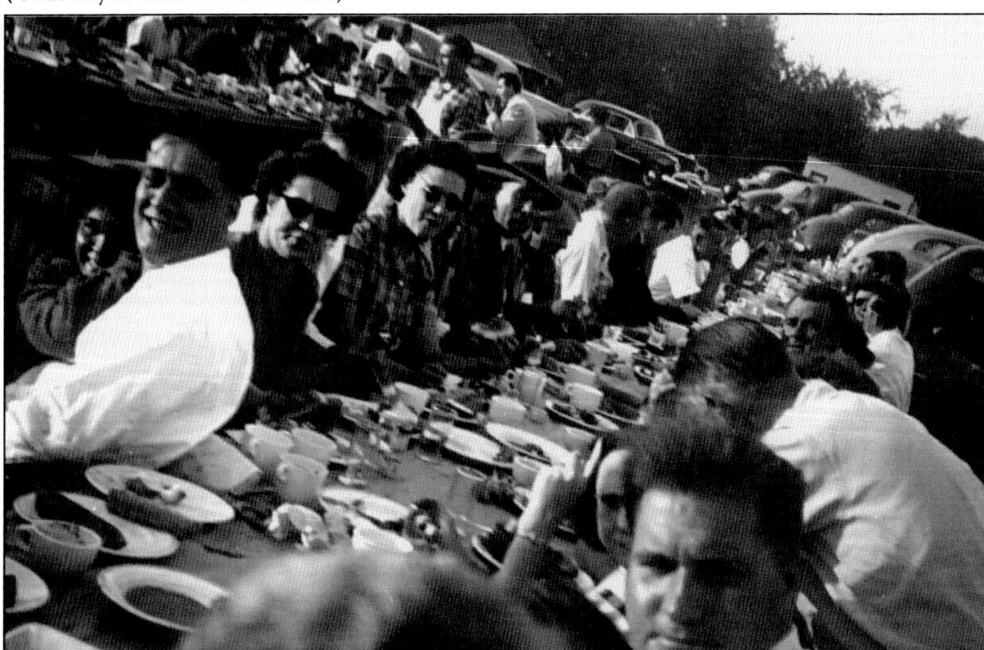

Scoutmaster Walt Davidson, left, and assistant scoutmaster William Ahlers are shown here in 1976. Davidson started Plattekill Boy Scout Troop 179 in Plattekill in August 1976 with six boys. The following year, he began Cub Scout Pack 79. More than 30 years later, both groups continue to meet weekly at the Plattekill Firehouse, under Davidson's direction. (Courtesy of Walt Davidson.)

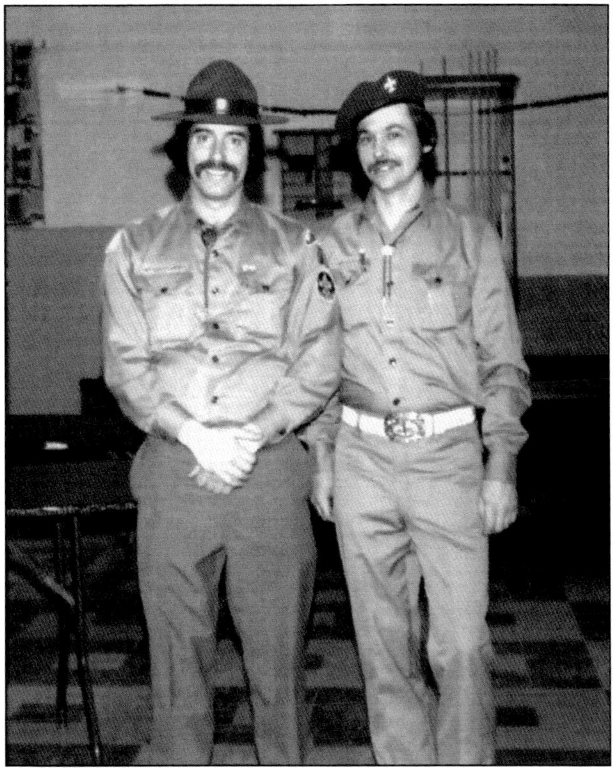

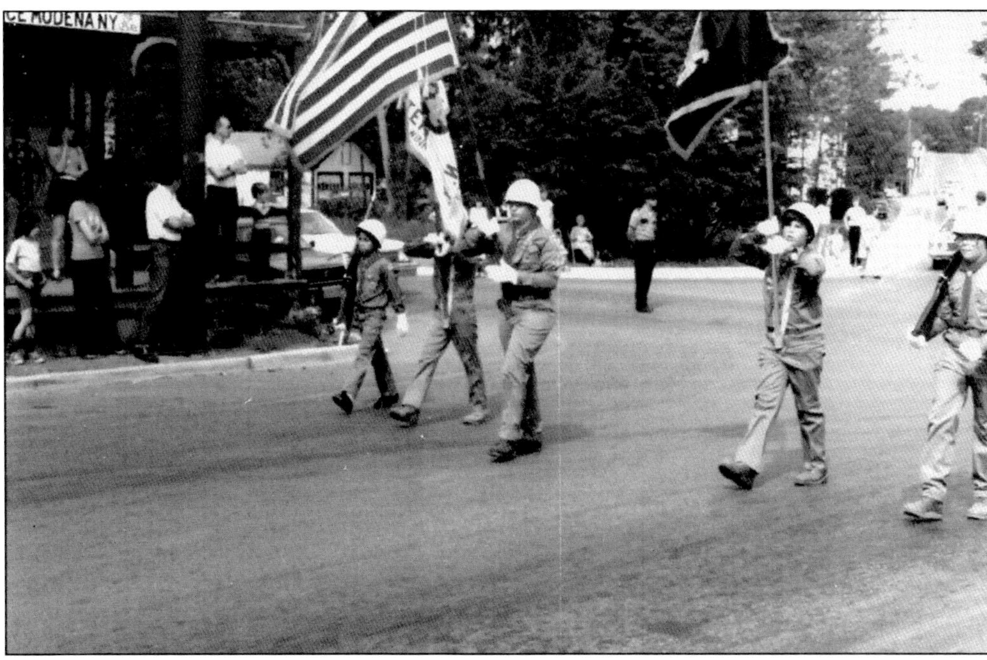

Boy Scouts from Plattekill Boy Scout Troop 179 march in a parade around 1978. The scouts are coming through the intersection in Modena and heading for the Modena firehouse on Route 32. The Route 44/55 bridge is visible in the background of the picture, and the former Modena Post Office can be seen on the left. (Courtesy of Walt Davidson.)

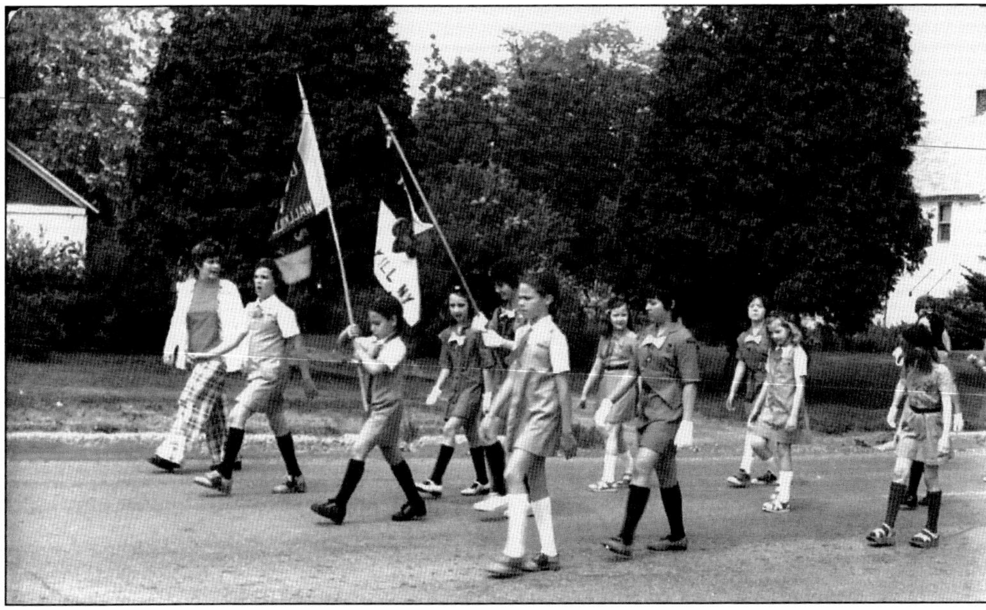

The Wallkill-Plattekill Girl Scouts and Brownies of Troop 221 are shown marching in a Memorial Day parade along Route 44/55 in Modena. The organization was active through the 1970s and early 1980s. The Roosa and Smith homes can be seen in the background. (Courtesy of Daniel and Carol Feldt.)

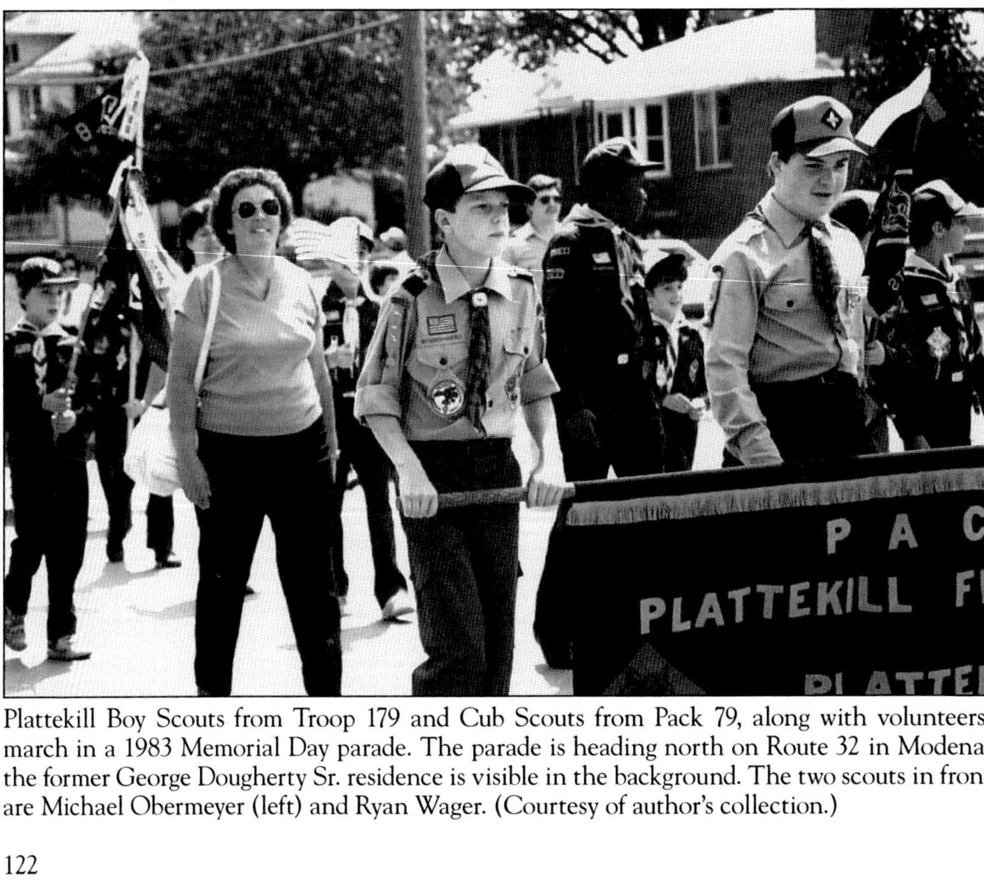

Plattekill Boy Scouts from Troop 179 and Cub Scouts from Pack 79, along with volunteers, march in a 1983 Memorial Day parade. The parade is heading north on Route 32 in Modena; the former George Dougherty Sr. residence is visible in the background. The two scouts in front are Michael Obermeyer (left) and Ryan Wager. (Courtesy of author's collection.)

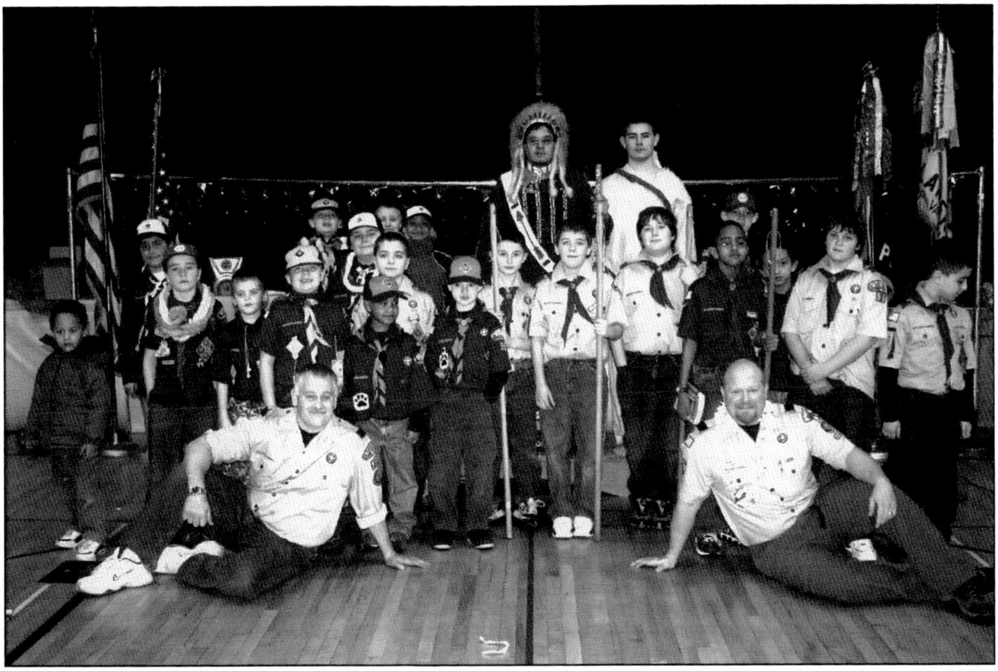

Members of Plattekill Boy Scout Troop 195 and Cub Scouts from Pack 95 get together for a Blue and Gold Dinner in the Plattekill Elementary School gym in February 2007. Webelos from Pack 95 "crossed over" to become Boy Scouts in Pack 195. (Photograph by Elizabeth Werlau, originally appeared in the *Southern Ulster Times*.)

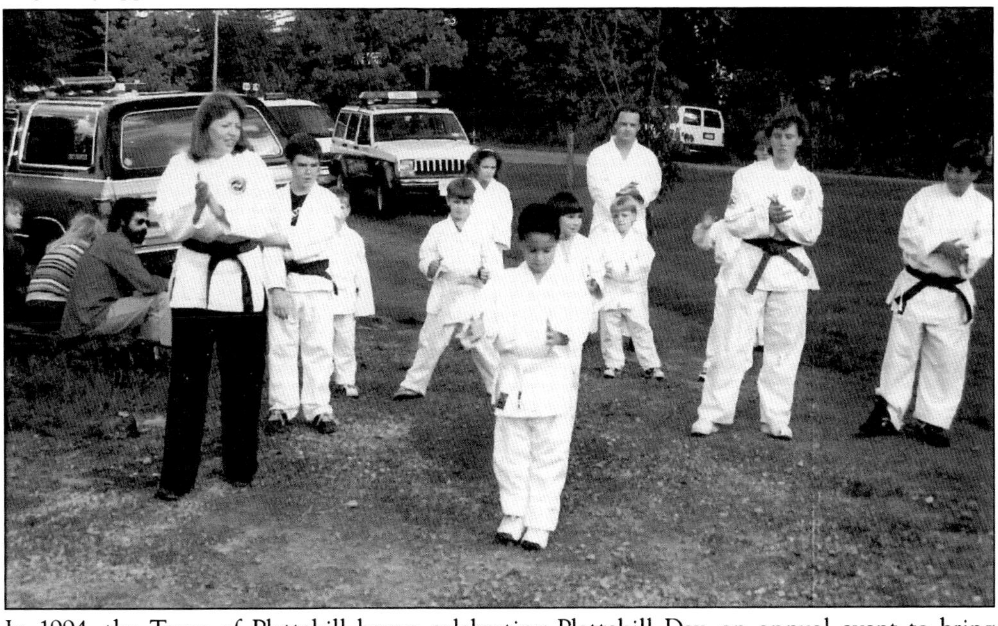

In 1994, the Town of Plattekill began celebrating Plattekill Day, an annual event to bring together the entire community. First held in the parking lot of the town hall, the event is now held each year at the Thomas Felten Community Park. Pictured here is longtime town clerk Barbara Dawes leading a karate demonstration at an early Plattekill Day event. (Courtesy of Office of the Plattekill Town Historian.)

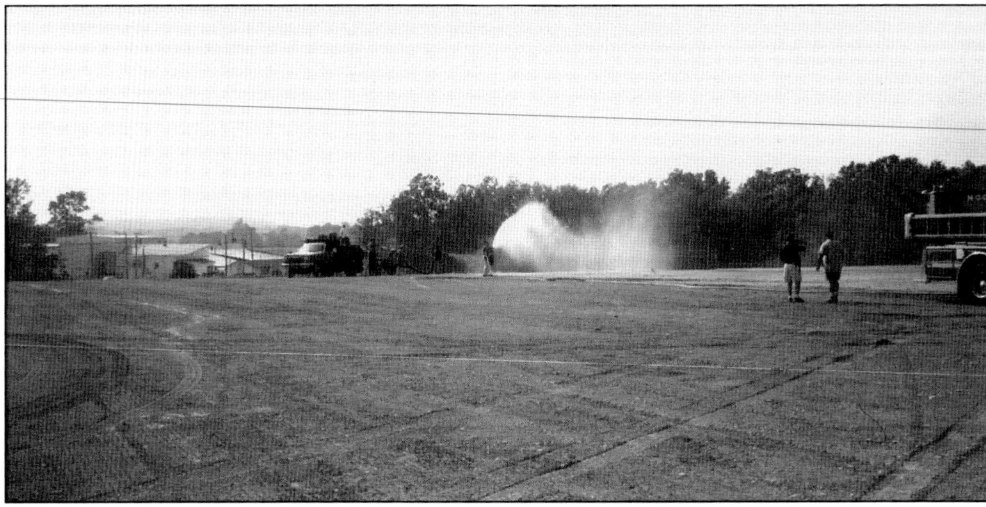

The Thomas Felten Community Park was established in 1996 and now provides a common meeting place for residents to enjoy. Shown here in 2000 are volunteers from the community helping to seed the new soccer fields at the park. This picture was taken on Sunday, June 25; early in the morning on June 26, the Stanley Orchards warehouse seen in the background of the photograph burned down. (Courtesy of Jeffery Zupan.)

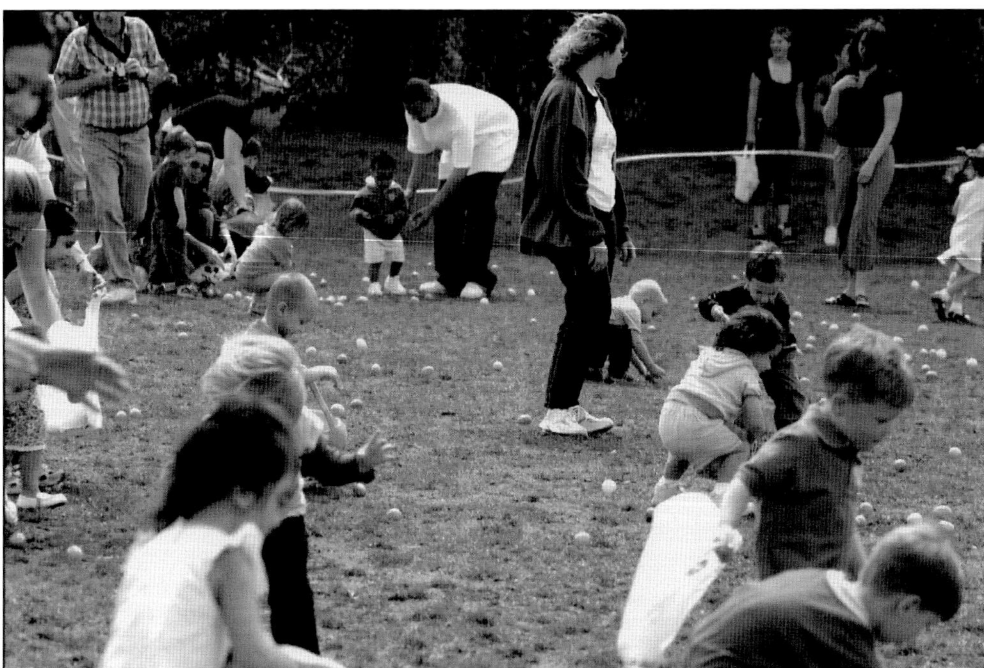

Numerous town-sponsored activities take place throughout the year at the Thomas Felten Community Park, including Easter Egg hunts such as this one in 2006. Additional land along Patura Road in Modena was purchased by the town in 2007 with the intention of enlarging the current park. (Photograph by Elizabeth Werlau, originally appeared in the *Southern Ulster Times*.)

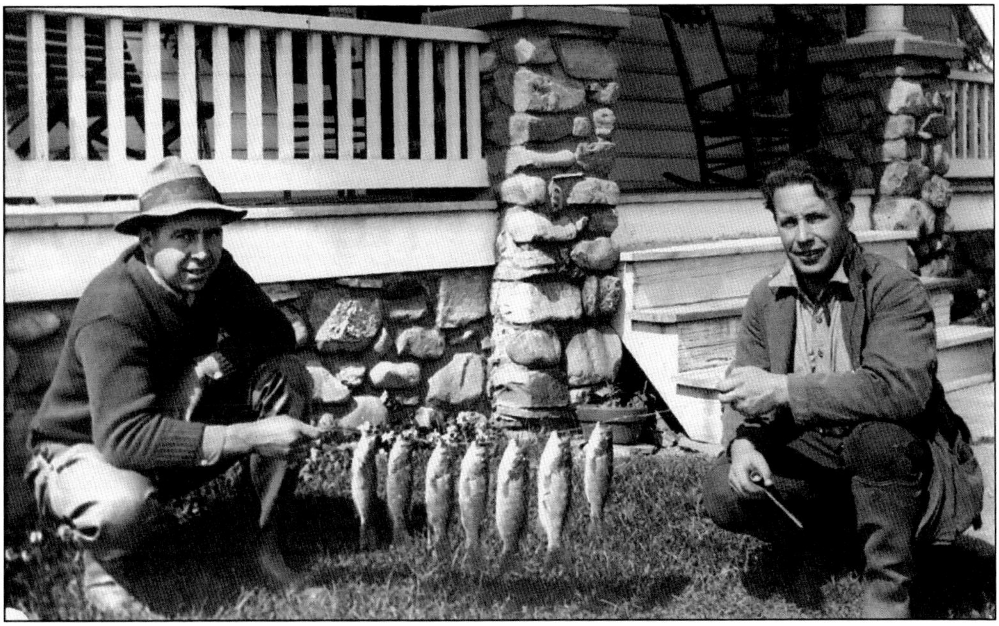

Plattekill resident Ed "Pop" Wager is one of many people responsible for documenting the history of the town. Wager, shown here on the left with Myron Fosler in the 1930s, was a member of the Plattekill Fire Department and a town constable. In 1995, he recorded his memories of the town, including growing up in the Cotter Road area and of being an officer during the active villa years. (Courtesy of Muriel Obermeyer.)

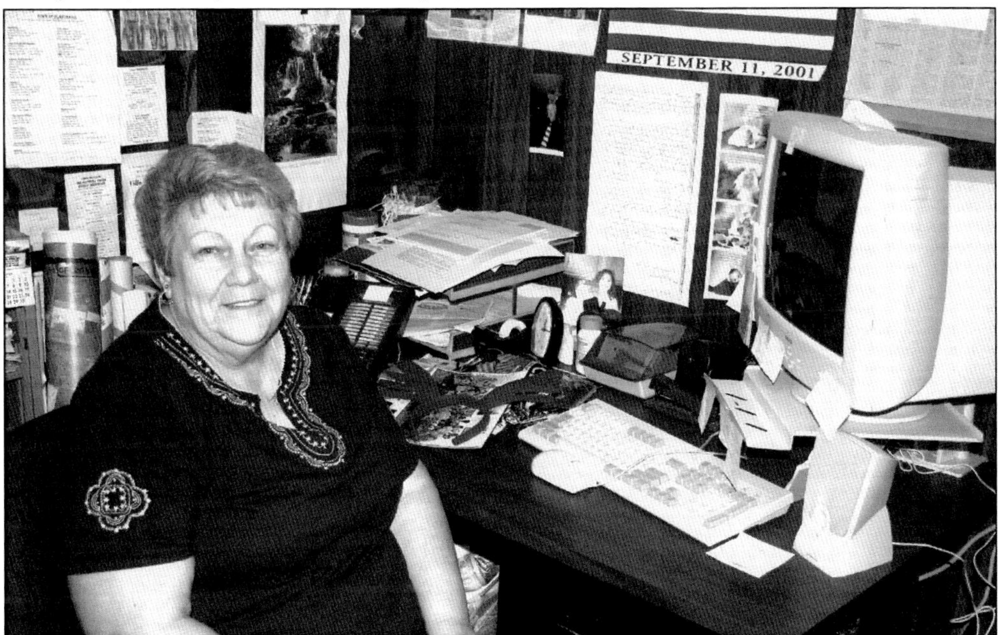

Town of Plattekill historian Muriel "Micki" Obermeyer is pictured in her Plattekill Town Hall office in 2006. The Plattekill Town Hall serves as the storehouse for all town records and historical artifacts, including Obermeyer's extensive collection of antique clothing. (Photograph by Elizabeth Werlau, originally appeared in the *Southern Ulster Times*.)

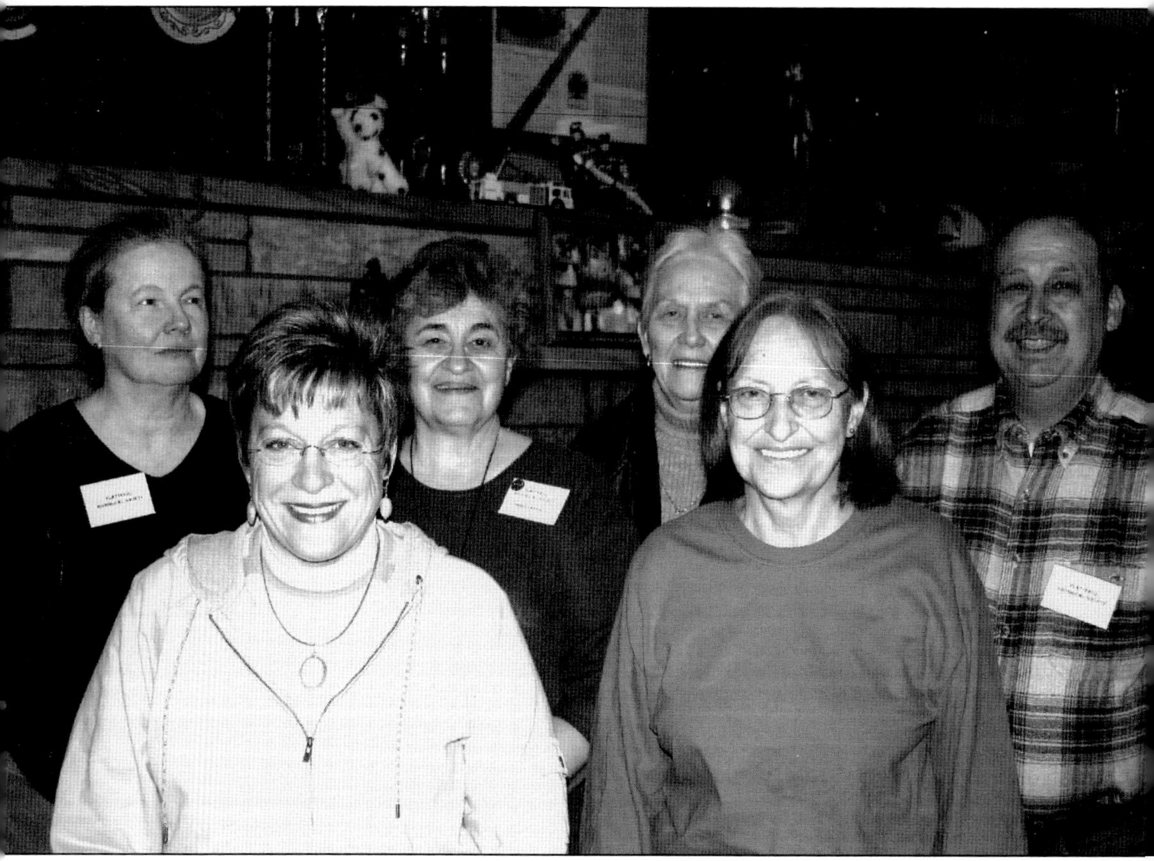

The Plattekill Historical Society is an active group that holds monthly meetings at the Clintondale firehouse. Guests are invited to bring "show and tell" items of historical interest, and guest speakers have included local historians, research librarians, artisans, and volunteers from area non-profit groups. In addition, the group organizes tours of local historic sites of interest and has begun to maintain a digitized collection of their extensive collection of postcards, photographs, and other documents through the Hudson River Valley Heritage Project (www.hrvh.org). Pictured in 2006, from left to right, are officers (first row) Sue Coy Doyle and Lynne Ridgeway; (second row) Valerie Smith, Shirley Anson, Marge Gardner, and Jonathan Ridgeway. (Photograph by Elizabeth Werlau, originally appeared in the *Southern Ulster Times*.)

Bibliography

Anson, Shirley V. *Friends and Neighbors: A Pictorial History of the Town of Plattekill and Southwest Lloyd, Ulster County*. Clintodale Monthly Meeting, 1989.

Anson, Shirley V. and Laura Jenkins. *Quaker History and Genealogy of the Marlborough Monthly Meeting, Ulster County, N.Y., 1804–1900*. Baltimore: Gateway Press, 1980.

Beers, F. W. *County Atlas of Ulster, New York: From Recent and Actual Surveys and Records*. New York: Walker and Jewett, 1875.

Hasbrouck, Kenneth. *History of Modena*. New Paltz, New York: self-published, 1949.

Hurd, Jerome, Elizabeth Hurd, Ralph Van Siclen, and Alice Van Siclen. *The Village of Clintondale from its Beginning to 1959*. Clintondale: J. and E. Hurd, 1959.

Mabee, Carlton. *Bridging the Hudson: The Poughkeepsie Railroad Bridge and Its Connecting Rail Lines*. Fleischmanns: Purple Mountain Press, 2001.

Mabee, Carlton. *Gardiner and Lake Minnewaska*. Charleston: Arcadia Publishing, 2003.

Mitchell, P. N. *History of the Village of Clintondale, Ulster County N.Y.* Self-published, 1894.

Wadlin, Beatrice Hasbrouck Wadlin. *Times and Tales of Town of Lloyd*. Highland, New York: 1974.

Sylvester, Nathanial Bartlett. *History of Ulster County, New York*. Philadelphia: Everts and Peck, 1880.